From Ceylon to Corsham

COMMANDER

PAT HOARE RN

First published in the United Kingdom in 2008 for the author by
The Hobnob Press, PO Box 1838, East Knoyle, Salisbury SP3 6FA
© Pat Hoare

British Library Cataloguing in Publication Data
A catalogue record for this book is available from the British Library.

ISBN 978-0-946418-82-4
Typeset in 12/15 pt Scala ; typesetting and origination by John Chandler
Printed in Great Britain by RPM Print & Design, Chichester

Contents

Foreword

A FTER REACHING RETIRING AGE, I went on holiday every February to the lovely island of Sri Lanka, where I was born, sharing the time which was spent by the sea between Serendip hotel at Bentota and the Ranweli at Waikall.

With time on my hands, I fell to thinking what a wide experience, compared with most; I had in the Royal Navy, and indeed subsequently, this being combined with a blissful personal life, which included near unique experiences by my wife.

Accordingly, I decided to record these experiences in autobiographical form for my family successors, and four years later it was completed, with just five copies within the family, and one with the Imperial War Museum.

Now, decades later, family and friends who have read it, have persuaded me to make it available to the a wider audience, as it might be of interest to a number of people 'who were there' or who have been associated with me in a long life.

So, before it is too late, here it is!

Holton House,
Corsham 2008

1
It Started from Here

J ACK HOARE was born in October 1885, the fourth child of John Hoare a cloth
manufacturer of Westbury, Wilts. and his wife Louisa. As business prospered, so they
moved in to Westbury House where the young family of eight were to grow up. He was a
very average boy both physically and scholastically, but backed up by a tinge of red in his
hair. he apparently had a short but strong temper. On one occasion his mother, hearing
screams issuing therefrom, rushed to the kitchen to find young Jack, brandishing a knife,
in hot pursuit of the cook round and round the kitchen table with the gap rapidly closing,
and affected an arrest in the nick of time.

Not long afterwards, he succeeded in locking his four sisters in the second floor playroom in a fit of temper and breaking the key off in the lock, necessitating the embarrassment
of the Fire Brigade having to be called to release the unfortunate prisoners. Soon after
these episodes, and no doubt, others, he was shipped off to a small private school in Clevedon
to start his formal education.

His father was a small pompous little man who had become Managing Director of
Laverton's Cloth Mill near-by, and was accustomed to keeping the whole family including
his wife very much in their place, and expected to be waited on hand and foot. An example
of this was their annual Summer Holiday, when they always rented a complete Preparatory
School in Swanage, taking with them all the servants. They journeyed thence by train
from Westbury, the father being taken alone to the station in a trap, and his wife and eight
children together with all servants and baggage proceeding separately in a large wagon.
On arrival of the train, he took himself alone to a first class carriage at one end of the train,
and the rest travelled third class at the other.

After private school, Jack and his three brothers all in turn went to Bradfield College
where they all appear to have achieved nothing very successful, but nor anything of
disadvantage; in fact a typical middle of the road path.

Almost opposite Westbury House stood the other big house in the middle of the
town called Fontainville, (now demolished to make way for a new shopping centre) where
lived the Fisher family, the offspring being all girls, and as the Hoare boys grew up it is not
surprising that the Fisher girls opposite played an increasing part in their lives; indeed
getting engaged to one of them became a family occupational hazard.

The eldest of the boys, Arthur, followed his father into Laverton's Mill and was later
to become Managing Director for many years, having first married the eldest Fisher girl!

The next son was Jack, and as there was no place for him in the family business, he was taken in by Mr. Fisher to assist him in his Dye works in the town, he having no sons. It is believed that this employment lasted a few years, before the works went bust, like most of the other Fisher ventures, and Jack, whilst taking a few temporary jobs, was somewhat at a loose end.

It was then that a family friend by the name of George Brown, who was a tea planter in Ceylon, managing an estate for James Finlay and Co. of Glasgow, came to stay, and he was able to arrange for Jack to come out to Ceylon in a similar capacity to learn the ropes and then make it his career, which indeed he was to follow until he retired in 1946. And so Jack sailed to his new life in 1910 and was soon to make great friends with Leonard Watkins-Baker who was an assistant in a neighbouring estate in the Ratnapura area.

Leonard was the son of a once prosperous solicitor in Clifton who had ten children, seven boys and three girls, who lived in a big house near the suspension bridge. They were well known in the area and six of the boys played rugby for Clifton and six of the family played for Gloucestershire on the same Saturday; three boys in the rugby team, one in the hockey team, and two girls in the ladies hockey team. However, one day in 1910, the father sent for his ten children and told them bluntly that he had lost every thing speculating on the stock exchange and was near penniless.

The sons, who were at various stages of qualifying for the professions, once having got over the initial shock, said 'Don't worry dad we will go abroad and restore the fortunes. ' Two things are unquestioned; firstly that they all went abroad, and secondly that none of them made a fortune. Four sons went to Canada, and one to South Africa and two to tea planting in Ceylon, whilst of the girls, two got married and the third, Gladys, went teaching in Prep school.

Returning to Jack and Leonard, it was their regular habit and weekly pleasure to proceed, two up, on an ancient motor cycle on a Saturday evening the fifteen miles to the Ratnapura club, returning, no doubt somewhat inebriated in the early hours of the morning. It was therefore with some alarm that Jack heard from Leonard one day late in 1913 that his sister Gladys was coming out from England to stay with him, for he foresaw the demise of the regular Saturday evening session.

'No problem' said Leonard ' I will get the estate blacksmith to weld a home-made reclining side-car on to the side of the bike, and nothing need change'.

Shortly afterwards the unsuspecting Gladys arrived on her first visit outside England; she was introduced to Jack, and the Saturday evening routine was explained to her. Come the first Saturday, she was loaded in to the side-car, and off they went on their fifteen mile drive to the Ratnapura club, arriving at the usual time of 9pm. What they had carefully omitted to tell her in advance was that the club was 'Men only' and so on arrival there they explained that she should sit in the side-car until it was time to drive her home. Surprised, but assuming that this was normality in this 'Somerset Maugham' like world, there she patiently sat until the early hours, when as usual the two tottered out of the club and drove her home.

This was to happen on Saturday after Saturday until the time drew near for her to return home, but meanwhile war broke out in August 1914 and it was decided the Gladys would stay in Ceylon. In the circumstances the almost inevitable happened and Jack and Gladys were married in June 1915, spent their honeymoon at Mount Lavinia Hotel and returned to live at Jack's estate bungalow, and the bachelor day were over.

2
Childhood in Ceylon

JILL WAS BORN in April 1916, and I followed one year later in April 1917 (christened Patrick Durrant). History has it that the baby Patrick was born weighing twelve and a half pounds, three week premature. The mind boggles at what would have happened if the full course had been run.

It happens that there was also a defect at birth which required liberal supplies of ice, which were certainly not forthcoming in the estate bungalows of those days, which were still so primitive that there was no running water, and only 'Thunder boxes and buckets' in lavatories. So, for some days ice was sent daily by train fifty miles from the Colombo Cold Storage Company in ice-boxes to Ratnapura, whence they were carried on coolies heads the fifteen miles to the bungalow. I am glad to say that this enabled the baby Patrick to survive.

In the autumn of 1919, the whole family came to England on holiday complete with Singhalese Ayah, and there was a family reunion of three generations at Westbury House, the family returning to Galbode Estate where my father had his first appointment as a Superintendent, and still in the Ratnapura area. Very sadly, shortly after this, occurred a major catastrophe, which is the first incident in my life which I remember very clearly to this day.

As has been mentioned, the bungalows then had no plumbing, and hot and cold water were to the bathroom in buckets. On the evening in question, Jill and I, who were inseparable, were walking along the passage, hand in hand, on our way to our bath, when as we came round the corner. Jill slipped and fell straight into the bucket of scalding water which had been placed there temporarily by the houseboy on its way to the bathroom, there to be diluted with cold. To make matters worse, as we were walking along hand in hand, I was pulled in on top, but escaped by only getting my leg in. All medical help was

Road transport, 1919: a visit to another estate

Arriving by water transport

Jill and Pat, July 1920: one week before the fatal accident

summoned, but of course in those days this was the doctor in Ratnapura fifteen miles away, and his only means of transport was horseback. Four days later Jill died aged just four years old.

Looking back, I can recall being very distressed, but also, perhaps naturally, getting over it much more quickly than if we had been older. It was of course absolutely shattering for my father and mother. One effect it did have on me was of memory, and although I was barely three years old, and can not remember some of my life that immediately followed, I can to this day draw out a precise plan of the whole house and all its rooms, and the place therein where the accident happened, but can not remember anything of the garden or what the house looked like from the outside. Shortly thereafter, James Finlay very wisely moved my father to another estate called Medakande at Balangoda, some fifty miles away.

Life there returned to an even tenor, and as before, I had a donkey and a donkey boy, and went out for a ride every day. Grown up relaxation was tennis and bridge at the Balangoda club where my father was secretary, and I was occasionally taken along and left at the rest-house for the afternoon whilst they played tennis. This is only mentioned because one wonders where, at the present time, it would be considered safe to leave a four year old child in such circumstances.

My parents, very understandably and sensibly, in light of their recent great sadness, decided that the right thing would be to have another child, which would also ensure that young Patrick would not now be an 'only'. And so in May 1921 was born John.

I recall being sent away to stay on a neighbouring estate when he was due, and being woken up in the night to be told I had a brother. Thinking the shock would be great I was offered a little brandy which I readily accepted; a taste which I was never to lose. On enquiring if my brother could play football and receiving a negative reply, I lost interest and went back to sleep.

In 1922 my father was moved again to Maddagadera estate, down in the south some ten miles inland from Bentota, and it was here that I began my first love for fishing. Every afternoon I would set off with my inevitable donkey and donkey boy to a nearby tributary of the Kalu Ganga with my bamboo rod, floats and worms and fish, and almost invariably had success. They seemed like whales to me but in retrospect were probably only little bigger than sprats. However, they were a welcome addition to the boy's family evening curry, and a small reward for the four times when he had to dive in and fish me out when I fell in, which seemed to cause no concern to anyone.

The family mode of transport had now become mechanised and my father was the

They catch them young

proud owner of an old B. S. A. motor-bike and side car complete with carbide lamps. Our only occasional outings used to be to Bentota beach for curry lunch on a Sunday, I sitting between my mother's legs on the floor of the side car, and John left behind with the Ayah. Bentota was then a lovely beach and a rest house, backed by the palm trees and a lagoon where the river flowed out to the sea. Now it is a concrete and chromium jungle, known as a holiday complex.

Early in 1923 as I was approaching my sixth birthday, my parents deemed it proper that I should be despatched up-country to boarding school at Haddon Hill, which was the English school at Newera Eliya in the hills and thence I went. I remember at the end of the first term, arriving in the evening by train with all the other boys at Colombo, and standing alone unclaimed, when my mother came up and peered under the vast topee that totally hid my face and said 'You must be mine; you are the only one left!' It was during these first holidays from school that I remember one particularly bizarre episode.

My mother had retired to bed early, and being very devout, was kneeling by the bed saying her prayers. My father, who was not a tee-totaller, and on this particular night, had been even less tee-total than usual, followed shortly afterwards, and as he entered the bedroom saw a tarantula on the wall above his wife's head. He tiptoed out and returned with his loaded shot-gun and shot the tarantula straight over the top of his praying wife's head. This resulted in his wife giving a scream and believing she had gone to heaven full toss, a huge hole in the bedroom wall, and a small portion of the tarantula going absent, for he very nearly missed it altogether. I particularly remember this, because the rest of the spider sat in a bottle pickled in spirit for a long time afterwards.

It was at about this time that I began to have a growing desire to join the Royal Navy. I can't think why, because. apart from the occasional visit to Bentota, I had never seen the sea, and had absolutely no naval connections, although from an early age I had always been interested in ships. Perhaps it was partly due to the propensity on the part of my mother to ram me into a sailor suit at the slightest excuse, which was rather a vogue in those days.

In 1925 my father was again due for home leave, and as I was now eight years old, it was inevitable that I should be taken home and left at boarding school, which was then the normal colonial practice. And so one April evening I lay in my bunk in the Ellerman Liner 'City of Cairo' at night, waiting to sail and through the porthole I saw lying in the next berth a cruiser of the East Indies Squadron. Up and down the quarter-deck by the light of the back-bone lights under the awning, walked the Officer of the Watch in white uniform, his sword belt hanging at his side and his telescope under his arm. 'That', I said to myself ' will be me when I grow up, a prophecy to be precisely filled in 1938, when I became Sub lieutenant of the East Indies flagship H. M. S. Norfolk.

Some three weeks later we steamed in to Tilbury, and a few days after that I was presented to the Headmaster of my preparatory school in Weston-Super-Mare. With a 'Goodbye darling; God bless you. ' my parents departed, not to be seen again for four years.

3
Education

Preparatory School

ALTHOUGH THIS PERIOD lasted over five years, and memory of much of it remains clear, the overall recollection is flat and uneventful, no doubt because the pattern of life grew more vivid as one gets older. There are certain things however that stick in the mind; trivia though they are: The smell of flannel blazers; the taste of lemonade, provided after games matches made from 'Eiffel Tower Lemonade Powder'; the weekly pocket money of three pennies, one put in the church collection on Sunday mornings, one at hymn singing in the evening and one for oneself. Oh! the bliss when just occasionally one of the pennies was dished out as two half-pennies which were surreptitiously inserted A. M. arid P. M. , thereby leaving tuppence for oneself!

Sundays had a special ritual, in that one dressed up in Eton Suits with stiff collars, that stuck out all the way round, over cut-away bum freezers. Before church, we lined up with our hair brushes and had the unruly mop stuck down by Matron with Pears Brilliantine, and then we lined up in crocodile and marched to church and back. In the afternoon we all sat down and wrote the compulsory letter home of the 'Dear Mum; I hope you are well; thank you for your letter. We beat St. Johns 1-0 yesterday: love Willie' type. Unchanging week by week! In my case the inward letter was written in in Ceylon three weeks earlier and arrived every Monday by courtesy of P and O.

In retrospect the scholastic standards and quality of assistant master got progressively worse down the the years, and the emphasis seemed always more to beat all the rival schools at games, which to be fair we nearly always did. However, the educational horizons were somewhat limited, and the idea that I should be coached for a Public School scholarship was abandoned. I am sure none of the masters had this ability, let alone the pupils.

I was still keen on only one goal, a cadetship to the Royal Naval College Dartmouth, the exam for which was less arduous than a scholarship but appreciably stiffer than common entrance. The education resources of the establishment bent themselves to helping me achieve this aim, and in October 1930 I reported to Queen Anne's Mansions in London for my interview and medical. Of the some, two hundred and fifty hopefuls who reported that day, all but 56 were ploughed, and I was over my first hurdle. These statistics are only mentioned to show what store their Lordships put on their subjective judgement of officer material for which they were seeking. In early December the lucky 56 returned to London

Beach fashions at Bournemouth, August 1925

for two days of exams from which the final thirty four were taken, and by Christmas, with a sigh of relief I knew that I had entered the Royal Navy, and to my parents great relief, at only half fees.

Before concluding Prep school memories, it may be worth recalling the problem of children of parents who lived abroad, and there were many at this time of Empire. In my case I was usually parked with relatives who, however kind, could never really be a substitute for one's own home, and however well meaning, could not extend the same affection as towards their own children. There was therefore an inevitable feeling of being in the second eleven. Also, since the privilege of looking after me was unselfishly shared round by a number of relatives, there was no one base or room where one could collect one's own clothes, toys and the like.

It did however teach one self-reliance, and I remember vividly at the age of eight, setting off from Weston-Super-Mare to stay with my Grandmother in a village in Nottinghamshire with a set of instructions and some money and going up to Paddington, across to Kings Cross, and placing myself in charge of the guards of three trains, whilst I changed at Peterborough, Grantham and Lincoln, and finally met 'Granny' complete with pony and trap at the little village station of Walkeringham. What was even more amazing was that my school trunk successfully negotiated the same trip! I wonder if any parent would allow their child to do that trip in this day and age.

Royal Naval College, Dartmouth

M UCH HAS from time to time been written about 'Dartmouth', but as the last of the
'Thirteen year old' entry are already turning sixty, and as the process, firstly of
joining and then of passing through all phases was, by modern standards, to say the least
unusual, it is proposed to record certain parts of it in some detail.

When the final 56 sat the work exam, which extended over two days, the ubiquitous
Messrs. Gieves asked all the candidates and their next of kin to a neighbouring hotel for
tea, and we were all measured for our uniform. As soon as the results were known, the
uniforms for the lucky 34 were then made, and the day before we were to join the college
we went to their establishment in Old Bond Street and collected our outfits.

Then one cold mid-January day, we first termers met for the first time, somewhat
self-consciously in our new uniforms, under the charge of our two Cadet Captains (prefects)
arid boarded the 1. 15 p. m. 'Torbay Limited' express to our new destiny. Some three hours
later, and still somewhat shy, we reached Kingswear, were transported by ferry to the other
side, and fallen in and marched up to the college, and through the doors of that magnificent
facade on the hill, across whose front is engraved 'It is upon the Royal Navy, under the
good providence of God, that the health, wealth and prosperity of this country do chiefly
depend'.

We were then shown round, firstly to the First term gunroom (Common Room) and
then to our dormitory, with a chest at the end of each bed with ones name on. Then began
the long palaver of having explained to us in detail how every single garment had to be
folded and placed even, as an example, the folded shirts being placed one on top of the
other, with the seams exactly in a vertical line, and every shirt of the same precise width.
This principle applied to all clothes from socks to reefer jackets, and with all our footwear,
cleaned and dressed by the right in a line by our beds. Having retired to bed, for which we
were given fifteen minutes, including having our open chests ready for inspection, an
order was then boomed down the dormitory on the subject of windows.

There was approximately one window per bed on each side of the dormitory, one
side being North and the other South. Someone well up in the hierarchy decided what the
rule that night should be and at the shout from the Cadet Captain of say, 'Windows quarter
open North', all those who slept on that side, clambered up on to the window sills, and slid
the windows to match the order. Meanwhile, the two detailed chest cadets, adjusted each
row of chests to form a precise straight line, and so the finale would then be enacted. To
the shouts of 'Attention in the dormitory', we all 'lay to attention' whilst the Duty officer
marched through on his rounds. Then out went the lights at what was now about 21. 00,
and the morning and the evening were the first day.

At 07. 00 next morning the stentorian voice of our Term Chief Petty Officer yelled

'Turn out' and 34 somewhat embarrassed young cadets stripped off their pyjamas arid ran naked to and through the cold plunge with which every dormitory was provided. We then emerged, dried ourselves and stood each. in front of his own labelled basin, above which was a rack where washing things were kept, again like one's chest, with a precise place for everything; the tooth mug in the middle with the brush neatly at right angles on top; soap to the right, toothpaste to the left, and so on.

On completion of washing there was a rush to get dressed, but half-way through the Cadet Captain shouted 'Say your prayers' and everyone then knelt by their bedside and did just that, standing to attention by their chest on completion. When all had finished, there was the order 'Carry on' and dressing was continued. We then mustered in the corridor outside our gunroom, were fallen in yet again, turned right and were doubled into breakfast a process which was repeated before every meal. The rest of the day was taken up in introductory lectures and geographical familiarisation, and that evening the rest of the four hundred cadets joined, and the new 'Benbow' term, for such was to he our name throughout our time, with all of one day's experience behind us, was integrated into the system.

The first day has been spelt out in some detail, because in fact it was to become the pattern of every day for the next three years, with the addition of a parade and prayers every morning and evening, and the fact that one doubled from one lecture to the next between sessions. In fact one virtually doubled everywhere.

Superimposed on all this was the tick system. One, or one's belongings or apparel were being endlessly inspected, particularly in the early terms, and if anything was found wrong such as a misplaced shirt crease in one's chest, or a button undone, or the lanyard on crooked or not doubling from A to B. the Cadet Captain awarded a tick, which was cancelled after one month. If, however, four uncancelled ticks were achieved, which in my early days I found singularly easy to obtain, then the dreaded summons 'Hoare turn out' was called after 'Lights out', and one trotted down the dormitory in one's pyjamas and out through the door to bend over and get beaten, after which the score sheet was put back to zero again.

The scholastic syllabus differed somewhat from the conventional public school and is perhaps worth mentioning. Although Latin was a requirement for passing into the College, no classics were taught once there, the only foreign language being French. Mathematics, Science and English were of a high standard, as was history, although, not unnaturally it was heavily biased towards Naval History. There were also of course periods of seamanship, signalling, engineering and navigation.

There was also a Divinity syllabus, and it will come as no surprise that in the fourth term everyone got confirmed. It was not quite the case of the Term Chief falling us in on one Sunday and ordering 'Left turn; double march; get confirmed', but I do not remember any of our term declining! We all in due course got the customary bible or the like as confirmation presents, except one who made the rest of us green with envy. His godmother was no less than the Princess Alice, Duchess of Athlone, and this splendid lady sent him a pair of roller skates!

Of course the main difference compared with conventional schools was that the 34 of us all stayed together, advancing to a fresh syllabus each term, until one passed out at the top after eleven terms.

The sociological aspect of the Benbow Term intake, which was probably typical of all the other terms, might be of interest, in that every one of us, without a single exception, came from conventional Preparatory schools, all but three from the south of England, and eleven of the thirty four had fathers or brothers who were already in the Royal Navy.

Today 1989 and fifty eight years on, of the original 34, ten were killed in action, five have died since the war of illness or accident, five fell by the wayside either scholastically of through illness whilst still cadets, and fourteen still survive. Of the fourteen, nine are executive officers, two specialised in engineering, and three became paymasters due to eyesight failure.

And so term followed term until the end of the fifth term, when one moved from Junior to Senior College, which made no noticeable difference, except that one was now a colt for games, until after the eighth term when one entered the senior year and received a

Benbow Term passing out, July 1934

few relatively inconsequential privileges, such as being allowed to put one's hands in one's blazer pockets, and being allowed to visit the local farms for cream teas on Sundays. The standard fare at the farms of two scrambled eggs on toast, and as much bread, Devonshire cream and jam as one could eat with tea and cake cost two bob a head!

Sporting activities were always very much encouraged, and competition to get into the top teams was particularly intense, because of course, by definition everyone was of a high medical standard. This grew to a head in the final year, and I was in the 2nd XV rugger, with an occasional game for the Ist XV in my ninth term, second XI soccer in my tenth, and the tennis VI in my eleventh and final term. Also, in our final year, four Cadet Captains were selected per term, making twelve from the term in all, and I was lucky enough to be one for our last term. Even at that level there were no studies or other exceptional comforts.

At the end of our final term there were passing out exams, which approximately equated the 'A' levels of today, but with the addition of specialist subjects such as seamanship, engineering and navigation, and one obtained either a first, second or third class pass, or failed. I passed out with a second class. The next horizon was the sea going cadet training cruiser H. M. S. Frobisher.

Of course, during the nearly four years at Dartmouth there were the leaves which matched the conventional public school holidays, and there still lurked the problem of what to do with the boy during these periods. After all those years, since I was eight, various relatives naturally were getting less and less attracted with fielding me for holidays except for very short periods, and then it was found that various impecunious parsons and their wives in over-large vicarages in different parts of the country were taking in children in the holidays, whose parents were abroad, for there were many such at the height of Empire before the Second World War.

I sojourned for various lengths of time at three such emporia, one in the Midlands, one in Gloucestershire and one in Sussex, but did not survive for many visits in any one of them. There was no feeling in any of them of warmth or affection or of being wanted for any other reason than that it was a convenient vehicle for increasing their stipend.

A favourite vehicle for getting rid of us young, for sometimes there was a gang of us, was to give us the price of the cheapest seats, and bung us off to the cinema. At one of the above establishments, two of us found that we could slip out through the fire exit after the show, and use the same ticket the next and following times, meanwhile pocketing the entrance fees for other attractions. However we overplayed our hand, and the management, finally gazing at tickets that had more punch holes than cardboard, tumbled to the ruse and reported us to the incumbent and his wife. They in turn, feeling that such goings on tarnished their ecclesiastical image, sent us packing. The end result of this however was to limit the sadness reaching the end of leave and the beginning of a new term, for there was little to choose between them, and there was but a longing for the end of the road where we would be at sea in ships and all as it were the same boat! However, all this was about to change . . .

James Bell, an Englishman, and a member of a prominent Anglo-Argentine family was ranching out there and was a particularly good horseman and polo player. Sadly in about 1924 he was killed in a riding accident leaving a penniless widow and five children under the age of ten. The widow returned to England with the children and settled in Minehead in Somerset in a small house provided by her late husband's relatives, and a small annual allowance. By 1933, with the children getting older and expenses increasing, Mrs. Bell took the courageous step of renting a larger house and taking children, whose parents were abroad, for the holidays, and I became one of the pioneer visitors.

However, there was one big difference from previous ventures. Here were already five teenagers straddling one's own age, with a large house and garden, an outside playroom, one's own bedroom, and above all a complete feeling of being integrated as part of the family. In short, there was a sense of coming home when one came on 'leave', that was markedly different from term time.

'Woodside', as the house was called, was for a few years from the age of sixteen, to be the place to which I always returned. There was, after a short time, a more potent influence that pulled me there. I had been increasingly aware for some time that the world was comprised of two sexes and not one and my increasing friendship with Peggy, who was the fourth of the quintet, and rather over a year younger than I, burgeoned ere long to being in love.

Suffice to say here not to jump too many hurdles in advance that after some vicissitudes, we were married eight years later.

The Cadet Training Cruiser, H.M.S. Frobisher

O N L E A V I N G Dartmouth after the eleven terms and the following summer leave, the next step was to join the cadet training ship at Chatham in September 1934. The ex-Dartmouth cadets spent two terms in Frobisher putting into practice what was learnt at the College in the environment of a normal warship, the result in practice being a mixture each week of working like an Able Seaman, having lectures on engineering and ship construction, and officers duties, both Divisional and watchkeeping, and keeping watch oneself.

Each morning, however, started with the same ritual. Reveille sounded at 05. 30 and we turned out of our hammocks which we had slung the previous night and stowed them away, we then fell in at our particular part of the ship in bare feet at 06. 00, and under our Divisional Petty Officers, we scrubbed decks for an hour until 07. 00, except on Fridays when we knelt down and holystoned the decks instead. All this was no doubt very good for our souls, but must have been the most inefficient means of cleaning decks yet devised!

Mediterranean Fleet, Malta, September 1934

The two terms that fell to our lot were the Autumn and spring terms, the former to the Mediterranean and the latter to the West Indies. To give their Lordships their due, the cruises were planned with considerable enlightenment in terms of providing culture and history for the cadets.

In the Autumn cruise, after the statutory stops at Gibraltar and Malta to introduce us to Naval ports, we then proceeded to Naples, with outings to Vesuvius and Pompeii, before going to Ragusa (now Dubrovnik) in Yugoslavia, arriving there fortuitously the day after the King had been assassinated. Thence we proceeded to Crete to view the ruins of Knossos and already, since in those days there was not the holiday travel abroad that there is now, we were getting a sense of privileged romance at seeing so much, but the highlight was still to come.

The next port of call was Haifa, whence we were taken, half at a time, for a three day pilgrimage of the Holy Land, covering not only Jerusalem and its environs, but Bethlehem, Nazareth, Jericho and the Dead Sea as well. In fact, hard work combined with a broader education such as the above, really led to a very enjoyable postscript to Dartmouth. We also received pay at the princely rate of six shillings per week, (we were not paid for Sundays!) and our parents were expected to pay us an allowance of not less than £50 per year, which precise sum I received.

We used to form ourselves into syndicates of six each pay-day, each member putting a shilling into a kitty and drawing lots for the winner. The net result was that one member got eleven shillings which was worth having, and the rest of us only had five, which hardly made any difference. I must surely have won the jackpot one week, for I remember bringing Peggy back for Christmas a kimono and an amber bracelet from Gibraltar, and a filigree silver bracelet from Ragusa.

The spring term started in January 1935 and was the West Indies cruise. Scrubbing decks for the first few days, until we entered warmer climes, was decidedly nippy, and it was the first experience for us of ten days continuously at sea. About half-way across the Atlantic, I remember the Captain stopping the ship, and the order was issued 'All cadets overboard for a swim'. and there was the somewhat uncanny feeling of swimming over a thousand miles from anywhere with 3000 fathoms of water below me.

The afternoons after work finished were sometimes enlivened by cockroach racing. We kept our steeds in matchboxes, each claiming to have a secret diet for our embryo champions. Mine, I recall, was ships biscuit to which was added a little rum. The cockroaches were steered by the tip of a pencil, and pushing led to instant disqualification by the stewards of the course. The trick of sticking a morsel of chewing gum under one's opponent's runner when he wasn't looking led to being warned off the turf for life! Races were for an entrance fee of one penny: winner takes all!

After calling at Bermuda, our leisurely cruise along the outer islands, using the beautiful trade wind weather to enhance our practical seamanship training, particularly in boats, was brought to an abrupt and dramatic halt. An S. O. S. was picked up from S. S. Valverda, outward bound from Cunacoa with a cargo of kerosene, which had a fire in the engine-room, which had killed one Engineer Officer and seriously injured another. The ship was a few hundred miles distant and when we reached her the fire had been extinguished, but the engine-room was out of action. We got excellent seamanship training taking the ship in tow and taking her some several hundred miles to Bermuda, and dropping her in five fathom hole before returning to our interrupted cruise in the islands.

This interlude was for me a blessing in disguise. In our Fore top division, we had a locker-man called Freddie Foad, an Able Seaman of great vintage, who could not stand 'they cadets', and who placed us at disadvantage whenever he could, resulting in desultory guerilla warfare. On the morning in question, just before the Valverda episode, it was my duty to clean the inside of the cutter hanging at its davits over the ship's side, and in full view of the door of Freddie Foad's locker. I had accordingly armed myself with a few potatoes from the adjacent spud store, and crouched down undetected in the bottom of the boat with intent at the appropriate moment to score a bulls-eye on our enemy. At last he emerged, and peering over the gunwhale I let fly.

It was indeed a cruel act of fate, that precisely at that moment the Captain chose to emerge from his cabin, which was opposite, and took the missile neatly under his starboard eye-ball. It was clear that this was not an intended act of mutiny, and private investigation apparently revealed the intended target, but not surprisingly it entailed two weeks stoppage of leave, the whole of which incarceration coinciding with the Valverda interlude.

The rest of the cruise went delightfully through the islands, which I was soon to visit again as a Midshipman, and we returned to Chatham at the end of March 1935, having wintered well, for another set of exams (and another second) and so to the end of our formalised cadet training.

As soon as we returned to Chatham, a list went up on the notice board showing all ships with Midshipmen vacancies which were to be allocated to our term. All those with Naval connections or influence had their or their parent's choices already typed in, but to my astonishment, for the four vacancies in H. M. S. Ajax, a brand new cruiser for the South America and West Indies station, only the name of Harold Dannreuther was typed in, and Michael Allison, Peter Davey and I quickly added ours. It would have been my first choice in any event. We all then went off on leave, and on 30th April 1935, my eighteenth birthday, the four of us joined the brand new gleaming H. M. S. Ajax in Portsmouth dockyard, proud in our Midshipman's uniform and Dirks. Our first real ship, and the start of two years in the University of Life . . . .

H.M.S. Ajax

4
Midshipman ~ the University of Life

WHEREAS OUR TIME in the Frobisher was entirely training, now for the first time, parallel to our continued training, we actually had authority, when for instance we were on watch, or in charge of a boat. By the same token, the officers above us were not just senior Instructors but people in direct line of authority in a chain of which we were the lowest link, within the over all aim of producing an efficient fighting ship.

Our living quarters was the 'Gunroom', a space under the quarter-deck about twenty feet long with a long table with a padded bench down one side and chairs on the other, and two armchairs in one corner, in which we lived and ate, three Sub- lieutenants and seven Midshipmen, although the former also had cabins of their own. One of the Sub-lieutenants, the Paymaster was W. S. Tute who was soon to leave the Navy and become a well-known prolific author.

One deck further down, and ill ventilated, was the chest-flat where the Midshipmen kept all their clothes, each with one chest in a space not much bigger than ten feet square between the lot of us, clothes in this context covering blue uniforms, white uniforms, civilian clothes, footwear, head gear, the lot. Our sleeping quarters was the 'flat' outside the gunroom where our hammocks were slung between hooks welded to the overhead bulkhead.

In this connection one boy seaman (aged 16-17) was allocated to each Midshipman as a hammock boy to sling our hammocks in the evening and stow them away in the morning for which, out of our pay, we paid them one penny per day, or to be precise half-a-crown at the end of each calendar month. We also had one Royal Marine Bandsman for three Midshipmen to look after our chests, and they received from each Midshipman the sum of ten shillings.

These emoluments may seem somewhat meagre, but it should be remembered that our total pay was only seven pounds ten shillings a month (five shillings a day), from which in addition to the above we had to pay our mess-bills including food, the contribution for which was nine pence per day, on top of the standard victualling allowance paid by the Admiralty for all members of the ships company of one shilling and three pence. For this sum which now seems scarcely credible, we received a large cooked breakfast, and three course lunch and dinner with a fourth course on the weekly guest night! The President of the Mess was the Sub-lieutenant for whom also a duty Midshipman acted as a quasi-fag.

The first two days after joining were spent entirely in what is known as 'slinging ones hammock', which meant that one was

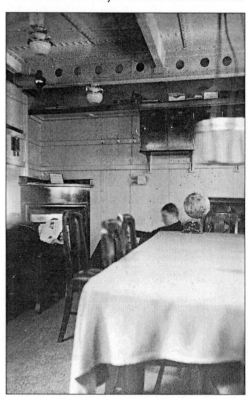

The Gunroom, our home for two years

given this length of time to be acquainted with all spaces in the ship, be they mess-decks, storerooms, machinery spaces or whatever. Then we were allocated our duties. Whilst the other three were each made assistant divisional officers of the three divisions of the ship under Lieutenants, I was lucky to pursue a somewhat different path.

Ever since Dartmouth I had always wished when the time should come, to specialise in Navigation, and as this had become known, I became assistant Navigator, colloquially known as the 'Tankie' from the sailing ship days, when one of the assistant's duties was to dip the fresh water tanks daily. One of the current tasks was to visit the chronometer room daily and wind and rate the three chronometers and weekly get an accurate radio time signal. The reason for having three chronometers was the obvious one that if there were only two and their rate of error diverged, one would not know which one was wrong!

The cardinal sin was to forget to wind them, although they went for forty eight hours because a very accurate knowledge of time is vital. The reason for this is because time and longitude are synonymous and without an accurate knowledge of the former, one can not by astronomic means obtain the latter.

The Navigator, Lieutenant Commander John Smyth, was a red head of easy going charm who taught me a lot, and I was soon doing all the chart-corrections and various other ancillary tasks. In addition, I was also made the Assistant Torpedo Divisional Officer which again was 'different', as the division was functionally oriented to maintaining and servicing the torpedoes, as opposed to a geographic division looking after a physical part of the ship.

There was a set of triple torpedo tubes amidships each side of the ship with a workshop between them, and they were trained and fired from a special 'sight' on the lower bridge where the firing angles were calculated and where the firing triggers were. It was the first such sight in the Navy and the first ship where the torpedoes were fired remotely and not at the tubes. This was to be my 'action station'. At the age of eighteen I was to be the one who pressed the trigger that fired the torpedoes! This romanticism somewhat palled with the passage of time, because torpedoes were expensive, and the business of recovering them so time consuming that they were very seldom fired for exercise, and of course never in anger! And so, having settled in, we took stock of those above us.

The Captain, who looked to us to be about a hundred, but who was probably only fifty, was white haired, purple of complexion, had a somewhat hunched unprepossessing manner and was known to us as 'old eyes down but looking'. The Commander was short, dapper and pleasant enough in a distant way, and intrigued us by having a large double photograph of his wife in his cabin, brunette on one side of the frame, and bottled blonde on the other. None of the Lieutenant-Commanders or Lieutenants made any lasting impression on us, and we were glad we were not as old as them, because life could not be any fun at that age!

Through May and the beginning of June, the ship was kept busy carrying out all the trials necessary for a newly commissioned ship, and in the gaps, we, the Midshipmen were under instruction and going ashore to various short courses to fill the gaps in our knowledge. The former included ammunitioning ship, aircraft catapult trials (for we carried two Hawker Osprey float-planes), direction finder calibration, a full power trial and streaming paravanes, to mention but some. The latter comprised, inter alia, anti-gas courses, wireless telegraphy, recognition signals, and painting lampshades for the officer's farewell ball!

On 11th June, we sailed for Gibraltar and Malta to carry out our operational working up, and our foreign commission had begun in earnest. Our cargo to Gibraltar included six couples of foxhounds for the Calpe hunt. Being kennel-maid for the trip was just another of the many and varied duties that came a midshipman's way!

For the next five weeks, all week days were taken up in repeated surface and anti-aircraft gunnery firings, seamanship general drills and other war-like activities in order to turn a scratch crew in a brand new ship into an efficient fighting unit, and in late July we sailed to Gibraltar and then on to Trinidad to become part of the South American division of the America and West Indies station. But storm clouds, although not directly connected with our country, were already beginning.

In 1896, the Abyssinians overwhelmed an Italian garrison and massacred 4000 men, and Italy with Somaliland and Eritrea separated by an Abyssinian corridor, had long waited for revenge, which would include the conjunction of these two territories. In the summer of 1935, Abyssinians attacked an Italian frontier post, and Italy had started to mass troops in Somaliland with clear intention of turning a retaliation into a full scale attack on the country, as soon as she was ready so to do.

We arrived at Trinidad on 3rd August for what was intended to be the start of an extended eight month cruise round South America, but it was not to be. After a short stay we moved on to La Guaira, the port for Caracas in Venezuela, and parties of us were transported to the capital for various functions, sometimes staying overnight at the recently completed Hotel Majestic: majestic in every way except that no water came out of the ornate gold taps.

Here was our first experience of the strictness of South American chaperoning. It was hard enough work chatting up one's young dancing partner with the few words of Spanish at one's disposal, but the task became Herculean when it extended to doing the same with formidable chaperones in the intervals.

It was at the end of my stay in Caracas that I was suddenly filled with the gripping fear that I had committed the ultimate navigational crime and had made no arrangements to have the chronometers would in my absence and they would all have stopped. Immediately on returning on board, I rushed down to the bowels of the ship to the chronometer room, and the evidence was all too real. With much mathematical calculation, and earphones from a ship's wireless set tuned to the modified rhythmic, time signal coming from Rugby on long wave, I finally managed to start all three so that it would look as they had never stopped, thus saving both my job as 'Tankie' from stopping and my backside from the ultimate indignity.

From La Guaira we proceeded to Grenada, a beautiful island and then the only one with no colour bar. At each stop the ship always gave a formal reception, thé dansant or informal evening function, as best suited the place and the occasion. Here it was the second of these together with drinks, and was the only place where the preponderance of guests were coloured, and included a number of large mothers and ladies of responsibilities in the community and not many attractive young ladies.

The Commander sensing that a problem might arise cunningly let it be known to the Midshipmen that an alcoholic reward would be given to the one who danced most with the largest and oldest of the 'Mammas'. We so entered into the spirit of the contest that the offer had to be withdrawn after a few dances, because it became too obvious that something was afoot when the attractive young ladies sat around like gooseberries whilst all the elderly heavyweights were never off the floor! I wonder what the present day Race Relations experts would make of the fact that our standard cocktail on these occasions was a "White Lady'!

After Grenada followed by St. Lucia, we arrived at Barbados which was to be our last stop before Rio de Janeiro, Buenos Aires and all ports south, but alas things turned out very differently. On 4th September we received a signal from C-in-C to come to short notice for steam and await further orders.

We had 150 of the ships company ashore, a number on all night leave, and at ten o'clock in the evening the commander sent for the Duty Warrant Officer and told him to back up the recall signals and go ashore and help round up those who were ashore. He requested an assistant and as Duty Midshipman and all of eighteen years old I accompanied him. It was of course an enormous eye-opener to an innocent young snottie, going round various establishments saying 'Come on; get up Jack . . . no you can't ask for your money back' and so on. Suffice to say that by seven next morning they were all back on board and I had gone ashore a boy and come back a man.

Another brick in the University of life. . .

The following day we sailed for Bermuda, took on war stores on arrival, and sailed on to Gibraltar, and all was revealed. In light of the continuing preparation by Italy for war, it had been decided that the Mediterranean fleet should be strengthened, and as part of this plan the two South American cruisers Exeter and Ajax were on their way to join in the fleet at Alexandria where we arrived on 25th September.

We almost at once sailed for Haifa and joined the Third Cruiser Squadron, where we were to remain, alternating with Port Said until late November, a period of relative dullness and much exercising. It was on 4th October that Italy finally invaded Abyssinia, backing a hunch that proved to be correct, that Britain and France would take no action. The League of Nations had applied financial and trade sanctions against Italy but it did not seem to make much difference.

During this period I ran the ships motor-boat instead of watchkeeping, and remember well the great pride one took in one's first command. The brass-work was polished daily, and when the Brasso ran out, we used to buy Daddies sauce from the N. A. A. F. I. which did just as well. The drab seats in the cabin were covered with white drill and blue piping at our expense, and if ladies were to be carried, (particularly the Commander's tough wife), we would buy flowers for the little vase in the cabin. The boat hooks were all decorated with fancy Turks heads and blue and white whipping, and if there were a lot of different ship's boats all leaving a jetty at about the same time taking officers on leave back to their ships, we would each plead with our mechanics to adjust the governors, so that we would be just that bit faster than our competitors.

Having arrived in Alexandria, we once more joined the main fleet in a round of exercises, but it seemed clear that we were some way below the standard of the regular members of the Mediterranean fleet. This led shortly afterwards to the Commander-in-Chief. Admiral Sir William Fisher (The Great Agrippa) announcing that he intended to proceed to sea in H. M. S. Ajax to witness her at exercises. He came onto the bridge at 8 a. m. where I was Midshipman of the watch, dolled up in my best suit. After a few minutes, whilst we were clearing the harbour at about 15 kriots, the C-in-C suddenly whipped round, pointed at me and said 'You are yawning boy, go to the top of the fore-mast'.

This was not a time for informing him that I was not yawning, I had my best suit on, and that I suffered badly from vertigo, all of which statements were true, and I left the bridge and proceeded to the foot of the mast to gaze up at respectively the fore-mast, the top mast and then the polemast, stretching up some 150 feet which is about 140 feet higher than the level at which I get dizzy. The fear of the great Agrippa was even greater than the fear of death, so up I started! To cut a long story short one long hour later I reached the top, not only petrified with fear, but with arms aching almost to the point of having to let go from pulling one's way up the wire ladder step by step. Life was not made easier by the fact that the ship having reached the open sea, she was rolling slightly, so one moment one was hanging out one side and a moment later on the other.

Desire for survival is a great spur, because if asked in cold blood, I would not have ever believed I could achieve it. Weird thoughts went through my mind during, the climb, such as whether my parents would have a claim against the Admiralty if I was killed; however two hours after starting I was back on deck again with my suit badly damaged. Pausing only to decide not to ask the C-in-C for the price of a new suit, I was back on watch on the bridge again, and having done my party piece was left in peace by the great man for the rest of the day.

And so 1935 moved into 1936 via a traditional naval Christmas and a seemingly continuous series of exercises to keep the Fleet at the highest level of efficiency, which description now even included us, and in early January we sailed to Malta to dry-dock and have a short refit, and then returned whence we started.

On 20th January, His Majesty King George V died and on the 28th, the day of his funeral, all ships fell in by Divisions for 70 minutes whilst a gun was fired every minute.

Much the same routine continued until mid-April when we returned to Malta for a longer refit. Continuous exercises interposed with some rugby and hockey, and, a Midshipman's pay being what it was, a recreational trip ashore about once every two weeks for a game of tennis and a good meal at a cheap continental restaurant.

Alexandria was an ideal recreational base for the fleet with two good clubs with every kind of sport, reasonable beaches, very good restaurants with a considerable French influence and a considerable number of night clubs, all except the last being relatively cheap.

Here, at Malta, the Midshipmen had their first real break since September, and we were packed off for nine days to a camp arid rifle range to the north of the island where we lazed, swam and played tennis. We also hired a small car and toured the sights such as Citta Vechia, the ancient capital of the island, the cathedral, the catacombs, and the old ruins purporting to date from when Malta was joined to North Africa. We returned in time to join the ship, with the intention of sailing once more back to the daily grind at Alexandria, but first we were ordered to proceed to Marseilles to escort the boy King Farouk in the S. S. Viceroy of India who had been pulled out of Harrow to return to take up the throne on the death of his father. The transition from innocent schoolboy to lecherous despot was not to take very long.

We were soon back in the old routine, and began to wonder if we would ever return to that South American lotus land that had been our objective when we left England a year ago.

By way of diversion, I note that on Wednesday 27th May, the Queen Mary sailed on her maiden voyage to New York; Mahmoud, owned by the Aga Khan won the Derby at 100-8, and Amy Mollison flew from Cape Town to London in 4 days 16 hours, beating the previous record by over two days.

At this time the Italian conquest of Abyssinia was nearing completion, because although the League of Nations applied sanctions, they excluded the one commodity, oil, which would have made the situation critical for the Italians. This decision by the League appears to have been due to the fact that the United States, which was not a member, refused to agree to apply oil sanctions, no doubt for commercial reasons, but also probably influenced by their isolationist tendencies. However, parallel to this quietening on the Abyssinian front brewed up the beginning of the Palestine trouble, which was to run and run, and indeed is still not solved.

These first rumbles of trouble started because the Jews who were scattered all over the World took the view that it was their original Holy Land, and as such they had every right to return to it, rule it, and make it as they wish. The immigration began to rise to thousands, and the Palestinian Arabs who over recent times had come to consider the area as their own, strongly objected to these large incursions and asked Britain to stop the flow which she has refused to do. This has resulted in strikes and riots, and the Palestine problem had begun . . .

By 10th June we had moved from Alexandria to Haifa as back up for the troubles and the Lotus Land seemed as far away as ever! We were sending guards on all trains and also guarding the oil tanks, and we heard that Fridays were likely always to be the worst days as this is the Moslem Sabbath and the priests at the Mosques rouse their congregation to a frenzy. This was, no doubt, the reason why we were given free tickets to the open air cinemas on a Friday, the theory probably being that if there were a lot of service people in the cinema, they were less likely to chuck bombs over the wall into the auditorium!

On 12th July 1936 the Fleet received news that it was dispersing from Alexandria, and that ships from other squadrons would be returning after ten long months away. The Australia and Sydney back to Australia, the Berwick to China, the Galatea to home waters, and last but not least, the Exeter and Ajax to South America. The reason was that the Government were lifting their ineffectual sanctions on Italy, and the permanent Mediterranean fleet together with the Army could look after the Palestinian situation. Two days later, in a high state of euphoria, we sailed to Malta for a brief period in dry dock and to take on stores. Here two of us went greyhound racing for the first time, arid having been told that the surest way to win was to bet each race on the dog that widdled the most, no doubt something to do with the doping, we followed this somewhat unusual advice successfully, and returned to the ship with an appreciable augmented stipend.

All these international events, which played such a part in our lives so long ago, seem so distant and insignificant over fifty years on, but this was not quite to be the end, before we were to get back to our station which we had left ten long months ago. A revolt had been smouldering in Spain ever since the Communists had won the general election for the first time, and on Saturday 18th July this finally broke out in the garrisons of Spanish Morocco, and at once spread to the mainland. Fighting soon broke out in the large towns such as Barcelona and Seville, and ships of the Mediterranean Fleet were soon busy evacuating refugees.

We arrived in Gibraltar on 28th July to oil and store and at last sail back to the West Indies, but it was still not to be. On arrival, our sailing orders were placed in abeyance and the C-in-C temporarily hoisted his flag in us, until his new flagship arrived from England. Gibraltar was full of Communist refugees, who could not be sent back because the border was held by Monarchist rebels who were gradually winning over many of the big cities.

On 3rd August we finally left harbour and sailed west, straight into the line of fire of units of the Spanish Navy, busy bombarding rebel strongholds. And so we finally said farewell . . .

The Spanish Civil war was to go on for a long time, with much cruelty and suffering, the Russians pouring in supplies for the Communists, and Hitler and Mussolini trying out their new aircraft and military weapons by supplying them to General Franco and his rebel forces, who were finally to win the day. Amidst all this, the Olympic games took place in Berlin!

We called briefly at Bermuda to smarten ourselves up to 'Showing the flag' standards once more and sailed again for the start of a memorable nine months cruise which would circumnavigate South America. We arrived at: Cristobal on the morning of August 21st, which is the U. S. Base at the Atlantic entrance to the Panama Canal, and immediately started a very different life to that which we had recently been used.

Time was spent in much sporting and social liaison with the local U. S. Navy and a very interesting tour of the full working of the Panama Canal, and although I was to traverse it a number of times subsequently, the speed and efficiency of its operation has never ceased to amaze me. It was intriguing to see that Cristobal which was part of the U. S. Canal Zone and operated by them, abutted Colon which was part of the state of Panama and the division ran right down the middle of the main street, with each country operating their own jurisdiction and currency on their side of the street. It was at Cristobal that the growing up process, retarded during our militant time in the Mediterranean, advanced once more.

Four of us Midshipmen were taken under wing of a couple of U. S. Naval Lieutenants and their wives and royally entertained during our free time. This initially entailed being given a traditional British Sunday lunch of 'Roast beef and Yorkshire pudding'. Where they got the beef I knew not; it was quite the toughest piece of leather I have ever eaten before or since and could only be swallowed whole in slices, since it was beyond chewing. This difficult process was however much assisted by the American traditional Sunday morning of 'Dry Martinis' of which we had imbibed several.

In the evening we were taken to either the Atlantic, or the Moulin Rouge on the Colon side of the street which were night clubs with dancing and a 'strip' cabaret. Commonplace in these days, such things were then unheard of in the United Kingdom, and our eye-balls were practically abandoning their sockets. On our last evening, the customary dance and cocktail party was given on board for all the locals, including our own hosts, and at the end, the Commander, who had noticed when ashore that the Midshipmen had been advancing their education faster than he deemed proper, announced that the Midshipmen were to keep watch through the night, ostensibly because he thought there might be a large number of inebriates returning from ashore amongst the ships company.

This gave cause for thought, as we had arranged a farewell night club run with our local hosts. It was accordingly decided that we would split the night up into two hour sections, and the first spell from ten until midnight would establish which of the two night clubs our superior officers were patronising, and setting up shop in the other one. Our hosts then ferried us back and forth to swap watches as the night progressed.

Culebra Cut, Panama Canal

I remember that I was on watch from midnight until 2 a. m. , and so was ferried back at the beginning and collected again at two and finally returned to the ship when the party ended at four, only to retire to my hammock until 6 a. m. when it was time to turn out and get ready for sailing, having had the, so far, latest night on the tiles of my young life! On reflection we must have used a certain degree of skill in our planning, for our masters never found out how we foiled their plan.

We entered the Canal at 11. 00 a. m. and traversed the three Gatun locks which lift the ship up to the level of the large man made lake, which was caused by flooding the central valley of the isthmus. After the lake is the most interesting part of the whole traverse, which is called the Culebra Cut. This is where for some ten miles the canal is cut through the continental divide, and is continually dredged, and so narrow that when two ships have to pass, they approach head on and at the last minute alter course slightly to pass on the diagonal. Finally we dropped down to sea level again through three locks, entered the Pacific Ocean at 5. 30 p. m. on 24th August, and headed for Buenaventura the Pacific port of Columbia, arriving there three days later.

Buenaventura, as far as I was concerned, really had nothing going for it except the first experience of a low lying hot poverty ridden town of the Pacific jungle, situated on a wide muddy river estuary. and perhaps to us its greatest claim to fame was that the chart of the estuary which was used for entering port, was surveyed by Captain Fitzroy of H. M. S. Beagle assisted by Mr Darwin, Gentleman! The port owed its existence to the export of Colombian gold and platinum. Perhaps now there are other Colombian commodities!

It was noted in my log at this time, that in the Mediterranean:-

(i)   The Spanish Civil War was at its height with argument and counter-argument between major powers on who was breaking the Neutral Pact and supplying one side or the other.

(ii)   Mussolini announced on the steps of the Plaza Venezia, that he had introduced a new conscription scheme and could mobilise a million soldiers in a day, never for war, but in the cause of eternal peace!

(iii)   Greece had declared Martial Law to stop the communists getting into power.

(iv)   The Arab general strike in Palestine continued.

Only a few months ago, we were in the midst of all this, but distance lends enchantment . . . and it all seemed very far removed.

We departed from Buenaventura without regret and arrived on Wednesday 2nd September at Guayaquil, the port of Ecuador, which again is up a jungle banked, fast running, thickly muddied river, but there the comparison ends. Guayaquil was a large prosperous bustling port, with the river rushing along at about six knots, which made one's task of driving the ships boats to and from shore, and holding the boat alongside the gangway whilst passengers embarked, a hairy and somewhat interesting experience.

Next day I embarked on one of the most interesting trips of the whole of my Midshipman's time, and perhaps its scale was a measure of the prestige of the British in general and the Royal Navy in particular. After all, we were just one of His Majesty's cruisers visiting a South American port. The Captain and eleven officers had been invited by the President to make a formal visit to Quito, the capital, some distance away, and entirely at the expense of the Government. The party included two Midshipmen, and I was lucky enough to be one.

We entrained at 10. 00 a. m. for what has, through television, now become to be known as one of the great train journeys of the world and for the first two hours we crossed the coastal alluvial plain through jungle full of myriad's of birds of every size and hue. By noon we reached the foothills of the Andes and began to climb steadily up through sub-tropical woods, getting ever thinner, and stopping occasionally at a little indian village, where each family has its own cow and pig and a plot of land, and manages to eke out a poverty ridden existence.

The climb up the Andes is so steep and riddled with hairpins that the train cannot get round the hairpin bends, but at each hairpin, drives into a siding, the points are then changed, the train reverses to the next corner, repeats the same procedure, then goes forward up the next stretch and so on. The highest point is 12, 200 feet and then there is a gradual descent to Quito which is 10, 000 feet.

Most officers were put up at the main, and for all practical purposes, the only hotel, but another Midshipman and myself were put up in a private house of remarkable interest.

It was a mini-castle with a lovely garden, looking right out on to the well known snow covered peaks of Chimborazo and Cotopaxi. It was owned by Don Frederico Stagg of British nationality, but partly Ecuadorian ancestry. An elegant and dapper man in his early forties, he lived in this large and beautiful spot alone with numerous indian servants and an old Rolls Royce as immaculate as himself.

It transpired that his grandfather was with Simon Bolivar when South American countries were winning their independence, and as far as can be seen, they invented Ecuador simply by drawing the area on a map! The grateful populace built this estate for his grandfather and heirs in perpetuity and there he was, young rich and lonely. It was particularly sad because he had a young beautiful American wife to whom he was devoted, who died of T. B. and in his bedroom was a large photograph of her in front of which was always a bowl of water with just one rose floating in it.

After a mild attack of altitude sickness, we were driven in to Quito in the old Rolls next morning to join the rest of the party, and to get our first glimpse of the oldest capital city of South America. It was delightful to see how unspoilt it still was and portrayed still very much one's National Geographical image of an old Andean indian town with many indians still walking about dressed in red rugs and funny hats.

All the officers were invited to Ecuadorian cavalry stables to go riding later in the morning, and it seemed that I was the only one who had never been on board any horse before, let alone a cavalry charger. Somehow the grooms cottoned on to this, and judging by the nodding and winking, I was allocated the most fiery of them all. We moved onto the adjoining plains and cantered off through the adjoining country side: at least the other eleven did. I soon realised that being aboard a stroppy horse that was travelling fast and did not speak English was no place for me. Accordingly, I removed my feet from the stirrups and pushed upwards, allowing the horse to continue its journey unhindered by the rider, and myself landed with a bump on Ecuador, painful but very much less so than the alternative. Having rejoined the party on their return, we adjourned for lunch at the cavalry club.

That evening Don Frederico gave a dinner party for his two guests and others. In those days, there were only two or three British residents outside the Embassy, but a small local exclusive set, the young of which all going to university in the United States, and the pick of them being asked to dinner. After dinner, the lights were dimmed and the curtains pulled back, and there before us was all the majesty of the Andes by moonlight. In came one of the servants and stood on the balcony in the dark and played the most haunting music on his pipes, and when he had finished and was coming in, I mentioned how very moving I found it, and immediately the pipes were given me as a present, and I have them to this day.

After that evening, anything had to be an anti-climax, but next morning we were taken to a ranch that supplied all Quito with milk and meat, whose owner was a friend of Don Frederico. The ranch had a swimming pool fed by a mineral water spring, and apart from the novelty of bathing in soda water, ones floating glass of 'Scotch' was topped up directly from a bath side tap. In the evening was the inevitable official reception at the British Embassy, at which were all the same 'young' as the previous night's dinner, and six o'clock the next morning we caught the train back to Guayaquil, sent off on our way, even at that early hour, by the same 'young''. And so ended a truly memorable visit to a then as yet totally unspoilt city, made all the more magic for us by our remarkable host.

Two day later we sailed overnight to a total contrast

We arrived in the morning at what appeared to be a piece of Peruvian Desert waste, but on closer inspection was found to be the Canadian oilfield installation at Talara, with a very hospitable and very thirsty population of some hundred Canadians, against whom we proceeded to play every sort of game, and with whom we proceeded to consume every sort of drink.

The community of Talara was a very good example of what one met over and over again in one's service career, be it here, Aden, the Andaman Islands, North Borneo and many others. Whenever one met a small community of this nature, and where one might expect a certain bitchiness one to the other, I always found the reverse to be true, and there was usually a very happy community spirit.

It was certainly true of this desert community, hundreds of miles from anywhere in a fairly trying climate. It may be, that the arrival of a cruiser in their midst was somewhat of an event in their lives; none the less, their generosity, with limited resources, warmed the heart, and made all the more for a very enjoyable visit, belieing completely the first impressions, as we gazed from the deck at the Peruvian desert.

We moved on to the port of Payta next day, yet another small and squalid Pacific town, only this time desert and not jungle based. It owed its existence to being the outlet for the considerable Peruvian cotton fields in the area. It was here that I first really became aware of the large number of little British owned Export/Import firms scattered in every little port all over the world.

The whole of the South American Pacific coast was the province of Duncan Fox & Co. colloquially known as Drunken Fox and serviced inevitably by a British Line, the Pacific Steam Navigation Company, and each port with its own little British club. Here in Payta, dirty and arid and miles from anywhere, were the handful of 'Brits' operating the trade and shipping of the area, with their typical little club and its tennis court and sipping their gin and ginger beers, for such was their local drink at sundown. Different views different drinks, but the same way of life in endless little ports in endless dreary places all over the globe. Perhaps Payta was even more English in this respect than usual in that its prime export was Panama hats.

Our next stop, on 19th September was Chimbote, on the boundary between the desert and the beginnings of cultivation, where the hinterland had large areas of marsh heavily populated with wild duck. Chimbote was a fascinating place, basically a large natural almost land-locked harbour, surrounded by the piled up excrement of masses of sea birds for many centuries, and collected and exported as guano, which was the best natural fertiliser known. The collection of sea birds offshore must surely be unique in the world, feeding on the mass of fish that congregate on the boundary between the cold Humboldt currents coming up from the south and the warm Equatorial current.

On the first afternoon, the wardroom went ashore for a giant duck shoot with every available gun, and the Midshipmen were ordered ashore to beat and pick up. Duck were being shot out of the sky in large numbers for some hours, and the shooters were mystified how difficult it seemed for we who were picking up to find where they landed. However, a fair number were turned over to them, and the rest were smuggled on board, and we ate duck until we were sick of it.

The following day was a good example of the enjoyment that can be found, even in the most outlandish places. In the morning we went away in the motor boat with some delayed fuse under-water charges and fired them off in the bay and collected enough fish that were stunned to feed the whole ship's company of some five hundred. Then the Midshipmen, sharing the only rod, went spinning behind the boat. When it was my turn, I had the most bizarre piscine situation of my life; I had turned round to talk momentarily to someone else in the boat, and when I looked back on feeling a jerk, I found that a pelican had dived down and taken the spoon, and I was busy trying to reel in the bird some fifty feet up in the air. After much tugging, the line finally snapped and the pelican flapped off, the spoon hanging nonchalantly from its bill.

In the afternoon, three of us climbed Mount Chimbote which rises straight up from one end of the harbour, and was only difficult in that the sides comprised of very loose shale. After getting back to the ship just as it was getting dark we were ready for a large dinner of – guess what – fish followed by roast duck!

Lest it be thought that the idea of coming to such a place was for rural jollification, it should be pointed out that we were here for a total of six days in order to have a period of drills and exercises after an absence from these for nearly a month and also to get the ship spotless before our next visit, which was to one of the major cities of South America, namely Lima.

We arrived at Callao at 09. 00 on 25th September. This is the port for Lima, and like so many of such ports, was as grimy and scruffy as Lima was attractive and well laid out, the two being connected by a non-stop fifty mile an hour tram service.

On the evening of our arrival we attended a reception at the British club, a few stories up in one of their taller buildings, although none are very tall because of the danger of earthquakes. In the middle of the reception it was noticed that the liquid was swilling around in one's glass and there was a slight swaying sensation. The natural conclusion was that our hosts were plying us with some pretty heady stuff, and it was only when they pressed us to join them in a hasty retreat to ground level that we realised that it really had been a minor earthquake, which had caused interesting sensations, but no damage.

The following day we played our first game of rugger since leaving the Mediterranean, just losing to the British colony, arid afterwards, another midshipman who had been in the team and I were invited to supper by the British leading archaeologist heading the team who were excavating the old Inca ruins on behalf of the Peruvian government. There were strict laws prohibiting the export of any of the finds, but notwithstanding this, our host gave me a lovely old piece of Inca pottery in the shape of a carved jug, which has a place in my living room to this day.

The following evening another Midshipman, Dasher Spriggs and I went ashore to look at Lima, have a quiet supper, and. return on board, blissfully unaware of what in fact was to ensue. We found what seemed a reasonable restaurant for supper, and were ordering our food, when our attention was drawn to two large and very tough looking men at an adjoining table, who each had in front of him on their plate a whole large fish which was being demolished head and all, in rather the same fashion that a cat demolishes such a meal. They beckoned us over to join them, and it transpired that one was a Russian and the other a Czech, and they asked us to be their guests firstly for supper and then for the South American middleweight boxing championship which was to take place later that evening for which they had ring-side seats. This invitation was readily accepted by two impecunious Midshipmen.

After supper, they drove us to the large open air stadium and it was soon clear that they were well known there. They took us straight to the dressing rooms of the evening's main contestants and introduced them to us, and after wishing them well, we were taken out into the open towards our ring-side seats. At this moment, a powerful spot-light was played on to us and the whole stadium erupted into a cacophony of yelling and booing, and all that Dasher and I wanted at that moment was for the earth beneath us to open up.

Worse was to follow, for our first sight, when we escaped from the glare of the spotlight, was of the British Minister sitting in the front row, flanked on one side by our Captain and the other by the Commander, all dressed in dinner jackets; our hosts could not muster a collar between them. On our asking for an explanation of this extraordinary reception, our hosts readily explained that the stadium had boxing and wrestling on alternate weeks and that on the wrestling weeks, they were the two dirty villains and well known to the assembled audience. We had clearly now passed the point of no return, and the only way was forward. In the event we had a very interesting night's boxing and were then taken to their hotel and given a whiskey and a sniff of cocaine before returning to the ship. In the euphoria that was then reigning, I asked my two new-found East European friends to formal guest night dinner in the mess two nights hence which they readily accepted!

Come the dawn, and the full horror of what happened and was still to happen filling my mind, I decided it was time for bold action, and so after breakfast I knocked on the Commander's cabin door, told him the whole story and waited for the thunder-bolt to fall.

To my relief, I thought I saw a slight twinkle in his eye behind the stern exterior and finally he said that there was to be no punishment, but that I was to learn that in true Naval tradition my two guests were to be received for formal dinner to which they had been asked, and treated with all the hospitality for which our service was famous and that I was to stand all the costs myself.

Two evenings later, precisely at the time I had invited them, arrived my two erstwhile friends, I in my full mess dress, stiff front and bow tie, they in turn still collarless, cauliflower-eared and unshaven, but beaming with delight. My mess mates played up magnificently, and everything was done precisely by tradition and the two chums totally unembarrassed became the centre piece of attraction. Finally after we had risen from the table, the curiosity of the wardroom had grown too great, and the two wrestlers were summoned thence. That was the last I ever heard of them.

The previous evening also witnessed an unusual occurrence. The British Minister had told the Captain that he would like two Midshipmen to come and stay the night at the legation and Harold Dannreuther and I, as the two most senior, were despatched somewhat trembling with fear.

We need not have worried; we were met by Mrs. Forbes the Minister's wife, a bizarre lady, who walked around a lot of the time with a parrot on her shoulder, rather like Long John Silver, only with a full complement of legs. We were then ushered in to the Minister who informed us that he would meet us for drinks shortly when we would be joined by the two most attractive young ladies from the British colony. He then gave us some money and told us to take them to the best hotel in Lima, where a table had been reserved, for dinner and dancing. After seeing them home, we were to return directly to our rooms in the legation without disturbing anyone.

This programme was followed with no little enjoyment, and the piece de resistance was when we arrived back at our room in the early hours, to find on a table between our beds, whiskey, soda and a plate of caviare sandwiches! Next morning after breakfast, we returned to the ship feeling we had met and stayed with the most human and understanding person ever to enter the diplomatic, service! I also awarded him further bonus marks for not recognising me from the stadium the night before!

It might be appropriate to digress here to mention that no account has been given in each port of the formal entertainment given and received by the ship to the local inhabitants, in order not to be too repetitive.

The Ajax, like all cruisers and above in those days, carried her own Royal Marine Band, which could play martial music, classical, suitable for dinner party accompaniment or dance music. At every port, depending on its size and the appropriateness of the entertainment, we might give a formal reception for any number from 40 to 400, or a dance or both and of course the ship was open to visitors for one afternoon in each stay when any number up to 2, 000 might look round the ship.

In addition we played the locals at every appropriate sport, and the ship's teams were usually, but not unnaturally, just weaker than our opponents, but not to the point of embarrassment. I represented the ship in the tennis, rugger and hockey teams, as appropriate and when required. In return, we were always entertained by the local dignitaries, and local organisations were very good at arranging outings, dances and the like for the ship's company.

As an example, in Lima there was a reception at the English Club on arrival, and there were matches against the locals at golf, tennis, rugger and soccer. The local British owned brewery arranged a large dance with free beer for the ship's company, and the local railway an all day trip in a special train complete with beer for everybody in the ship who could be spared up 12, 000 feet into the Andes and back again.

In return our ship's concert party gave a show to a packed house in the local theatre; we were open to visitors on one day, and exclusively for the Peruvian Navy on another, and on our last evening gave an official reception for 250 people, followed by a private dance. Quite separate from the above, the Captain would be paying and receiving official calls and giving and receiving lunch parties and the like.

Of course, on top of all this, normal ship's life went on; Midshipmen either kept watch or ran the ship's boat, did their divisional work, and received instruction. If any commodity went short in all this, the first casualty was always 'sleep'.

And so, after four ports and four weeks in Peru, in the great diversity of desert in the north to sophisticated city in the south we sailed for the even more diverse country of Chile, thousands of miles long, but never more than a few hundred miles wide, ranging from desert in the north to almost antarctic, desolation in the south, and from the sea in the west to some of the highest peaks in the world to the east.

The people were to prove to be fiercely pro-British, having to a great degree owed their liberation to Admiral Cochrane, and whose Navy which was their pride and joy, was not only precisely modelled on ours but was in the main comprised of ships that had started life in the Royal Navy. The cruise through Chile was to take twelve weeks finishing at Punta Arenas in the Magellan Straits at Christmas time.

Arid so it was that we left Peru and arrived at the North Chilean port of Iquique, once more in the desert, on Monday 31st October, only two months after having left our duties in Alexandria with the Mediterranean fleet, but light years away in geography and experience. Iquique showed in every way the fate that had befallen it: a town of many thousand inhabitants, it was the derelict ghost of its former self. Once the greatest exporter of nitrate for fertiliser and explosives, the discovery of synthetic means of production had left the town isolated and poverty stricken.

Like so many other places round the world where the British had come and enriched themselves and their environment, only to be stranded when the tide of prosperity ebbed, there was still a British colony of a hundred and fifty, with nowhere to go and no financial means of getting there anyway! Some were, no doubt, of second and third generation and had resigned themselves to play out time where they were. There was nevertheless the inevitable British club, and no less inevitable, the head of the British community, Colonel Le Fevre, and the annual visit of the British Cruiser was the red letter day in their lives. Both at the club and in the Colonel's house, considerable hospitality was dispensed, and all the customary games were played against the locals.

This led to one near catastrophe: the programme arranged before we arrived included a basket ball match between the local team and the Midshipmen of H. M. S. Ajax. Our team in the event were three who played it once before and two, including me who had seen it once but had never played, and we assumed the enemy would be much the same. We were duly bussed to the stadium dressed in our assorted sports clothes, and our embarrassment on arrival can be imagined when we found ourselves in a packed stadium of yelling fans, two brass bands and our opponents who were one of the leading professional teams of North Chile.

Something had gone seriously wrong in the planning, and luckily both their team and the supporters realised this, and the evening turned into a hilarious success. with all our feeble efforts being cheered on wildly by the fans, and the opposition only scoring when we did, and even then helped by them and the final score reading 12-10 to our opponents! Having done our best to turn a sow's ear into a silk purse, we then asked our opponents on board for a drink, and by the end of the evening there were even stronger bonds of Anglo-Chilean solidarity, and an evening that at one time looked as if it was heading for disaster and ridicule tuned into an occasion of much good humour.

The standard cocktail party and dance was given to the British colony and leading Chileans, and we landed a full church parade on the Sunday, with the service at the English church taken by our own Chaplain, and the following day we sailed away. The last act was one to be witnessed at various times during one's Naval career. The ship edging slowly off the jetty, the Royal Marine band on the quarter-deck playing old sentimental tunes of far off Blighty, and the British colony on the quay almost to a person waving their handkerchiefs and then returning to their hum-drum marooned lives until the next ship, next year.

Our next stop south, at which we arrived next morning, had some of the hallmarks of Iquique, but not to the same extent because some of the reasons of Antafogasta's existence were still in place. Bolivia has no outlet to the sea, and all sea-borne trade travels via the Antafogasta-Bolivia railway, needless to say British owned, and this gives rise not only to a limited prosperity, depending on the abundance of Bolivian trade, but also the presence of a British population of some hundred, engaged either in railways or shipping.

There is little more to say about this visit which was virtually a duplicate of our last port, less the basket ball match. We were along side a jetty here for the first time on the Pacific coast, and so access to the ship was easier on 'open to visitors' day than elsewhere. A measure of the popularity such a visit as ours engendered was that the ship was open from 4 p. m. to 6 p. m. , and two thousand one hundred people tried to come on board, saved from a near riot by the excellent Chilean police, using successful, but by our standards, somewhat unorthodox methods to control the crowd. Once again we sailed away, a week after our arrival, waved off by some four hundred English and Chilean people on the jetty.

I never understood why we went to the next place called Coquimbo some two days later. We spent five days there, with little social activity except for the annual spring festival known as the 'Fiesta de Primaverra' which was in fancy dress, the locals ignoring us, and we reciprocating, and perhaps this break was a blessing for it enabled us to have a few days normality before three weeks in Valparaiso.

We arrived there on Wednesday 28th October to stay until 14th November and was one of the highlights of the whole two year commission, without anything particularly dramatic taking place. The town itself is of no great beauty, but has a most attractive residential suburb, Vina-del-Mar, made up of fine avenues and houses and clubs and casino. The inhabitants were very pro-British and most spoke English excellently. In addition, whilst the official exchange rate was 40 pesos to the pound, it was perfectly acceptable to exchange the pounds in which we were paid for 140 pesos.

The result was, that even on a Midshipman's pay, one was able to go ashore, take a young lady out to dinner and dance at the Vina-del-Mar casino and arrive back on board only about a couple of quid lighter. As far as the Midshipmen were concerned, there was a considerable liaison with our opposite numbers in the Chilean battleship Almirante Latorre, the only snag being that there were fifty six of them and only six of us. We lost heavily at athletics, won at tennis and drew at water polo, but where we were sunk out of hand, but

The Patagonian cruise

going down with all flags flying, was when we were asked to their mess for a guest night dinner, being poured back to our ship at a late hour, whilst our senior officers looked discreetly the other way.

During our stay, Dasher Spriggs and I visited Santiago, the capital, for two days and a night, travelling by express de luxe pullman train that would have put any British railway to shame. Santiago is a very well laid out modern town at the foothills of the Andes and we stayed at new Hotel Splendid. Apart from goofing around, we played a round of golf at the inevitable English country club, and returned to the ship at Valparaiso the following day.

Lest it be thought that we young gentlemen were living pretty high on the hog, it is worth pointing out that our pay was £90 per annum augmented by an allowance from our parents of a further £50; out of this we had first to pay our mess bills, and a measure of how much we could do with the small change is an indication of the cheapness of our environment.

On leaving Valparaiso, we were to have proceeded to the Chilean Naval Base at Concepcion, but they had a severe outbreak of typhus and so instead were diverted to the Chilean owned island of Juan Fernandez, immortalised as the Island where Alexander Selkirk was marooned, and some consider as the island on which Daniel Defoe based Robinson Crusoe, although the island itself ill fits the description in the book. Its more modern fame is that the German cruiser Dresden lies in the harbour, where it was sunk in the First World War, and it exports some six thousand lobsters to the mainland every week. The island rises, covered in thick vegetation, to some three thousand feet, and near the top is a plaque marking Selkirk's look-out post.

Our main social attraction was to rig flood-lights at night to shine in the water which attracted swarms of fish, weighing in excess of three pounds each, and these could be readily abstracted by a fish-hook baited with bread on the end of a piece of string. The drawback was that the messman served up this somewhat gustatorily unattractive diet so frequently to save money that in the end we cut off his source of supply! The island also gave us the opportunity to carry out drills and exercises before returning once m ore to the social round.

We left Juan Fernandez and picked up our original cruise again as planned at Puerto Corral which is at the mouth of the Valdivia river, for which town it is the port. Valdivia has a very large German population, owning all the main businesses. A lot of our time during our stay was spent in going up and down the river in ferry boats to carry out various liaison activities with the populace of Valdivia, interspersed with one bizarre episode.

Admiral Cochrane, based on Puerto Corral, had achieved a splendid victory in Chile's struggle for independence, and it was arranged that the local dignitary would unveil a bronze plaque to his memory in the presence of our Captain and a ship's guard of honour, and all went well until the moment of unveiling, when it was found that some felon had nicked the plaque in the night, to the horror of the dignitary and the scarce concealed mirth of the guard of honour.

It was now, of course, the beginning of the southern summer in December, and with it began a bleak but awe inspiring cruise for over a thousand miles threading through the islands of the Patagonia channels from Puerto Montt in the north to Punta Arenas in the south.

Puerto Montt indeed was to be our last civilised stop and it was from here that we had an expedition into the south Chilean lakes and rivers. The longest lake, Lake Llancuhue is twenty two miles long and a hundred and fifty fathoms deep with a mountain rising to a snow capped peak on one side, and the volcano 'Osorno' rising similarly on the other. This is but one of a chain of lakes, albeit the longest, joined by fast running rivers, partly cataract, and of a bright green colour, believed to be due to an exclusive origin of melting snow, and together with the surround of majestic Andean peaks, must surely stand comparison with any scenery of this nature in the world.

After leaving Puerto Montt the real wildness began, and continued for a whole week as we went slowly south, pausing here and there to examine various anchorage's for suitability for use in war, and to ensure that there were no signs of other nations already having had the same thought. As we went south, so the vegetation got less and the ever present snow capped Andes ever more lowering with here and there a glacier coming down to the sea.

The geographical nomenclature showed the influence of the early British cartographers, not least Captain Fitzroy of H. M. S. Beagle assisted by 'Mr Darwin, Gentleman'. Such names followed one another as for example Kelly Harbour, Farquhar

Island, English Narrows and Alert Harbour. One wonders who Kelly and Farquhar were.

On our fifth day and well south and miles from any civilisation or habitation as we thought, and whilst at anchor, to our astonishment out paddled from an inlet, a Patagonian Indian family in a very crude home made craft. They were rightly considered to be almost the most basic human beings extant on earth, and how they survived with only ragged clothes made from old washed up sugar sacks and the like in that hostile intemperate climate is amazing.

Our typically warm hearted sailors immediately almost sunk their boat with volleys of corned beef tins and loaves of bread, the former being incapable of being opened, and the latter causing puzzlement as to what should be done with the bread. Attempts at eating the corned beef tins prior to opening them were soon discarded.

Finally on 21st December, after an enthralling week, we rounded the southern tip of the continent into the Magellan Strait and came to anchor in the civilised and prosperous town of Magellanes, now better known as Punta Arenas.

One never ceased to be amazed at the far flung nature of British influence and emigration, and here, thousands of miles from anywhere, in a Chilean town, complete with Army barracks and a Naval base, was a vigourous British colony, mainly Welsh, engaged in extensive and prosperous sheep farming, a branch of a British bank, the ubiquitous Duncan Fox, busy on their export-import business, and all the trappings that went with the British when they settled overseas. Whilst here we carried out a ceremony that was typical of the sort of unusual tasks that crop up on such a cruise from time to time.

On 26th April 1881, H. M. S. Dotterel was in this harbour, when its powder magazine suddenly blew up, there being only four survivors. The dead were laid to rest in the local cemetery, but now this was required for a new playing field, and so the dead had to be moved to a new cemetery. And so on Christmas Eve we landed a Royal Marine and Naval Guard and an official mourning party, which joined up with Chilean Army and Naval detachments and their band. Everybody marched to the cemetery where all the coffins were laid and covered in Union Jacks, and these were placed on three gun carriages; these were then pulled, one by our sailors and two by Chileans to the new cemetery through crowded streets. On arrival they were re-interred and our Chaplain conducted a short service. On conclusion, , the Chilean Mayor made a long speech saying how Chile mourned with England at this tragic disaster, whether it was the original explosion or the new playing field was not clear, and then, the ceremony over, we returned on board and continued our Christmas preparations.

We left Magellanes on 29th December crossing through the fascinating straits of that name, where the currents run at five knots in one direction, and then quickly turns to five in the other direction, in order to spend New Year in the Falkland Islands, spurred on by the fact that our Christmas mail had missed us and was probably waiting for us at Port Stanley.

It might be of interest to digress briefly here to a subject which may have become obscure with the passage of time. All through our Chilean cruise we were reading in the American press of the liaison and activities of our, as yet, uncrowned King Edward VIII with the American Mrs. Wallace Simpson, and we were only partly aware of the unwritten agreement amongst the British press not to publish any of these stories. Finally on 7th December, Mr Stanley Baldwin, the then Prime Minister announced in the House of Commons, the arrival of a constitutional crisis when he put to the cabinet. a request from the King that a bill be passed to allow him to marry a lady who need not be Queen of England. Mr Baldwin then informed the King on behalf of his own and Dominion parliaments that it was impossible to comply with his request.

It transpired that the Prime Minister was increasingly disquieted by the gossip in the American press, and so on 20th November had interviewed the King, Mrs. Simpson's divorce having been completed on the 18th, and had informed the King that the marriage he was contemplating was not practicable, and would not hold the approbation of the people. And so it was, that on 7th December, the Prime Minister pointed out to the King that, morganatic marriage being impossible, there were only two alternatives; one was to renounce Mrs Simpson and still remain Head of our Empire, and the other was to marry and leave the throne. The King, on 11th December finally announced that he wished to renounce the throne of England, and the rest is well known.

It might be interesting to record here the final words of Stanley Baldwin that formally closed the whole sorry affair. 'Whilst there is not a soul among us who will not regret this from the bottom of his heart, there is not a soul who wants to judge. We are not judges. I appeal to you for restraint and remembrance of our revered and beloved figure of Queen Mary. We have after all, as guardians of democracy in this little island, to do our work to maintain the integrity of Monarchy. Let us look forward and remember our country, and the trust reposed by our country, and let us rally behind our new King and help him. '

And so back to the Falkland Islands . . . . where we arrived on 30th December 1936.

The islands are very similar to what had been in one's mind's eye. A long low vista of wind-swept peaty tussock grass, like much of the Scottish Highlands, heavily grazed over by sheep. The town of Port Stanley (which is the only town) with a population of about 1, 500 is made up of a Cathedral and Government House, joined together by little bungalows in different colours with corrugated roofs. All cooking stoves and heating are from the unlimited supply of peat, coal and wood being virtually non-existent in these wind swept islands.

On New Years Eve there was a large dance in Stanley to which large numbers of our ship's company and officers went and which followed along normal lines, but the next day we gave a children's party on board which did not!

The children's party on the visiting warship is the big annual day that all the kids look forward to and each ship tries to out-do the one before. Indeed we put on a magnificent show with roundabouts, swings, slides and many other activities. In warmer climes the Midshipmen's contribution was normally to be pirates, with a plank over the ship's side along with we sent unsuspecting victims off the end and in to the sea, whence they swam back to the gangway to the great delight of the children. However, it was too cold here for this, so we borrowed the blacksmith's shop and turned it into a pirate's cave, complete with a cat-o-nine tails and handcuffs, which believe it or not, were still carried in ship's stores. Visiting children were supplied with imitation rum and other goodies. Our downfall was to be that we thought it would be a good idea in order to help our animation, if we gave ourselves real rum.

During the course of the afternoon we were visited by the local guide leader in her uniform, a Miss Hoare no less, though no relative, and we, and she, thought that it would be a good idea to handcuff her to the metal stanchion in the middle of the cave, and all the assembled children could dance round her with the pirates uttering blood curdling threats.

So far, so good. Alas when the novelty wore off and it was time to release the prisoner, the real rum had had its toll and none of us could find the key of the handcuffs. Finally, after much searching, we had with some embarrassment to find the duty Artificer to come with a hacksaw and saw through the handcuffs in order, finally, to release a by now somewhat irate captive whose sense of humour had long since deserted her!

The greater part of the following week appears to have been taken up in the seamen going ashore daily to manhandle an old 6' gun, taken from H. M. S. Lancaster in 1916, up Sapper Hill at the back of Stanley and mounting it as defence against any invader in some future war, although what protection this old piece would have given is open to conjecture. There were also opportunities to visit the large penguin rookeries and seal colonies which were of course new to us and of great fascination. Two penguins were brought back to the ship as pets and fed on a diet of herrings in tomato sauce which offended their taste as much as it did the humans, and since they were not settling down they were released at South Georgia which was to be our next stop.

Indeed, we sailed there on 8th January and for the first time got the real feel of the Southern Ocean. There was an almost lonely feeling as one steamed through these grey, rough, windswept seas, passing the typical flat-topped Antarctic icebergs which had calved off the continent's glaciers to the south and drifted up on the currents, whilst round us wheeled the wonderful albatrosses, with their vast wing spans and effortless flight. Periodically, in the sea around us, would be the spouting of various schools of whales, the Fin wales being predominant.

Two days later, we anchored in Cumberland Bay in South Georgia with its Argentine owned whaling station at Grytviken, and the few houses that accommodated the British Administrator of the island . The island is a truly magnificent sight, outstripping even what we had recently seen. The mountains came straight down to the sea from about 4000 feet, with snow lying all the way down to the lowest levels and in the valleys are fine glaciers.

The whaling company operated six catchers, all Norwegian manned, and although the season was only about three months long, the captains, mates and crew made very large sums of money and went home and did nothing for the rest of the year. Two of us were lucky enough to go out in a catcher, and briefly the system was as follows:-

The Captain was on the bridge and the mate in the crow's nest, and as soon as he sighted a school, he would come down to the bridge and relieve the Captain who went to the harpoon gun right in the bows. Then began the really skilful co-operation, the mate steering the ship to the Captain's hand signals, he trying to anticipate precisely where the whale would momentarily surface to blow. At the critical moment, he would fire the harpoon into the whale, which would immediately sound to a great depth. Attached to the harpoon

Whaling Factory, Grytviken

was 500 fathoms of 7' hemp which went through a pulley on a very strong spring at the mast head and thus down to the hold where it lay in coils.

In essence, therefore, the mast and the ship itself acted as a fishing rod. The line was then brought to a winch and the whale, which was either killed almost instantly, or struggled for a brief period, was winched to the surface. When the whale was surely dead, compressed air was blown into it to increase buoyancy, an identity flag was stuck into it, and the hunt was on again for another one. Once two or three had been caught, they were collected in, secured alongside and taken to the factory at Grytviken. Here each whale was hauled up on to a flensing plane and a big cut made by the tail on each side to which is fixed the eye of a wire. The other end was taken to a powerful capstan and the whale blubber peeled off in one operation and chopped up and put into vats for melting down to abstract the oil. The head and guts are then removed and the rest of the body chopped up and put into different vats to provide a lower grade of oil. In a very short time, one more magnificent creature had disappeared only to be followed by the next one.

The island provided magnificent walking with colonies of seals and penguins and myriad kinds of sea-birds, including vicious skuas, one of which dive-bombed me on a cliff when I was photographing a nest, causing me to drop and break my camera beyond repair. Against this backdrop, stood out of course, in a magnificent position the cross marking the grave of Sir Ernest Shackleton.

On the way back to the Falklands to return the Governor, who we had taken to South Georgia with us, we picked up an S. O. S. from the Discovery, who was carrying out research and surveying in the South Shetland Islands in the Antarctic, and turned south and increased to 28 knots. It transpired that a party of surveyors were missing from the island upon which they were based and were long overdue. When we arrived there, extensive searches were carried out in the vicinity of King George's Island.

By that night (for it is daylight until late) the men had been found on a small island, their boat having broken down and then sunk, and they had kept themselves alive by killing a seal with a pocket knife, which had sustained them for eight days. They were taken back to the Discovery suffering slightly from exposure, and dietary irregularity, but otherwise none the worse, and we in turn, with mission completed, headed for the Falklands.

Arid so drew to a close a truly fascinating five weeks through some of the earth's wilder shores and seas, and given to few to witness, and having sailed from Falkland, we headed to the opposite extreme in the form of the bright lights of the big cities of South America's Atlantic seaboard and back to the social whirl that went with 'showing the flag'.

Our first stop was Buenos Aires, and at the entrance to the River Plate we made rendezvous with our Flagship, H. M. S. York, flying the flag of the Commander-in-Chief Admiral Sir Matthew Best. In all our time on the station this was the first time that we had met the boss! We took station astern of her and entered harbour and berthed, one astern of the other.

In this day and age when of course the place is held in some contumely, it was worthy of note that then the British population of 30, 000 had considerable influence and ran much of the railways, commerce and estancias, with its social life based on the Hurlingham Club, then one of the finest clubs in the world. Buenos Aires was then the fifth biggest city on the globe.

Peggy was of course born in the Argentine and I had the opportunity of meeting a number of her uncles, aunts and cousins, including Douglas King who used to stay for his holidays with us all in Minehead, and who sadly was to be killed in the war when his aircraft was shot down in the Middle East.

There is little purpose in repeating the same social round in each port, but of course in a city such as this, the scale was much bigger and our joint reception with the York comprised all guests going there to be received by the C-in-C and where there was a reception area and two bars, and then, if so inclined, stepping across to the Ajax where there were another two bars, a band and dancing followed by a buffet. On the day that the ship was open to visitors, over three thousand came on board. As we were now in company with York between ports, and opportunities had been so few, all daylight hours were taken up in exercising together.

Our next stop was a day away at Mar del Plata, which could fairly be described as the Brighton of Buenos Aires; a big modern sea side resort, with every bit of sand covered in groups under bright umbrellas. The hinterland is the haven of the very wealthy, and I was asked out to lunch by a family I had met, only to find that their home comprised a large house approached by a long avenue of poplars and surrounded by beautiful old world walled gardens, a large private chapel, and an eighteen hole golf course with luxurious club house.

After leaving Mar del Plata, we were joined by another cruiser of our squadron, H. M. S. Exeter, and all three ships proceeded to Montevideo, the capital of Uruguay, which must have been quite an impressive sight for the locals. We then together sailed on to Rio de Janeiro, carrying out endless exercises by day and night on the way and on Thursday 18th February we approached one of the most famous harbours in the world, and the beauty of the setting certainly lived up to all that one had previously seen and read.

For the next few days, we combined the charms of Rio in the evening with receiving our annual inspection by the Commander-in-Chief by day, which ensured that there was no time for idleness. Having been on our own for so long, it was also very enjoyable catching up with old friends in the other ships, and swapping experiences of where we had been.

From Rio we sailed in company to our final South American visit, though why it was chosen I know not. This was to the port of Ceara in northern Brazil. It is a town of about 100, 000 people exporting coffee, cotton and hides and there is a perpetual strong swell coming in off the Atlantic. We had to anchor one and a half miles off shore and the swell was too bad to lower any of our boats, resulting in all communications with the town being by local lighters. There was no great sadness when we departed, in order to carry out a series of major exercises at sea and finally to anchor in Barbados to complete our never to be forgotten seven month circumnavigation of the South American continent.

The next three weeks were very different to all that had gone before. We were joined by the other two cruisers of our squadron, Appollo and Dragon, and we entered an intensive period of exercises and gunnery and torpedo practices to knock all the rust off that had accumulated during our lotus eating period! This terminated in our all gathering at Tortola and anchoring in two lines for the annual pulling regatta. This is one of the highlights of a squadron year, and races go on at half-hourly intervals for two days, the crews having practised intensively beforehand for weeks. The races vary from the veterans skiff with a crew of two to the big cutter races with crew of twelve. There is much rivalry and ribaldry and also much wagering, and all ships go 'out of routine', all day so that there can be plenty of cheering and water-borne support, and this is followed by much social interchange in the evenings in the officer's mess.

On 20th March, we finally arrived back at our base in Ireland's Island in Bermuda and had a quiet spell for a couple of weeks, only remarkable as far as I was concerned in that I was lucky enough to be picked to represent the island of Bermuda, together with two other Naval representatives in their annual rugger match against the combined teams of Harvard and Yale Universities, thus gaining the only international cap of my life. Furthermore in a nine all draw, I scored our only try!

My selection might have been helped by the fact that our new Gunnery Officer, who had recently joined and was in charge of Midshipmen, John Forrest, had recently retired from being a regular member of the England second row. He was a giant of a man with cauliflower ears and a very genial disposition who quaffed vast quantities of beer at the slightest excuse. Sadly this simple taste was shortly to lead to the beginning of his demise.

The whole of April was taken up in the main squadron exercises for the year, which included the Easter period. On Good Friday at about 11p. m I was on the bridge as Midshipman of the watch and the Captain was also there, when an apparition covered in a white sheet appeared up the ladder at the back of the bridge. An astonished Captain asked what the hell was going on, when from under the sheet came the unmistakable and heavily beer-laden voice of John Forrest, announcing that he was the Holy Ghost on his way to his resurrection! This charming and splendid character finished his days as a market gardener in Bath.

When April moved into May each cruiser dispersed to a separate colony to represent his Majesty King George VI for coronation day. We drew Trinidad and arrived there on 10th May in time to get in one rehearsal before the main parade on the actual day which was the twelfth. The following day we returned to Bermuda to hear that our passing out exams, which are the culmination of one's Midshipman's time were to be on the 27th.

These exams are oral, taken by a Captain and three Commanders on every aspect of seamanship, together with written papers on ship construction and signals. Not only was the exam itself stiff but out of a thousand marks, one needed 850 for a first class, 700 for a second and 600 to pass at all. I got 812 for a good second, and once the exam was over, things were different. Not only was there somewhat of a festive mood, but we were allowed to keep Officer of the Watch on our own and generally have other more responsible duties.

In mid-June we finally steamed out of Bermuda flying our paying off pendant and headed for Portsmouth after over two years away from England. Peggy and her mother were to meet me on arrival, and although we had kept closely in touch during those two years, one could not help wondering having left a girl in gym slip and bobbed hair, who one was going to meet two years later! The answer was a slim smart young woman with a fresh perm, smart red blouse and even smarter blue coat and skirt, and there was not even any mutual shyness, as might have been expected, but we more or less picked up where we left off.

Next day, all Midshipmen, with our belongings packed, were discharged from the ship, and the University of Life had come to an end. We were indeed lucky in the ship to which we went, and the experiences that came our way, which are given to but few. It now only remained to go on two months leave and then in September, proudly wearing our Sub-Lieutenants stripes to join up again with all erstwhile Dartmouth term mates to do a series of courses that were the Naval equivalent of conventional university time.

5
Back to the Classroom

AFTER OUR TWO YEARS AWAY, we all had two months leave, which in my, case was spent mostly in the Minehead area. Peggy's mother, long before I returned to England, had sold the big house, where at school age we all congregated in the holidays. The eldest daughter Joan had emigrated to Bermuda to look after the only child of a prosperous doctor, where she subsequently married and made her home; Jack the only boy, having completed his apprenticeship was an engineer in the North Metropolitan Electric Company in North London; Molly, the next daughter, was 'doing something in horses' on which she was mad, and Madeleine, the youngest, was helping on a farm near Taunton.

That left Peggy, who was both the brainiest and most ambitious of her family. It was her wish to get Higher Certificate in order to aim for more satisfying later employment, but her mother could not afford to pay for her to stay at school. Mrs. Bell, accordingly rented an enchanting cottage on Horner water.

Horner comprised eight cottages in a row by a green on the edge of Exmoor. Seven sold cream teas to the tourists in the summer and hers was the eighth. The green in front, and the Horner brook, full of little five inch trout, gurgling its way past the cottage and down to the sea at Porlock. The cottage did have water sanitation, but no electricity, and lighting was by oil lamps, and cooking on a magnificent coal range. The stags would come and bell on the green outside the window, and the setting was of blissful romance. It was also a wonderfully quiet place for Peggy to swot at Higher Certificate by correspondence course, allied to her always determined spirit, and after one year she had passed English Language, English Literature and two French papers with very high grades. Just as well, because shortly afterwards, I would be returning to the scene to widen the horizons of her concentration. Horner was to have one major drawback, which was that it was one hell of a place to get to and from Portsmouth without a car for a weekend!

Arid so, after two months of relaxed summer weather had drifted past, the Benbow term came together in September 1937 for the last phase of intensive formalised training since we first came together in January 1931. The five who opted for engineering specialisation, and the three for becoming Paymasters, these latter three because they had failed their eyesight test, had now left us to go their separate ways, and so of the original 34, after a few drop outs, there were but 21 of us still on the executive ladder.

Various of us had spent our Midshipman's time in the Home or Mediterranean fleets, on the China station and on the South American and the swapping of yarns on coming together once more after two years was formidable, but after hearing them all, I was confident that none had had such a varied experience as the four of us from H. M. S. Ajax.

The period from September to April comprised a series of short courses in Gunnery, Torpedo and Electronics, Navigation, Signals and Staff course, which, together with the Seamanship exam already taken, determined, depending on the results, when one was promoted to Lieutenant. 85% was required for a first class, 70% for a second and 60% to pass. Each first class earned four months seniority, and each second earned two months. I got one first and five seconds which was just above halfway.

A friend, Peter Davey (who had been a Midshipman with me in the Ajax) and I worked to a fixed routine. Monday, Wednesday and Thursday we swotted far into the night, but Tuesdays were different. We had two seats for that night for the sixth row, centre gangway, permanently booked at the Portsmouth Hippodrome, which was one of the leading centres for variety in the country, when variety was very popular. Over the months we saw such fading stars, pathetically at the end of their careers, as Harry Lauder and Nellie Wallace, all the current stars such as Tommy Trinder, Max Miller and the like, including Gracie Fields, and also those who still had to make their name, such as the nineteen year old Vera Lynn, teeth and all.

The routine was always the same: in the long interval we stepped across to the 'Yorkshire Grey', which was the Theatre pub opposite, and had two pints of bitter at the public bar for the princely sum of fourpence a pint (old money!). It was a penny more at the private bar. After the show the ritual continued by adjourning to the 'Cut Loaf' in Southsea for a giant fry-up spread, and so back on board ready for the morrow. In those days nudes, by law, had to wear a G string, and to remain on the stage without moving. One week, seeing that there were going to be some such in the show, we enlisted two allies and reserved the box nearest the stage. Armed with a pair of braces and some bullets of wettened and compressed blotting paper for our makeshift catapult, we awaited the appearance of the statuesque nudes, with the intention of delivering a stinging blow, which should ensure their instant mobility.

The moment came, and the first bullet winged its way, missed its target, and landed with a splodge on the stage, to the total surprise not only of the girls, but also of the audience in the front rows. It was soon clear that we were better at more conventional forms of gunnery, because two more salvos missed the target, causing the girls to do nothing more than blush all over, and the audience to start mumbling threats. The management were by now cognisant of the situation and we were warned off, and marched to the street, to a somewhat more extended session in the Yorkshire Grey. Alas, the pub and the Hippodrome are no more, having both been flattened by the bombing in the war.

As mentioned earlier, the great administration problem was how to get back to Horner at the week-ends without a car. Luckily Ollie Moore, another of my term, who had spent his Midshipman's time in China, lived near Taunton and had a car. Accordingly each Friday, after work, I shared expenses, and he dropped me at Taunton. If we were punctual, I could get a train from Taunton to Minehead, the last bus for Porlock there on, and walk the last mile and a half from the bus stop. The reverse process took place going back on Sunday.

The handicap as to journey time was due to the fact that we tried to have a drink at every pub on both sides of the road from Portsmouth to Taunton once during the months we were to do the journey. We quickly had to abandon Portsmouth in our plans, because there were so many pubs there that if we had stuck to our plan we would never have got any further. We did however achieve our aim excluding the few major towns. Every Sunday evening we would arrive for supper at a pub in Salisbury called 'The Haunch of Venison' which gave excellent cheap food, and which I see is going to this day, but now as a fairly exclusive restaurant.

Almost at the end of our courses, Peggy's mother left Horner and bought a semi-detached house in Potters Bar, not a very salubrious resort, in order that Jack, who was working there, could live at home, instead of in digs, and thus make a contribution to the exchequer. At the same time, Peggy could make a somewhat unlikely try for the one annual scholarship at St James' Secretarial College in Kensington, which was considered the tops in the country. To her intense surprise and to all our delight, she achieved it.

Not long afterwards I received my appointment to H. M. S. Norfolk, as Sub-Lieutenant on the East Indies station based at Trincomalee, my father having pulled a few strings through naval friends to get me out there, and thereby fulfilling my ambition at the age of eight as described in an earlier chapter. This was all very exciting, but alas, in the event, was to lead to my one and only unhappy year in the Royal Navy.

Suffice at this stage to say that having recently had my twenty first birthday, I sallied forth in the 'Bibby Liner Yorkshire' headed for Colombo, Peggy headed for her course at St James' College, and our ways for the time being parted. Since nearly all the passengers were from Ceylon or Burma, there were a number who knew my family, and the liner life for nearly three weeks was very pleasant. However, the ship received a signal to say that I was to disembark at Aden, where the Norfolk would be, so the plan to have a few days at home before joining the ship at Colombo, came to nought.

6

Sub-Lieutenant at Sea

S OMEHOW, ONE SENSES the feel of a ship as soon as one comes on board, and somehow this one did not feel right from the start. I was the Sub in charge of the gunroom, with a nice crowd of Midshipmen; had a cabin of my own, was Boys Divisional Officer, and one of the four Officers of the Watch: all straight forward and nothing to complain about. The Captain, Jack Mansfield was a delight to serve, and over him the Commander-in-Chief was James Sommerville, the most genial of Admirals, and yet . . .

It all boiled down to the Commander and Gunnery Officer. The former J. Hughes-Hallet, universally to become to be known in the Navy as Hughes-Hitler, had a considerable analytical brain, no sense of humour, and a very low ability to lead subordinates. He was supported by the latter, who was sly and ingratiating. The Commander had the habit of suddenly flaring up and ordering the Officer of the Watch to be relieved and go below, and on one of these occasions when it happened to me, it at least had the merit of enabling me to read 'Gone with the Wind' from cover to cover, a task which I would not otherwise have undertaken!

On sailing from Aden, we proceeded to Colombo, where I met my parents for the first time for five years at the old Grand Oriental Hotel on the quay. My father did not at first recognise me, but having established communications, he then fished out his cheque book and said that he was afraid he had not been able to do much for me because of the slump, but he was prepared to rectify that in small measure by writing me a cheque for £20. I then made one of the stupidest remarks of my young life by replying 'Oh no Dad, £10 would be ample', and before my very eyes he did just that!

The ship did one cruise to the Persian Gulf and another to East Africa, but somehow there was little sparkle, and when we returned to Colombo I did manage to get Christmas day off to visit my parents. When I returned, I was met by a deputation of officers from the wardroom, who asked if my father would ask the Commander to come up and stay for a week on the estate, so that everybody could have a break! This was duly arranged, and for a few days all was peace, but once he returned all normality was soon resumed! Shortly after that a very sad accident occurred, which in the event was turned to my considerable advantage.

The other cruiser on the station was H. M. S. Manchester, and whilst visiting Goa, her aircraft flew into overhead electric, cables and the pilot and passenger, who was the Sub-Lieutenant were both killed. Norfolk was due to sail home shortly anyway, and so the Admiral and Captain, who knew I lived there, arranged that I should transfer to Manchester and the new Sub-Lieutenant from England would join Norfolk. Accordingly, I transferred to Manchester, and began once again a very pleasurable ship-board experience.

I was again Sub of the Gunroom with a nice crowd of Midshipmen, and also was in charge of the 'Top' division and also one of the main triple 6' gun turrets. The Captain and Commander were both very pleasant and indeed she was a happy ship.

Munich had come and gone and the war clouds were gathering, so we adjourned to Trincomalee to prepare. The East Indies Station cruisers had by tradition always been painted white with yellow funnels, and very smart they looked too. Over this lot went dull grey matt paint and later camouflage.

We then moved to the Bombay area in late August 1939, and on 3rd September came the dramatic signal 'Open envelope X' which read 'Commence hostilities against Germany'. This was followed almost at once by another signal to the fleet which simply said 'Winston is back', as indeed he had been immediately appointed First Lord of the Admiralty.

We immediately moved to Aden, and proceeded to escort merchant ships up the Red Sea. There was not the slightest chance of any warlike activity taking place out there, but we went through the motions, and it gave us good practice at following zig-zag patterns, darkening ship, going to action stations and the like. On our return to Aden after our first trip, the local Royal Artillery signal station solemnly challenged us and we duly responded. The local Battery Officer, well known to us socially, promptly ordered a shot to be fired across our bows! Our Captain was not amused.

This was no time for a ship as valuable as a modern cruiser to be sculling around in the Indian Ocean, and in late September we were ordered back to the United Kingdom, reaching there, via stops en route, in mid October.

Owing to our movements, we had no mail for nearly two months, and so there was a great pile waiting for us on arrival at Portsmouth. I saw with horror that there were no letters in Peggy's handwriting, but one in her mother's and instantly assumed that she had decided to break up our relationship. Nothing could have been further from the truth.

It transpired, that, returning daily on the Green Line bus to Potters Bar from St James', where she was now on the staff, Peggy, who was naturally athletic and good at games, although of slim build, felt her joints getting a bit stiff and aching and so jogged home from the bus stop. It was the worst possible thing that she could have done, for in fact she had got an acute attack of Rheumatic Fever and her health very rapidly deteriorated.

On September 3rd, the very day that war broke out, it was imperative to get her to a major hospital with top specialist care, if her life was to be saved, but all hospitals had been evacuated except for serious cases, because it was feared that there might be heavy air-raids and many casualties immediately hostilities had started. Luckily Peggy's brother Jack played rugger with a brilliant up and coming young surgeon, (who was later to become an honorary surgeon to the Queen), and he in turn gave honorary service at Queen Mary's Hospital for the East End at Stratford E15. Also attending there was Claud Elman, an eminent Harley Street heart specialist. Thence Peggy was rushed and placed in an oxygen tent, with her aortic and mitral valves badly damaged and with her life despaired of.

When we arrived in England and I was given leave to see her, she had won the battle to live, but was still in the oxygen tent and weighed under six stone. The specialist's forecast was that there was only limited hope that she would ever be able to get out of bed and lead any semblance of a normal life. How wrong she was to prove them in time.

I got one more day's leave from the ship, and at the same time my mother had come to England for a brief leave to make arrangements for my brother who was leaving Bradfield, and would in due course join 'Shell'. I went to see my mother and floated a loan from her on H. P. to be paid back over twelve months and proceeded round to Benson's in Ludgate Circus and purchased one sapphire engagement ring. Thence to Queen Mary's Hospital and place it upon Peggy's finger, pausing to wonder if we were the first couple to get engaged formally in an oxygen tent! We were not to meet again for another two years.

Soon after I returned to the ship, we sailed to Scapa Flow to join the formidable Home Fleet there assembled, and became part of the 18th Cruiser Squadron under Admiral Leyton, whose function was to establish the Northern Patrol between Iceland and Faroes, in order to intercept any shipping that might have cargoes for Germany.

The principle was that all ships bound for European ports had to get a 'Navycert' from the British Authorities showing that no part of the cargo was destined for Germany. If any ship of any nationality was stopped by one of our cruisers on patrol and was shown not to be fully covered, she was taken into Kirkwall in the Orkneys and the offending cargo off loaded. The rewards for slipping through the patrol were great.

All through the winter of 1939/40, we steamed up and down on patrol, in gales, driving rain and rough seas, keeping watch on the open bridge in all weathers. It was, of course, before the days of radar, and the range of detection was that of the Mark 1 eyeball.

On 1st January, I had been promoted in the ordinary course to Lieutenant, and pausing only to celebrate with a serious overdose of Drambuie, I moved from the Gunroom to the

Wardroom, a fully trained executive officer, with my watchkeeping ticket and a Commission signed 'George RI'. In the event another Lieutenant and I were the lucky ones, for we were made Boarding Officers, and were to take it in turns to board any ship, other than British, which we intercepted, to check her Navycert, and if incomplete, to take the ship into Kirkwall. The boarding party consisted of one of us armed with a revolver and four sailors armed with rifles. I am not sure which of us would have been the more nonplussed if we ever had to use our weapons!

The routine was to be on patrol for two weeks, then return to Scapa for three days for fuel and provisions, and then back on patrol again. The great wish as a Boarding Officer was to find an un-navycerted ship at the beginning of the patrol, steam it into Kirkwall, and relax in the local hotel at Kirkwall and wait for the ship to return from patrol. In the event, I only had to bring in two ships during our three months patrolling and both luckily produced good timing.

The first was a Norwegian ship S. S. Tyriefjord, and was without incident, and the second was a Swedish ship named 'John'. It was commanded by a very grumpy bearded Nordic, who at every meal, for I dined in his saloon, looked up at me and said grace which consisted of saying 'God bless our food and protect us from these grave dangers into which we have been brought. '

Although we had an armed sailor in the wireless office to stop any outside communication, and I stayed on the bridge as much as possible to ensure that we kept pointing in the right direction, I was never sure what we could have done if a ship decided to make a bolt for home.

Now being a Lieutenant, I was due for re-appointment and on the 1st April 1940 was duly appointed to H. M. S. Warspite, which was itself at Scapa Flow. It had never occurred to me that I might ever go to a battleship and it was with some trepidation, in the event totally unfounded, that I crossed with my luggage in a pinnace to start the next phase of my career.

Before leaving the days of H. M. S. Manchester, I must make a reference to one John Corby. He was President of the Warrant Officer's mess and indeed was the Senior Warrant Officer in the whole Royal Navy, having signed for extended service and having entered the Navy as a boy in 1897. His was an august presence before whom lesser mortals trembled, but underneath great kindness and a sense of mischief. He was the proud possessor of the Distinguished Service Medal which he was awarded in the early part of the century when a Petty Officer in a sloop in the Persian Gulf.

It appears that he was sent ashore in charge of a platoon of armed men complete with bugler to chase and capture a party of armed Arabs who were illegally running slaves in from East Africa.

It transpired that the Arabs were much more heavily armed than his party, so to protect them he ordered the bugler to sound 'The Retreat'. At this precise moment an Arab bullet passed through one cheek of the bugler and out through the other, and as hard as he tried to sound the retreat, the air went out through the holes in his cheeks and none went down the bugle. As a result, his men stood their ground and the Arabs finally retreated and John was awarded the D. S. M. ! That was his story and he swore every word to be true but . . .

On another occasion, he got fed up with a Midshipman who was for ever whistling. John Corby was, amongst other things, in charge of diving, and tests were periodically carried out in the, what are now old fashioned, diving suits with big brass helmets and supplied by an air pump with two big wheels turned by hand.

He asked the Midshipman if he would like a dive which was readily accepted and down went the lad to about thirty feet, Corby then ordered the handles to be speeded up to build up the pressure, and the young man was soon screaming to be brought up because of the agony on his ears. When it was decided that he had had enough, Corby picked up the inter-com and said 'Now whistle, you little bugger'. The poor boy was brought to the surface and never whistled again.

John Corby was of a rare breed, and taught us all a lot.

7
H.M.S. Warspite

T HE WARSPITE, which had been the Flagship of the Mediterranean fleet, with her original crew and pitched to the highest level of efficiency, had been sent to strengthen the Home Fleet, but with the rising danger of Italy entering the war, it was intended that she should return to her original role. But first much was to happen.

Hardly had I stepped on board, than Germany invaded Norway, and high priority was placed by us on stopping them having access to the iron ore trade from Narvik in the very north. It was known that there were some large German destroyers already in Narvik, and a division of our destroyers was despatched to enter the fjord to attack them. However the enemy were much too large and heavily gunned and our force was forced to retreat with heavy casualties. Meanwhile, part of the Home fleet, which included us, patrolled off the Norwegian coast to prevent any German invasion and here I had my first taste of real war, as we were subjected to continuous high level bombing during daylight by the German Air Force. Luckily, apart from being trying on the nerves, it had little effect, as that sort of attack had little chance of success except by random chance.

It was then decided that Warspite should steam up Narvik Fjord escorted by destroyers, and destroy the enemy destroyers which had recently had success, chancing the counter attack by enemy bombers and submarines, which threat was considered to be considerable.

The Captain accordingly addressed the Ships Company on the plan and also the attendant dangers that were to ensue on the following day, which started with a special Holy Communion at 8 a. m. , attended by some three hundred, the average on a Sunday being about twenty. How often was one to see in the future celestial insurance policies being taken out before impending danger! Accordingly on the morning of 13th April. we closed up at action stations and started steaming down the fjord.

I should say here that on joining the ship my duties, apart from watchkeeping, were to be Officer in Charge of the Forecastle division of about 150 men and in charge of the forward 15' turret of twin guns. It was of formidable dimension, each gun weighing 90 tons, and the whole turret, whose revolving structure went down five decks to the magazines, weighed 900 tons. The rate of fire was two rounds every three minutes, as it threw a shell weighing a little over a ton over twelve miles. Luckily it was the same turret's crew as in the days in the Mediterranean and were very highly trained, and so the fact that I had only recently joined and was relatively inexpert hardly mattered.

The fact that we were steaming straight up a narrow sea-way meant that the enemy could only be attacked by my turret and the one just above us, as the after turrets could not bear. Furthermore the range of any enemy would only be a few thousand yard and so the trajectory would be almost flat. At about 11. 30 we were given the standard constipating action stations lunch of two hard boiled eggs and a thick corned beef sandwich and by noon were waiting for things to happen. As we went even further up, so the enemy destroyers began to appear and each one in turn was destroyed by our very superior fire power. By 5 p. m. we had reached Narvik town with not only the destroyers sunk, but a submarine in the bag as well.

And then came a majestic moment; we had not received any air attack or seen any sign of activity, and we anchored off the town on a beautiful spring evening surrounded by the snow capped hills, and all the turret's crew clambered through the man-hole on to the roof of the turret and in a state of high elation ate our post-action tea of guess what – two hard boiled eggs and a Corned beef sandwich! As it got dark, we sailed away up the fjord towards the open sea under protection of darkness and on the following day to Scapa Flow.

The time had now arrived to prepare to sail for the Mediterranean and as a first stop we sailed round to Greenock on the Clyde. The day after we arrived happened a tragedy some five hundred yards from us which is only mentioned as an example of so many little cameos of disaster that were to happen all over the war zones with little or no publicity. The French destroyer Maille Brese lay in the peaceful Scottish sunshine that afternoon, when a torpedo, which was being worked on on deck suddenly exploded, and the ship very quickly became a raging inferno. A large number of her crew were trapped below decks, and the port holes were too small for escape. Men could be seen at every one screaming and scrabbling whilst the heat got ever- more intense. Ships including ours rushed cutting gear to her, but the heat was so intense that little was achieved. After some two hours the

H.M.S. Warspiute and destroyer escort

Grounded German destroyer

German destroyer abandoning ship

ship sank, sending, perhaps mercifully, all those trapped to their grave.

We arrived at Alexandria in early May and immediately became once again the Flagship of the Commander-in-Chief, now Admiral Sir Andrew Cunningham. This also presented logistic problems for the Wardroom for with him came a staff of five Commanders and at least 24 Paymasters, mostly reserves, who were the cypher watchkeepers, and our mess suddenly became populated by a lot of strangers, whom one never saw except at meal times, and who belonged to a different world from the ship's officers. This resulted in one bizarre situation, because there was soon a muttering about the quality of the food.

The Commander, Charles Madden, who was then President of the mess accordingly announced that all officers names would go in a hat, and whoever's name was pulled out, would arrange the menus for the following week, thereby presumably ensuring at least one satisfied customer. Alas, the first name out of the hat was a newly joined young Surgeon Lieutenant who the previous season had been a Scottish second row rugby trialist. On the first morning at breakfast, all these newly acquired Senior Officers sat down to breakfast and had an acute seizure when they found they were being offered mutton chops and beer! The experiment proceeded no further.

The new Mediterranean fleet was being assembled from stations far and wide and began to represent a formidable force. Alexandria was recreationally the perfect base. There was excellent food, two large clubs with a race-course and eighteen hole golf course in the middle and endless tennis courts, games pitches and the like. The night clubs and night-life generally was sufficiently varied to suit all tastes! There then followed a period of phoney war in the Eastern Mediterranean, whilst dramatic events were happening in Europe. Norway was subjugated and Denmark over-run. The low countries fell, and finally France was over-run, culminating in the evacuation at Dunkirk.

Through all this our fleet led a normal life, listening on the radio, and culminating in Churchill's famous speeches we heard live over the wireless. Then Italy declared war and life once again began in earnest.

Soon afterwards, the C-in-C took the whole fleet to sea to sweep the Eastern Mediterranean to make clear to the Italians who was master of the area, notwithstanding that on paper their Naval forces were superior to ours. It is extraordinary to think in retrospect that even then, there was no radar in any ship and our total fighter cover was two Gloucester Gladiator bi-plane fighters in the even older aircraft carrier H. M. S. Eagle.

On the first occasion, and on many others to follow, as we steamed further away from Alexandria, so we were picked up by Italian reconnaissance planes, and one could always, by day, be seen as a little black dot on the horizon. Immediately up went our two faithful Gladiators and more often than not the dot on the horizon would drop in a pall of smoke. However, we were subject to fairly constant high level bombing by Italian aircraft, and although there were a few near misses, one of which bounced off the flukes of our anchor, no ship was ever hit. They also occasionally carried out raids in harbour on moonlit nights, and so we were split into two watchkeeping groups, the conventional Officer of the Watch, and another Lieutenant and a Midshipman forward on the bridge as Air Defence Officer to sound the alarms and take action in the case of raids. I remember one night in the dark hours my Midshipman producing a pre-war Fortnum and Mason catalogue, so to pass the time we devised our perfect meal from it, priced it, provided half the money each and despatched our order.

As Italy had now come into the war, all mail had to go to England round the Cape of Good Hope and all replies back again the same way. We soon therefore forgot all about it, and were astonished and delighted when several months later the parcel duly arrived, and we sat once more in the night watches and guzzled it. Memory does not recall the menu other than that the main course was tinned whole roast grouse!

The mails had been coming steadily and quickly until the entry of Italy into the war, but thereafter everything went round the Cape other than one aerogramme which one could send each week, which was a mini version of the modern air-letter card, which I think was micro-filmed and sent by air. Sufficient good news however was reaching me that Peggy was continuing to confound the doctors and had been discharged from hospital and was able to do things slowly on the ground floor and go for short walks on the flat, but could not yet do stairs.

As mentioned earlier this narrative is not military and so reference to episodes of that nature are only chronologically approximate, most events having been fully accurately reported in official histories and biographies. They are only recorded here where human aspects played a part.

In this connection, in the early summer the fleet left harbour once again to sail westwards, still without radar or fighter cover, and once more getting slightly punch-drunk from Italian high level bombing when our reconnaissance aircraft, an old bi-plane Swordfish from Eagle, spotted the Italian fleet at sea off Cape Spartivento. The only other Battleship which was with us, the Barham, who could do a bare 20 knots, was left behind as we worked up to full speed and at the maximum 12 1/2 miles range we opened fire on the Italian Battleship Littorio who returned our fire.

Once again, as we were giving chase and pointing straight at the enemy, only our forward turrets would bear, and in an early salvo the Littorio was hit in the bridge structure. Immediately, the Italian fleet, which was of lighter construction and much faster than us, turned for Taranto and that was that. A small episode, but I think the first time since Jutland that one capital ship had struck another in anger!

And then . . . not long afterwards, we went to sea again for, as we thought, another sweep west down bomb alley, but as we reached the area, suddenly over the horizon flew a string of modern mono plane fighters, presumably as we thought to strafe us. And then over the horizon came H. M. S. Illustrious, our most modern aircraft carrier complete with radar and the modern Fulmar fighters which we had seen, and life in the alley and subsequently, became a lot more peaceful.

During all these sorties I was one of the four Officers of the Watch, and one realised when say keeping watch on the bridge for the four hours of the forenoon, what a special privilege it was to share it with the C-in-C and his staff and actually listen to all the discussion and decision making, whilst carrying on one's ordinary work of running the zig-zag, seeing to the ship's routine, helping the Navigator, keeping a look-out on the escort and all the other little jobs that fell to the lot of the Officer of the Watch.

In between sorties we occasionally went to carry out bombardments; one was in the Tobruk vicinity during the siege and another on Valona in Albania, which had just been over-run by Italy. On these runs, we always took to sea Larry Allen, the very flamboyant and pro-British war reporter for Time and Life, of course long before the United States had entered the war. As soon as we left harbour he was officially briefed as to our mission, and thereafter stayed by the bar drinking large scotches. Before returning to harbour he had completed his always highly entertaining despatch, I suspect without ever venturing outside. I remember, after the Valona trip that his despatch ended 'Twenty-four hours after the bombardment ended the 15' guns of the mighty Warspite were still red-hot, arid so was Valona!'

He was a wonderful, larger than life character, and it was very sad to hear years later of his death during the campaign in Malaya against the communist rebels. The British reporter whom we often took to sea was Alan Moorehead, who wrote excellent accurate reports in a somewhat less lurid key.

Our two most dramatic, sorties in the latter part of 1941 were the Battle of Matapan and the torpedo attack by the Swordfish aircraft from Eagle and Illustrious on the Italian fleet in Taranto. In the former case, reconnaissance aircraft reported that an Italian unit comprising a battleship, three cruisers and attendant destroyers were in the Southern Aegean. A Swordfish torpedo attack was carried out on the battleship in order to slow her down, but although she was hit once, she made good her escape taking most of the screen with her. However through consistently good sighting reports, the fleet were able to stalk the three crack Italian cruisers Zara, Fiume and Trieste until we crept up on them in the darkness, at action stations with 15' guns loaded, and they quite astonishingly totally unaware of our presence.

Then suddenly at only a few thousand yards with guns already pointing at them, and with us taking the two leading cruisers and the Valiant the other one, we illuminated them with searchlights and let fly. Within a very few minutes all three were burning wrecks and subsequently sank. Meanwhile our destroyers picked up two of theirs before the rest fled.

In the morning our destroyers stayed around to pick up survivors, whilst we drew away a little in case an Italian submarine had been sent to the area. On the destroyers rejoining the fleet later, our Captain in charge of them signalled by light to the C-in-C that he had rescued from the sea his Italian opposite number who was suffering acutely from piles. The C-in-C replied that he was not a bit surprised, and then we all trooped back to harbour. Our total casualties in the operation had been sadly the loss of one Swordfish crew during the torpedo attack on the battleship Littorio on the previous day.

Much has been rightly written about the remarkable success of the Fleet Air Arm attack on the Italian fleet at Taranto, and there is little to add here, except to recall the tense excitement at the time as Illustrious at dusk turned west towards her intended target, whilst the rest of us waited to the eastward, knowing that great things were afoot for that night, and waiting to greet her and cover her in the morning for the return to Alexandria. Great was the next day's jubilation as the news of the success came through.

There was of course much opportunity for recreation in the gap between these goings-on, and one of these was the Inter-service Inter unit seven a side rugby tournament. H. M. S. Warspite, of whose team I was a member, drew some obscure New Zealand Army unit in the first round, which became rapidly less obscure when we met on the field of play, for it transpired that the whole of their team had been members of the last All Black touring party. It seems hard to believe, but we achieved, in a game that only lasted eight minutes each way, losing by over sixty points to nil!

As the months went past and we listened to England on its own being pounded by air raids and yet winning the Battle of Britain, yet the active theatre of operations was in the Mediterranean. We had twice advanced along the Western Desert and been repulsed back to our starting point; Albania and Yugoslavia had both fallen to the enemy, and Malta was still standing in the middle under siege; but except in exceptional cases, the Mediterranean route was barred to us due to enemy air power and all stores and military equipment had to come round the Cape. One rumour had it that a million sand-bags were ordered for the Western Desert from England, and that they were sent out already filled with sand! Meanwhile news from home was of very slow improvement and Peggy could now manage a flight of stairs on her own by walking up them backwards one step at a time.

Then in the spring of 1941 Germany invaded Greece, and General Wavell sent troops, whom he could ill afford, from the Western Desert to help the Greeks. It was to no avail, and within a few weeks they were all being evacuated back to Egypt with much loss of material, as now Greece fell to the Germans. Next came Crete -

Having digested Greece, Hitler now turned his attention to Crete, but here we had in advance set up a Military and Naval Base in preparation. As usual the situation started with heavy bombing, but to forestall a seaborne invasion, the fleet put to sea, and steamed between Crete and the Greek mainland. In fact we were so close that we could see the German aircraft through binoculars land on the airfield after a raid, re-arm and come back again all in a space of a few minutes. As long as they were on high level bombing we were relatively safe, but in the afternoon along came the JU87 single engine Stukas. They carried one single 500lb bomb and could go into an incredibly steep dive, releasing the bomb with great accuracy from only a few thousand feet and then pulling out.

I had the afternoon watch on the bridge, when we all spotted a Stuka absolutely dead ahead going into his dive straight for us. I immediately ordered the wheel hard over, which is the standard practice to put the pilot off his aim, and at that moment he released his bomb. Of course, if a bomb is coming straight for your nose, there is no relative speed, so it is clearly visible and simply gets bigger and noisier and noisier.

In those few seconds the ship had just begun to answer her wheel and with a whoosh, a roar and a whistle, the bomb went about ten feet past the bridge, passed through the upper deck between the anti-aircraft guns, and exploded on the armoured deck in the six inch gun battery. Ten feet one way and I would not be writing this now; ten feet the other way and over 60 lay dead or dying and another 120 injured.

One of the dead was my good friend the Bosun Mr. Harding who worked with me on all the anchors and cables work in the ship for which I was responsible. A fine gentleman, a fine seaman, and a great mentor. It was the first time in the war that people I knew well had been killed close to me, and whenever it happened, then or subsequently, one was much humbled by the thought of the narrowness by which one was spared and others not.

As the sun set, we set course for Alexandria, with almost every ship in our unit damaged from aerial bombardment to some degree.

It was not to be a seaborne invasion that was to win the Germans the day but their huge airborne drop which secured the airfield and key positions prior to the follow-up seaborne landings. Our adventure into the cauldron was the first time the C-in-C did not come to sea with us, remaining ashore with his Army and Air Force counterparts dealing with the overall strategy and so Admiral Rawlings, the Second in Command hoisted his flag aboard us for the operation. In hindsight, our steaming the fleet so close to the enemy was magnifique but I wonder if it was 'La guerre'.

The defence of Crete, which Hitler thought would fall into his lap almost at once, lasted some three weeks, and then once again was the wholesale evacuation back to Alexandria. It was amazing once again, what a large proportion of the army were rescued, but of course, on each of these occasions, there was a critical loss of arms, vehicles and equipment.

And by now a very high rate of damage to the ships of the fleet. There was a bare handful of ships of the size of destroyer and above who were not damaged to some degree and indeed many were sunk. Kelly was not the only ship to be lost at Crete!! It was during this evacuation that his fellow service Commanders urged Admiral Cunningham to call it off, because so many ships were being lost, to which he replied 'It takes three years to build a ship, but three hundred to build a tradition; the evacuation goes on'.

During the days immediately after returning to harbour, much time was taken up in writing hand written personal letters of sympathy to the next of kin of all those in one's division who had been killed and attending their funerals in the military cemetery, and writing re-assuring letters to the next of kin of those who had been wounded.

Two months earlier, prior to the evacuation of Crete, three others of my term were in ships in Alexandria and also a reserve officer who was a relation of mine by marriage. Now John North had been lost in Neptune, when she hit a mine and blew up off Tobruk, Ronnie Davies was lost in the Wryneck during the Greek evacuation, Nick Acheson was lost in the Hereward at Crete, and John Osbourn was in the 'A' Turret of Orion when a German bomb came through the roof and blew him and the turret to bits when off Crete.

There was I, with my ship being temporarily patched up, playing tennis and eating sticky cakes on the verandah of the Sporting Club, the only one left. To cap it, I heard that my cousin, Ian Hoare, who had joined the Sappers and thence the Bomb Disposal Squad, had been blown to bits in London whilst de-fusing a bomb.

As the days went past, we ordinary mortals began to wonder what would happen to us and our ship, and then the startling news broke. After transferring our Midshipmen and one or two officers and a few ratings to other ships, and when patching up was completed, we were to sail the ship to Bremerton Navy yard in Puget Sound opposite Seattle to be fully repaired. Although the United States was not yet in the war, she had given facilities for our ships to be repaired in her Naval Bases. After a year of fairly close engagement with the enemy, this seemed to us like Shangri-La. And so in July we set sail for America, and it would be idle to pretend we were sorry.

There was one final happy occasion before departure; one of our Lieutenants, Derek Edelston got married to a local English girl and we all trooped off to the wedding at the local English church, followed by a reception at the Cecil Hotel, after which the happy couple left for their honeymoon in the lift! There was nowhere else to go.

We recaptured Derek at Suez and set off down the Red Sea, into the Indian Ocean and to our first stop, which was Colombo. The Captain, with great consideration, knowing my parents lived in Ceylon and that I had not seen them for three years, said I was to go ashore on arrival, and he did not want to see me back until 11 p. m. Accordingly, once more after all these years, I found myself at 11 a. m. in the Grand Oriental Hotel trying to get hold of my parents.

I managed to get through on the ancient telephone to the estate to get a message through to my father, who apparently jumped in the car and drove straight to Colombo arriving at about 2. 30 p. m. , having for the first time in his life passed Avisawella Rest House without stopping for a drink. Meanwhile I luckily recognised a planter's wife in the Hotel, from before the war, and she informed me that she had just seen my mother who was down shopping in Colombo, but who when she did so, always reserved a table for herself for lunch at the Sunday tea rooms. I accordingly adjourned there and sat at her table and waited until she arrived and walked to her table and sitting there was her son whom she imagined was many thousands of miles away! We then met up with my father in the afternoon, and had a very enjoyable time together until I returned on board.

Next day we sailed via Singapore, Manilla and Hawaii to our final destination. The Pacific ocean seemed endless, but we didn't mind. No darkening ship at nights or defence watch stations, or any of the other appurtenances of war.

Bremerton Navy yard in Puget Sound was a large yard set in a most beautiful spot with spacious grounds and living quarters, and we soon made friends with the locals. I in fact was given the, in the event, somewhat arduous task of being the ship's liaison officer with the local community, and in Seattle there was a large active British-American war relief association. Invitations poured in for any number from 2 to 200 members of the ship's company for afternoon tea in private houses to large dances. It was very difficult not to give offence by sending refusals to the very well meant invitations, but fairly soon after arrival, those who so wished, had already found friends among the very kind local community, who welcomed them in almost as a second home.

Another Lieutenant and I became particularly friendly with the Captain in charge of the base and his wife (and two daughters!), Captain Dunbar and for two months it virtually became our second home. Whilst there, young friends of the Dunbars wished to get married, but the bride's parents refused to sanction it and were thoroughly disapproving, whereupon the Dunbars arranged a sort of quasi-elopement, fairly usual in America, but virtually unheard of in this country. The couple were married by a priest in the Dunbar's sitting room, and somehow I got inveigled into being best man, without really knowing what I was meant to do.

After the marriage we moved straight into a champagne reception for the dozen or so who were present, and then came the moment when the happy couple were due to leave for the airport for their honeymoon. It was at that instant that they all looked at: me and asked what time I had ordered the car for. Not realising that this was part of my duties I had of course done nothing, but it was a time for quick thinking. I nipped off round to the house of the bride's parents and told them as they sat there glum and forbidding that their services were urgently required. I drove back with them and made them drive the newly-weds to the airport, which I believe was carried out in stoney silence; but perhaps it began to sow the seeds of a final rapprochement.

A problem that arose early in our stay was that the pay of a Lieutenant was £20 per month out of which had to be paid a mess bill. Furthermore only a fraction of this paltry sum could be drawn in dollars. The State of Washington was dry, except for purchase of complete bottles at the State liquor stores for consumption at home. The only places where one could go out for a drink, other than in people's private houses or on board were the supposed illegal 'speak-easys' which were like large log cabins with the statutory grille in the door in order to cage the arrivals. The hooch, including Scotch, was good but expensive, and we had virtually no money.

Then I hit on a simple scheme. I spent a day learning the then forty eight states of the United States like a parrot until I could write them down as fast as I could write. I then set off for the nearest speak-easy to test out my theory, and having been allowed in, bought a cheap and innocuous drink.

It was very easy to get talking to one's neighbours who were always interested in the Limey just back from the war. It only took a moment to work the conversation round to patriotism, and how limited appeared to be the knowledge of the average American of his own country. 'Why, ' I said 'I would not be surprised if I could name the forty eight states of your country as fast as you, and I will back myself for a half a bottle of Scotch. ' My neighbour looked at the Limey with incredulity at such a soft touch.

By now, everyone in the bar was intrigued; out came the paper and pencils, the starting gun was fired, and before he was half way through I had handed in my completed prep. There was much merriment, from all except one, that one of their number had been taken for a sucker, and I gave the victim a stiff drink and the rest of the half bottle did me for the evening. I never knew the ruse to fail, and hardly paid for a Scotch on an evening out for the rest of my stay!

I remembered that my four uncles had left England during King Edward VII's reign to seek their fortunes in the Vancouver area, (see chapter one) and as I had the address of one of them, as no relative had seen them from that day, I felt it incumbent to fly up from Seattle for a couple of nights, meet them and see how their fortune seeking had progressed. So I managed to contact Dudley, whose address I had, and who was something not very important in local government, and he met me at the airport in their old jalopy and took me to their little house. So far not very impressive!

The next day I was to be taken to meet my Uncle Tom, who was the eldest of the ten children, and I earmarked this as my highlight as I was always told from an early age that I was the living spit of my uncle Tom. Accordingly we journeyed forty miles down the beautiful Fraser river valley to Haney where he lived. As we got into the main street of the small town, the car stopped and an old man shambled up to the car window and there was a brief conversation. He had a few days stubble on his chin, no collar and his trousers tied up with string. He was also my Uncle Tom! Another illusion shattered!

It transpired that he owned a small pool room and haircutting saloon, and we were directed to his house for a drink. This transpired to be a small log cabin, conspicuous for its cobwebs, with some rickety chairs on the verandah where we had our refreshment, and then departed back to Vancouver. So, far from my original dreams of perhaps extracting a small financial contribution from these supposedly rich uncles, my only surprise at the end was that I was not held upside down to see if a coin might fall out of my pockets.

The other two uncles I did not meet. Eddie, who had left England, almost qualified in medicine and an England trial wing three-quarter, was now a forest ranger in the north near Prince Rupert, and Cecil who had been about to qualify as a solicitor, I believe ran a butchery near Vancouver.

The interesting and really rather pleasing thing was that all four of them, from a position of some substance and professional qualification in Clifton, had settled thousands of miles away in occupations on a totally different plane, had no ambitions, and they and their offspring were all completely happy and contented with this totally different and modest environment.

I was able to return to the ship surprised but unworried and write a full report to my mother on her four Canadian brothers. One might almost say the first report on them to reach the outside world for over thirty years!

Soon after return to the Warspite came the great news. The first British merchant ship to sail from the Pacific under the new lend/lease act was to sail home from San Francisco with a cargo of tinned goods for the new points ration scheme and a deck cargo of six Mustang aircraft. She, now named ' Empire Fulmair' and lately a new ship of the Matson Line on the Honolulu run, was to be manned by a Naval crew disguised as Merchant service, and drawn from Warspite and the Orion who was re-fitting at San Francisco.

The criterion was who had been away longest or who was specially required back in the United Kingdom. I qualified on both counts and found myself the new prospective Third Mate and Navigator and one September day found myself at Seattle station boarding the San Francisco express, and sent on my way by Mr. Thomas, the Consul in Seattle and his wife who had been very kind to me throughout my stay. Their farewell present of a large baby's bottle complete with teat puzzled me, until I peered inside after departure, to find, in this dry state of Washington, it actually contained a liberal dose of whiskey.

8
Homeward Bound to Holy Matrimony

A CCOMPANIED by Nigel Hooper, another Lieutenant from Warspite, who had once served in the Merchant Navy, and who was to be the First Mate of the Empire Fulmar, I set out for what was to be an eventful three months.

The first problem to be overcome after we had consumed the contents of our baby's bottles, was the ghastly American Pullman Car sleeping system. On either side of a central corridor were, on two tiers, bunks of small dimension with the curtains pulled across for privacy. As the whole arrangement was heterosexual, the only solution was to lie down behind one's curtains and undress, with considerable contortions, whilst in the prone position, and then do the reverse the following morning. The following day was of considerable interest, as we steamed south through the state of Oregon, and as evening approached we were not a little interested at a crowd forming outside the door of the observation car and bar, which had so far remained firmly closed, as we progressed through the dry states of Washington and Oregon. Then suddenly, through the carriage window we saw a trackside signpost with an arrow pointing in one direction saying 'Oregon' and in the other 'California', whereupon the bar door opened and the awaiting queue fell in and made up for all the lost time.

That night we arrived at San Francisco, were met by Consular officials, and taken to the Sir Francis Drake Hotel and to rooms of such luxury as we had never known. We slept well, and next morning our movements were only handicapped by a strike by the Hotel Bell-hops who were walking round the Hotel with placards demanding more pay. As the pay was well in excess of that of a Lieutenant in the Royal Navy, we took placards and did a couple of laps round the Hotel before proceeding to see the Empire Fulmar. She was a splendid almost new ship, and had been chartered to the Royal Mail Line to load and prepare for sea to sail for England.

As Naval Officers, we knew nothing of the business of loading Merchant Ships, and so were tactfully asked to keep out of the way for the time being by the Royal Mail officials, which we readily agreed to, the more so having found out that some mysterious benefactor, which was presumably either Lend-Lease or the British Government, was paying for all our accommodation, including as it transpired any of our guests as well.

The elder of the two daughters of Captain Dunbar, whose family had looked after me so kindly, whose name was Ruth, was studying at the nearby University of California at Berkeley. The poor girl had met and fallen in love with a fellow freshman very soon after joining and having decided to get married, and as he was reading Mechanical Engineering, it was agreed that she would take the five year course in Civil Engineering and that would make a great team. By the time I knew Ruth and her family, the chap had made other arrangements for his future, and Ruth was left with some four years of Civil Engineering ahead of her; a prospect which she found less than exciting. I rang Ruth up and was quickly asked for the following day to a Sorority lunch at her Sorority which was, I think Phi Chi Omega which I duly attended as the only male present, and a real live Limey Lieutenant straight from the war at that! It was intriguing to be treated as a freak, and a much sought after one at that.

After lunch I was shown round the vast Sorority building, and as we reached each floor, so Ruth would shout 'Man on first' and then at the next level 'Man on second' and so on, the other girls scuttling to safety as we ascended. Finally, after some ten days of lotus eating, we started our voyage back to Britain via in the first instance Los Angeles and the Panama Canal.

Fearing Japanese sabotage, because the time of their war was rapidly approaching, each ship traversing the canal had United States armed guard on the bridge and in the engine room, in addition to the Pilot, to monitor each order and the action taken upon it, and they were intrigued to find that the whole crew in reality came from the Royal Navy.

On passing through the canal, we anchored at Colon and were boarded by the local British Control of Shipping Officer, who astonishingly turned out to be the husband of Joan, Peggy's eldest sister, they having got married in Bermuda where she worked the previous year. As Joan had also come out to Colon, I was allowed to go ashore for an hour and see her, none of her own family having seen her for three years.

Next day we sailed on to Newport News in Virginia which was also one of the American terminals for the Transatlantic fast convoys. Here we again met a long suffering Royal Mail representative who whilst we went into town for a farewell bout of shopping and entertainment on U. S. soil, arranged for the ship to be fuelled.

Next morning the U. S. Customs Official came on board to clear us before the great moment of heading out to sea for Britain, but there was one last setback before making it that went something like this:-

Customs:- Where's your God damn Plimsoll line?

Captain:- What Plimsoll Line?

'The one on the side of your ship of course, the damned thing is under water and you are overloaded and can't sail'.

'Oh dear, lets come to my cabin and discuss over a whiskey what the best thing to do is'.

A couple of hours and two bottles of Scotch later, the customs man was placed gently at the bottom of the gangway and we sailed!

It seems that we were given too much cargo back at San Francisco, and when we filled up with fuel at Newport, our Plimsoll line coyly descended out of sight.

Soon after leaving we joined up with five other fast ships and formed a sixteen knot convoy homeward bound to the Clyde. We were escorted by what seemed like half the United States Atlantic Fleet, but only as far as 25° West which was where danger might be encountered, because of course they were not yet at war. When we reached the longitude of 25° West the mighty armada turned back and the British escort took over to escort us through the danger zone to the Clyde.

This comprised four old ex-American four funnelled destroyers which we had obtained from the United States in exchange for 99 year leases on bases in our Caribbean colonies such as Bermuda and Trinidad, and colloquially known as 'packets of Woodbines'. Not knowing that we were an all naval crew, the Escort Commander soon signalled to us congratulating us on our good station-keeping to which we replied that he did'nt do so bad himself! And so to the Clyde, after years away and it was a wonderful feeling steaming up the Firth on a lovely November morning.

Soon after joining the Fulmar, Nigel Hooper had told me that he wanted to get married at short notice on return to the the United Kingdom and it was certainly my intention so to do, and not being quite sure of the rules, we persuaded the Captain to read our banns every Sunday for three weeks on board. However this was to prove of no avail.

As soon as we secured alongside, we got the Wren Officers at Naval H. Q. at Glasgow to pass a message to Nigel's fiancee to get up to Liverpool the following day, and meanwhile we left the ship for good and likewise headed for Liverpool, where he began to show a certain coyness, even unto booking a double room for their wedding night at the Adelphi Hotel. However, we managed to get a Special Bishop's Licence, a church, a witnessing Verger and his fiancee all by mid-afternoon and they were duly married with me as best man and were sent off to the Adelphi. I followed after a discreet interval to find a still coy Nigel reading the evening paper with his puzzled wife sitting opposite drinking a cup of tea! We had a bit of a party in the evening and I sent them off to their connubial couch, and called again the next morning before heading South to see Peggy for the first time outside an oxygen tent since June 1938, three and a half long years before.

In 1940 Peggy's mother had been lent a cottage in Birdham, south of Chichester where she was living and looking after Peggy who had reached the point where she could walk a few hundred yards on the flat and climb stairs on her own by going up backwards, one step at a time. It was of course a great moment for us both, and we set about arranging our own wedding. But first, I had to take her to see Claud Elman the Harley Street Heart specialist who had saved her when she was first taken ill at the beginning of the war. I had a long private talk with him and he finished by saying bluntly that it would not be right for us to get married, as Peggy could never get any better, we could never have any children and it would not be long before I was a widower. We were married on 9th December 1941 at Birdham church which was to be the start of a wonderfully happy thirty three years.

There were however plans still to make, not least our honeymoon, and in the circumstances it seemed best to plump for a place where there was not likely to be any bombing and where there would still be largish hotels open complete with lifts. Accordingly we chose Bournemouth, and not having been in Britain since before the war, I sat down with a 1939 A. A book and phoned the top hotel which I still remember was called the 'Imperial', and a young lady answered the phone. I accordingly asked if I could have a double room for two weeks for my wife and myself and was curtly told that this was not possible. When I enquired the reason she was quick to inform me that 'They had been taken over by the W. A. A. Fs for the last two years'! However, undaunted we pressed on and booked at the 'Norfolk' which was excellent in every way.

For the reception after our modest wedding we had all the food I carried back from the States, the like of which had not been seen around for some time, and then on the way to the station we had to call round at the Police and turn Peggy into an English citizen. The reason for this was that having been born of British parents on a ranch in the Argentine, and not having been registered at birth, she was in the eyes of the law an Argentine and therefore subject to a wartime restriction order until we were married.

Militarily we were married in dramatic times for two days previously had been Pearl Harbour, and having spent the first night of our wedding in London prior to moving on to Bournemouth, on coming down stairs the following morning I read on the ticker tape that the Japanese had sunk the Prince of Wales and the Repulse. It is interesting looking back to think that we were married on 13/4 a day Lieutenants pay + 4/8 per day marriage allowance, making 18/- or £325 per annum.

My parents cabled a present of £100 from Ceylon as a wedding present, which paid for our honeymoon, and I had an odd £10 in the bank, and on these meagre resources we set off into Holy Matrimony, and furthermore, for the first year or so saved for the first and last time in our lives! We returned to Birdham just after Christmas and had to set about the nigh impossible task of finding accommodation where I could commute to the Navigation School at H. M. S Dryad at Southwick at Portadown Hill and whence Peggy could walk on the flat to do the shopping and gradually exercise more independence.

We luckily found half a house furnished in Cosham which fitted these criteria and moved into our first independent house in early January when I started my specialist Navigation course which was to last until late April. It was quite amazing that given new purpose and horizons, how Peggy's ability and self confidence grew, always providing things were on the flat, and she took over almost all cooking, catering and shopping.

In April I passed out as a specialist navigator and our stipend increased by the princely sum of half-a-crown a day. When the results were announced I was third out of a class of eight and I was appointed as my first specialist job to be the Flotilla Navigating Officer and staff officer to the 4th minesweeping flotilla. They were the oldest but also the biggest minesweepers in the Navy and were coal burning and at first I was somewhat disappointed by the appointment, but in the event it was to prove an extremely eventful and intriguing time that I would not have missed.

9
Minesweeping

I N A P R I L 1942 I joined H. M. S. Fitzroy, the Flotilla leader, at Yarmouth, on the next rung up the ladder, leaving behind the normal general duty functions, and taking up my first specialist appointment, and it could hardly have been amongst a more varied collection.

The Flotilla Commander, who was also my immediate superior, was a regular Royal Navy Commander, and apart from the two of us, every other officer in every ship, excluding the engineers, was from the reserves. Amongst the eight Commanding Officers was a Barrister, later after the war to become a Judge, a P&O 2nd Mate, a Southampton Liner pilot, a New Zealand sheep farmer and a London socialite of no previous occupation. Their officers were of no less varied hue, and as the Flotilla Staff Officer and supposedly general friend and consultant of all, I got to know many of them well. Indeed, when the Flotilla was tied up alongside the wall in pairs, one behind the other in port and I went ashore, having to pass them all, it needed extreme will-power to get to the other end still sober!

In this context it might be of interest to mention our own wardroom. The First Lieutenant was David Tudor-Evans, who had been London Manager of the Calico Printers Association and a leading light in the London scene. He was too old for compulsory call-up, but as all his subordinates were conscripted, he felt he ought to do his bit too. Aged nearly fifty and with some wealth, he was none the less an excellent officer in charge of the sweep-deck which needed a considerable level of seamanship prowess. He did not totally change his peacetime habits, for when he kept a night watch at sea, he would insist on the Chief Steward keeping watch with him, so that he could fetch him a glass of champagne and a chicken sandwich at intervals.

The Gunnery Officer had been in peacetime a successful commercial traveller in silk stockings, and the Sub Lieutenant, only lately out of public school, was the scion of a prominent Gloucestershire land owner. Last, but not least was our Engineering Officer, called out of retirement and with only one eye, his patch matching his piratical nature. His sister ran a chorus team on the variety stage called the Academy eight whose path we were to cross from time to time in bizarre circumstances. Life was never going to be dull with 'Joss' Hodges as our engineer and David Tudor – Evans as No. l. This lot together with myself, made up the Officers Mess, which was also visited from time to time by the Captain, who was in fact quite normal, though even this was to change ere long, but more of that anon.

And so came the first time when I took the flotilla to sea out of Yarmouth to start the sweep of a minefield. I had known nothing of the particular navigational problems of minesweeping which call for exceptional accuracy, but had a week's overlap from my predecessor to learn, not least the adage that 'Minesweeping is absolutely safe as long as you remember that it is dangerous'!

The daily routine was somewhat controlled by the sun, since sweeping could only take place in daylight, and so it made a long day, the ships leaving harbour in time to be in the sweeping area an hour's steaming away by sunrise, and getting back alongside on the last of the light, and it was a seven day a week job. Since sweeping was very much working as a team, and the hours were long and thirst provoking, it may have been the reason, as soon as we were secured, for much inter-ship fraternisation. This was particularly easy at Yarmouth because we used to secure alongside the road, right outside the Star Inn, where we used to book a private room for the ships when possible.

Occasionally one ventured further afield socially, as Yarmouth was also the home for an M. T. B. flotilla and ex- fishing trawlers used for inshore minesweeping. The Captains of two trawlers were none other than Earl Stanley of Alderly whose favourite parlour trick, when inebriated, which was usually, was to eat the fresh flowers out of the vase, and Francis Freeman, the heir to the Plymouth Gin distillery, who consistently showed a marked loyalty to the family products.

One night I was having a drink with the pair of them in the Freeman trawler, the noble Earl munching his way through some tulips by way of 'small-eats' when there was an air-raid. Francis gazing out through the porthole at the high octane storage tanks for the M. T. Bs, saw an incendiary bomb land on the top of one, and immediately nipped ashore, removed the offending bomb and returned to his drinking. I believe it was some months later that he received a bravery award, totally oblivious of the occasion or what he did.

In mid-May, we were deputed to cut out an old British defence minefield, so that it could be re-laid with fresh mines. We accordingly carefully marked the edge of the area in which the line of mines lay, using taut wire measuring gear, and started sweeping in strips. By the third day we suddenly reached the line, and in one sweep cut over 140 mines. The problem now was to dispose of them, the normal method being to puncture them with rifle fire, so that they filled with water and sank. However as darkness began to fall, some half of them were still floating and so the only solution was to leave them bobbing about on the surface and come back and continue the work the next morning. They should all be safe because International Convention requires, once a mine mooring has been cut and the tension released that the mine should render itself safe.

Next morning, we all streamed sweeps at daylight and ran down the line to make our next sweep. As we approached the start of the line there was a large explosion and up we went. We were mined between the engine and boiler rooms and rapidly stopped and took on an appreciable list. As it happened, the First Lieutenant was sick on shore and as I was the next senior officer, I had to leave the bridge and superintend the lowering of the boats, and setting free the Carley floats and other life saving equipment. After about five minutes, with an increasing list, it was clear that the ship was about to sink and the Captain gave the order to abandon ship, and it was good to see that everyone who was not killed by the explosion or trapped below appeared to get away safely. That left the Captain and myself.

The Captain was standing on the bridge with a resolute look that seemed to indicate that he had every intention of going down with the ship, which seemed to me to be a rotten idea. I made my views very clear to him, and then dived into the sea and swam clear: looking back I was pleased to see that the Captain had followed suit. Although fully clothed, it was surprisingly easy to keep afloat and watch the ship slowly turn over to be keel up, and as she sank there was a woosh of warm water as her boiler exploded.

We only had to hang around in the water for about ten minutes before being picked up, because of course all the other ships in the flotilla were astern of us and had immediately stopped and lowered their boats and started picking up survivors. I was picked up by a boat from H. M. S. Ross and after arriving on board was given a bath and lent some clothes whilst mine were dried and pressed, and this was followed by a large rum. We had sadly, it subsequently transpired, lost twenty two of our company, all lost in the actual explosion.

'Up spirits' in the last of the Coal Burners

When all survivors were picked up, the flotilla abandoned sweeping and returned to Yarmouth. A subsequent Court of Enquiry established that what probably happened was that, when we were trying to sink the mines by rifle fire on the previous day, water must have flowed into a mine, trapping some air inside and giving the mine neutral buoyancy, so that it was bobbing just below the surface. Furthermore, the mines had been laid so long ago that the safety device had got barnacled up and been rendered inoperative.

Normally, after being sunk, everyone gets a fortnight's survivors leave, but sweeping had to go on, so the Captain and I were given seventy two hours to sort ourselves out and get on with the sweeping. Accordingly, next morning I went down to Gieves in London in my still somewhat crumpled suit to order some fresh uniform and other clothes and went on home where Peggy was back staying with her mother.

I remember taking the bus out from Chichester to Birdham, and was walking the last half mile home, when I was stopped by an old lady who we knew. She asked me what on earth I was doing, and so with the thought that I might get a bit of sympathy I mentioned that I was coming back home as I had just been sunk, 'Oh well' she said 'those who are born to be hung will never be drowned', and on that cheerful note I walked on home.

Peggy was naturally delighted and relieved to see me as this was her first intimation of the recent goings-on, but after two days of rest and shopping I was on my way back. My remaining regret was the realisation that in the sinking I had lost my wedding present from her, which was a pair of ivory backed hair brushes with my initials on in silver.

The richest claim I remember for things lost in the sinking was from David Tudor-Evans who was not even on board at the time. He put in for sixty silk shirts and was rewarded by the price of two issue shirts from Naval Stores. By the same token the compensation for my wedding present was one standard normal hairbrush value 4/6!

And so one returned again to go on where we left off. The Captain, First Lieutenant, Engineer Officer and I transferred to what was the Divisional Leader ship, the 'Kellett', and off we went to sea again. It should be mentioned, in case it is thought that there was never a break, that because the ships were coal-burning, each ship in turn remained in harbour for one week and boiler cleaned and gave leave, and there was nearly always one ship away on refit. In addition, it was necessary for the whole flotilla to stay in harbour for a day every ten days or so to coal ship.

When our work at Yarmouth was finished, we were transferred round to be based on Portland. Enemy E-boats had taken to coming over in the night and laying mines on the channel sea-routes, and the areas could be roughly delineated by shore based radar, and so for a few months we were busy trying to sweep fields as fast as the E-boats could lay them.

It was here in September 1942 that I changed bosses and the last regular officer other than myself departed to be replaced by an R. N. V. R Commander as Flotilla Commander and a remarkable character he was. His name was Herival and he was the Alderney equivalent to the Dame of Sark, and was reputed to have made a lot of money by running booze into the United States in the prohibition days whilst doubling as the Commodore of the Royal Channel Islands Yacht Club.

On the evening of the day he took command he sent for me and sat me down and said that he had never done anything like this before nor had he ever commanded anything of any size. Two hours and a bottle of whiskey later I retired to bed with his self confidence, if not his health, slightly improved.

Next morning at 8am we coaled ship and then stood off the jetty whilst another ship berthed inside us to coal, and then re-berthed outside her. On completion of this brief and simple operation he sent for me in his cabin again and said 'Pilot (for that is what all Navigators in the Navy are called) let us celebrate my first sea trip in command', and this time the best part of a bottle of gin disappeared. Life was never going to be the same again!

Thereafter for a short while we had an intensive period of sweeping, and there is no doubt that not only did Herival learn fast, but in fact he had a natural sense of seamanship and ship handling and also a delightful sense of fun. When our next break of a week for boiler cleaning and leave came, I was duty on board and Herival adjourned to Boodles club in London for his week's break. On his return on a Sunday evening, he sent for me to ask if all had gone well and to exchange pleasantries about his leave. He then proceeded to recount to me perhaps his most bizarre and yet completely true episode of his time as my Commanding Officer.

Apparently there was, and is to this day, a wager book in Boodles, and on the morning of the day he was due to return to the ship, some young blood wagered him a fiver that he could not make a complete stranger eat a raw turnip during the train journey from Paddington to Weymouth. The wager was at once accepted. He duly obtained a turnip, leaves and all from the club kitchens, set out to catch the afternoon train from Paddington, whose first stop was Castle Cary, and carefully selected a first class carriage, occupied only by one old gentleman.

Soon after the start Herival enquired of the old gentleman if he would care for a piece of raw turnip, and the old boy, looking at him with puzzled astonishment, declined his kind offer. Whereupon Herival undid his case on the luggage rack, took out the strop for his cut throat razor hooked one end on the luggage rack, sharpened his razor, cut off a slice of turnip with it, pronged the piece on the end of the razor and said 'Are you sure you wouldn't like a piece of turnip?' The poor old chap, now convinced that he was in the presence of a mad man, accepted the kind offer, and to cut a long story short had eaten the whole turnip leaves, and all by the time the train reached Castle Cary.

Apparently, as soon as the train had stopped, the hapless victim rushed out of the carriage, found the Station Master, and vehemently said that there was a lunatic in his carriage who had made him eat a raw turnip under threats of grievous bodily harm. He led the Station Master to the carriage and pointed Herival out, who immediately looked at the Station Master and put a finger to his forehead and pointed to the poor unfortunate as if to indicate that the poor old boy was a bit touched, and the Station Master led him away to another carriage, whilst the gallant Commander, his wager won, proceeded happily on to Weymouth.

E-boat activity laying small clusters of mines in our channel shipping route was increasing, and we were kept very busy rushing up and down trying to keep the lane clear. The Germans had altered their E-boat laid mine moorings so that when the mine was cut by the sweep, it automatically exploded in a hope that this would be a deterrent. In fact it saved us trouble, because, instead of having to stop and sink the mine, we simply had a spectacular explosion in our wake, although it was sometimes annoying when the explosion damaged our sweeping gear and we had to stop and stream a fresh one.

We were using various South coast ports as a base for these operations, and one beautiful day in the autumn of 1942 we were sweeping off Dartmouth when three aircraft flew in from seaward at almost sea-level. The usual instant debate concluded that they were 'ours', but in a very short time our views were to receive a major adjustment, as they swooped up over the hill at the entrance to the harbour and delivered their bombs on the Royal Naval College which had once been my Alma Mater. It was puzzling that they chose a time when the college was on holiday, and in the event there was only one casualty; a Wren who was caught on the loo.

We were shortly afterwards presented with a sweeping problem of a quite different magnitude. The Germans had for long been laying magnetic mines on the sea-bed, actuated by the magnetic field of a ship when it passed over the top, but these were only effective in relatively shallow waters. To overcome this, the Germans produced aircraft laid moored magnetic mines which could be laid in deeper water. Furthermore they were designed to explode when the mooring was cut, again as an anti-sweeping device. The big difference however was that these mines carried several times the explosive of the E-boat laid mines which we had previously been sweeping.

And so we sallied forth from Devonport to sweep the first field ever of this new type of mine. By the afternoon of the first day we had cut our first mine and up she went. The power of this greatly enhanced explosive going off in our wake was to give the ship such a judder and whip that everything that was china or glass broke, and away went our plates, cups, saucers, glasses, wash basins and lavatory pans. Luckily no steam pipes fractured. The dockyard soon had relief supplies ready nightly and the sweep went on.

And so we came to Christmas Day, when we swept the same as any other day, but on return to harbour that evening our Christmas mail awaited us, including a large parcel from Peggy in which was a present for every officer complete with a hand painted card, none of whom she had ever met, but which she deemed appropriate from the various descriptions I had given of them. They were indeed touched.

In early January came our turn for boiler cleaning and I had to remain in the ship. One of the functions of the Flotilla Navigator included, after every sweep, the very accurate construction of a chart of every field swept, and the precise position of every mine, and showing on it each sweeping lap undertaken, and this was forwarded to the Director of Navigation at the Admiralty to be examined to ensure that no gaps had been left in the field, before they issued a Notice to Mariners cancelling the field. We had swept so many small fields recently that I had got behind in these charts and had to do some catching up.

During this period, Joss Hodges, our Engineer Officer, who always had to stay on board for boiler cleaning, found that the chorus team 'The Academy eight', which was run by his sister, were performing in 'Aladdin', the pantomime at the Exeter theatre. The pair of us accordingly took the Saturday off to look at the phenomenon.

It was an absolutely appalling show with geriatric comedians, all the younger ones having been called up, playing to an empty house, and it was no great honour that we were given a free box for the afternoon and evening shows. However, we alleviated the monotony by going back stage to chat up the girls, interspersed with liberal libations of alcohol. Suffice to say, that by the time the evening show was drawing to its close, the pair of us, strengthened by quite a lot of vitamins sloshing around inside us decided that the show needed livening up.

The final scene was of two Chinamen carrying Aladdin and his Princess on a sedan chair, and we persuaded the management that we were just the couple to do the portering on this occasion: hardly an exacting role! And so we appeared on stage carrying our load, the top half Chinamen and the bottom half clearly naval uniform. We deposited our cargo and so far so good, and it only remained for us to turn and bow to the audience, pick up the chair and depart. However, this attempt at synchronisation proved too much for us and every time Joss bowed I was upright and vice-versa. So we gave this up and set about getting the chair off-stage. Alas the same problem occurred again and every time he lifted his end, mine was still on the ground and again vice-versa. By this time the meagre audience decided that this was the first funny thing they had seen in the show and roared encouragement and advice, until finally amidst loud applause our mission was completed, and my first and last professional thespian performance had drawn to its close.

Sweeping continued along the South coast, off South Wales and the southern coast of Ireland and then finally off the east Dorset coast. On the last trip up channel, we got a signal to say that it was thought that E-boats may have laid mines in the shipping lane up which a large American troop convoy was due on its way to disembark troops at Southampton. Accordingly we waited until the leading ship was sighted, streamed sweeps, and asked them to form single line, reduce to seven knots and follow in the middle of the swathe we would sweep ahead of them.

As well we did, for, probably to their complete astonishment, we detonated three mines ahead of them, before they turned to Southampton and we to Portsmouth, where my totally absorbing minesweeping year came to a close.

One could not have had a better introduction to accurate navigation in an environment of enriching human variety, and now with the flattering background of being cheered off the ship by the whole ship's company, and their Lordships having kindly twice mentioned me in despatches, once when the Fitzroy was sunk and once near the end of my time, I went back home very tired for a little leave for it had all been very exhausting work with long hours.

Before leaving minesweeping it may be worth mentioning two 'human interest' stories. Soon after joining Fitzroy, Peggy's hairdresser in Chichester heard of my appointment and she ran a knitting circle for the forces. They accordingly adopted H. M. S Fitzroy, and, after we were sunk, H. M. S Kellett, and I was the go-between who received monthly their kind gift of old magazines and newly knitted garments, mainly balaclava helmets and jerseys and distributed them to the ship's company. It was not long before I found out something which I clearly could not relay back to the kind providers, namely that the recipients of these garments which had been so lovingly knitted, were busy in their spare time unravelling them and re-knitting them up as presents for their girl friends!

H. M. S. Fitzroy was also adopted by the Fitzroy Tavern in Soho, a tavern of not wholly pure repute, upon whose walls hung inter alia my photograph. A limited amount of free beer was dispensed to any member of the crew who called together with a warm welcome. I occasionally looked in if passing through London going to and from leave in order to help keep the liaison going. On one visit I was approached by a gorgeous young blonde who gazed into my eyes and asked if I could help her. Being a chivalrous type I said that I would of course do anything I could.

'Could I help her boy friend?' she said, 'He is a deserter and hiding behind the piano over there and the red caps are about to come in to look for him and arrest him and are outside now'. Suddenly the girl looked less attractive, the tavern less friendly, and the great outside highly desirable, and thence I took myself at great speed. It is worth remembering that during the war, even when on leave or travelling one always had to wear one's uniform wherever one was.

So now the burning question was 'What happens next?' First however I felt we had earned a break and that Peggy was now well enough for us to try and have a couple of day's fling in London. It was very hard to get into a West End hotel at short notice, but I knew 'Scottie', the commissionaire at the Park Lane Hotel slightly and he got us a nice double room. Again it is interesting to look back on prices. Here was a prestigious hotel where bed and breakfast was twenty four shillings per night and a suite could be booked for two guineas!

For the first evening I booked us at the Savoy Theatre to see Robert Morley in 'The Man Who Came to Dinner' only to find that the stalls were down three flights of stairs, and it was a long haul carrying Peggy up them afterwards. We then had a light supper at the Savoy afterwards, and under the eating out rationing rules one could only choose one starred item. Peggy chose an omelette and when it arrived, found that it was made of dried egg! So much for the Savoy!

After a couple of weeks on leave I was posted to H. M. S. Dryad, the Navigation School and my specialist base, and did odd tasks for a short time which enabled me to get home every night, and then came the news that I was to be appointed to join the staff of Admiral Vian at Norfolk House, St James Square, London in a task which I then had to keep secret, but in fact was to plan one section of the Invasion of Sicily, namely to take the First Canadian Division direct from the Clyde to the beaches of Sicily for H hour on D day.

As this was the first opposed invasion of the war, Vian wanted an assistant to his three main planning officers namely Operations, Navigation and Intelligence, both to ease the load and to be an immediate stand-in if any of them fell ill. In the event as will be seen, I had later to take over the Navigational role; meanwhile I was given the nickname of Trinity and assisted all three.

10
Under Vian

I T WAS WITH SOME trepidation that I journeyed forth to Norfolk House to join the staff, in an environment of which I had limited previous experience. I did, however, know of Admiral Vian's reputation for eating Midshipmen for breakfast with a liberal sprinkling of iron filings, and of giving short shift to any subordinate who did not match the standards he demanded. Equally, however, if one did survive, he gave his staff loyalty in return and furthered their careers.

One could go home every weekend which was very enjoyable, but the problem was where to stay in London through the week, particularly as we worked late on most evenings and so could not stay far out. This was solved in a very pleasant way by the discovery at the bottom end of Piccadilly of an old hotel which had been taken over as an Officers Hostel for those working temporarily in London, and staffed by a lot of Dolly bird Debs doing their war work.

By the time I had joined there was only about three weeks planning left to do before embarkation, and during this time the landing craft for the invasion were under training at Roseneath at the top end of the Firth of Clyde under a large bearded piratical Commander called Colin Maude who feared nothing and no person including Vian.

The admiral went north to view the dress rehearsal by the landing craft and was met at Glasgow by Maude on his best behaviour and attending to Vian's every need. On completion of the day's rehearsal Maude brought Vian back to the station and put him on the night train to London, saw him into his sleeper receiving congratulations from a somewhat surprised Vian, and then walked across and put the Admiral's overnight case into the train for Aberdeen!

The time finally came to move to the Clyde and embark. In our case, the Admiral and his staff embarked on the 'Hilary' which was a newly converted Headquarters ship which had originally been a passenger ship plying between England and the Amazon. The ship was full of the latest communications and operational gadgetry, but only carried one Browns compass on which everything depended with no reserves. The First Canadian division was embarked onto their troopships and the Army staff under General Simmonds, the Divisional Commander, joined us in Hilary. The whole organisation was then sealed in its ships for three days with no communication with the shore until the time came to sail non-stop for the beaches of Sicily.

Through all this time of course, not even our wives knew what we were planning or where we were going, although they could know when we embarked, that they would not hear from us for a bit.

The armada comprised ourselves and six troopships in two lines all escorted by a number of destroyers on an anti- submarine screen, with everyone else keeping station on us, and we of course carried out the prime navigation with the responsibility of getting the whole shooting match to the right Sicilian beach at the right time. Whilst the Staff Officer Navigation was the prime functionary, the ship's Navigator and I also independently checked the position as we went along.

The main problem was speed as the Hilary had one large screw which was slow turning with 72 r. p. m. representing twelve knots and so even a variation of a couple of revolutions made a big difference to the speed. As there was no rev. counter I used to check the revs. and thus the speed, by appearing in the Officer's mess, which was in what used to be the after hold, over the top of the propeller, complete with the stop watch much to the astonishment of the inmates of the bar, and count the revolutions by ear!

Finally on the appointed day at the appointed hour, non-stop from Clyde we delivered the First Canadian Division on Bark West beach on the South Eastern tip of Sicily. The American Divisions from Tunisia were going ashore to the Westward, and the British 5th and 50th Divisions from Egypt and Libya were disembarking round the corner to the north and East.

We stayed off the beaches for a couple of days until the Division and all its accoutrements had been put ashore, and sailed for Algiers. Here, the Admiral and all his staff were transferred to the large commandered University buildings on the hill above Algiers at Bouzeria.

During the previous few days the Staff Officer Navigation had incurred the Admiral's displeasure, and as happened on these occasions, he quietly disappeared back to England. The result was that I was now elevated to that position, which was very nice for me, but I was in a slightly awkward position, because I was much younger and junior to the rest of the staff.

The scenario now altered and staff planning set-up was introduced to plan the next move after Sicily had been vanquished. Accordingly our staff under Admiral Vian combined with staff of 5 Corps under General Allrey to make a plan for invading Italy through the instep using Taranto as the main base port of entry, whilst the staff of Admiral Oliver planned with 10 Corps under General Horrocks to plan an alternative invasion up at Salerno.

Time none the less weighed heavy and a lot of the mornings were spent playing staff cricket using rulers as bats and India rubbers as balls with every wall a boundary, before moving on to swimming in the afternoon and playing bridge in the evening!

The decision was made that the Salerno invasion plan should be adopted, so our staff became the planners for the developing of Naples as the main army back up base as soon as the port had been captured and time weighed even heavier on our hands as we waited after the invasion to go forward as soon as Naples was freed. Just before we transferred thence, it was announced that Admiral Vian had been appointed the British Naval Commander for planning and executing the invasion of Normandy. Accordingly he left us to return to England shortly to be followed by most of the staff who would continue to serve him. Sadly but understandably I was far too junior to continue with him in his new very elevated appointment, and he sent for me and explained the situation with great courtesy and was kind enough to give a very good report to help my future. And so, in the event I had a very enjoyable time on Admiral Vian's staff and one that taught a young Naval officer a considerable amount.

Rear Admiral Morse was now appointed Flag Officer Naples and of the old staff only two of us remained to join him. The other one besides me was Jock Cameron, an R. N. V. R. Lieutenant Commander who was the Staff Officer Intelligence and who was in peace time a well known Edinburgh Barrister. A man of great charm, and nearly old enough to be my father, he was always very kind to me, and I was delighted to see after the war that he rose to head the Scottish Judiciary.

We moved into Naples the day after it fell and the first job was to get a proper berthing and unloading organisation going on the wrecked quays to accommodate the large number of ships waiting to enter harbour to discharge their badly needed cargoes. I then got the minesweepers to sweep a safe passage into Capri for the American rest and recreation area and into Ischia for the British. When Ischia was cleared I met a very interesting trio of the S. O. E. who had appeared from nowhere and had set up their base there.

In charge was an R. N. V. R. Lieutenant called Simpson-Jones, who previously had been inserted into Madagascar by submarine, had been captured by the French, and and was about to be shot when he was saved by the British invasion. His army confrere dressed in a kilt and the insignia of a Major in the Argyll and Sutherland Highlanders turned out to be a multi-lingual Swede called Malcolm Munthe the son, no less of Axel Munthe, the author of the story of San Michele. The third member was an R. A. F. Squadron Leader. They had some captured Italian fast patrol boats and were busy inserting trusted Italians behind the lines, blowing up railway lines, giving prominent Roman Fascists Mickey Finns and other delightful school-boy antics. They were a law unto themselves, appeared to be beholden to no one, and none of us bothered them any more!

By now Italy was out of the war, and their destroyers were used to provide an anti-submarine patrol off the port against German submarines. It was deemed advisable always to put one British officer on each Italian ship when it went on patrol and I went myself on one occasion. One fed (and drank) with the Captain and it seemed somewhat incongruous to associate in this way with someone who had been one's enemy a couple of weeks before.

I remember entering into an argument with the Captain about their invasion of Abyssinia in 1936 and he was quick to point out that they were only doing somewhat belatedly what we had been doing continually throughout the nineteenth century all over the world and in particular Africa!

Our staff was housed in a large house with a vast gilt ball-room whose owner had left in a hurry before the surrender, not even taking with him all the black shirts which still hung in the wardrobe. We retained his excellent chef whose skills were much appreciated, for in the early days we had nothing but corned beef seven days a week, and he was a master of variegated presentations of this simple basic food.

Very soon there came the time when there was nothing left for me to do. The port was operating, the minesweeping was finished and the staff were turning their minds to planning the interdictory invasion of Anzio. Accordingly, I suggested, and it was agreed, that I should return to the United Kingdom to take up a fresh appointment. I got a lift in a destroyer down to Catania in Sicily together with Jock Cameron who was also returning and we joined the troopship Almanzora which was returning to U. K. with an assortment of troops from the middle-east, a contingent of Polish A. T. S girls, some nurses from a hospital ship and two troupes from E. N. S. A. who had finished a tour of Egypt.

And so in early December 1943 we steamed up the Clyde whence I had departed in June. It seemed hardly credible that in that short six months I had helped plan the invasion of Sicily, delivered the troops, returned to Algiers to help plan the next phase, gone to Naples to open up the port and returned to where I started.

It was great to be home again and to find that Peggy had made steady progress, and we again stood ourselves a one night stand in London, but otherwise had a quiet and restful leave before reporting once more to H. M. S. Dryad to see what would be in store next.

11
Brief Interlude

O NE OF THE ADVANTAGES of specialising was that one always had a professional home to which to return, and one's appointments were always carried our by one's own specialist school. On arrival at Dryad on this occasion, my next sea appointment was not immediately in place, and so like others, ashore between appointments, I was allocated a Sub-Lieutenant's course to instruct and take through for their four week course, for as in peace-time, Sub's courses still went on although slightly truncated, for they still needed to be trained to fit them for more senior service.

Although having carried out a fair amount of instructing, this was the first time I was going to teach in my own not so long ago acquired specialist subject. The master of this skill was one 'Harry Still' he was a much retired and purple faced Navigating Lieutenant Commander of unquenchable thirst who was called up and appointed for the sole purpose of taking Sub-Lieutenants courses through Dryad. Not only was he a brilliant instructor, but as he set nearly all the papers and therefore knew in advance what questions were to be asked, his classes always did far better than any of ours.

The stories of him in his active career were legion but one that appealed to me was when he was Navigator of a battleship carrying out trials, and was standing on the bridge recording with a chronometer watch in his hands. These were very expensive, and were kept wound and measured daily and could only be replaced when the measured variation exceeded one second per day. On this occasion, Harry was startled by a sudden broadside and dropped the watch over the front of the bridge on to the roof of the turret where it disintegrated.

'That's going to cost you a lot of money' said his Captain, who was his bitter enemy, with intense delight.

Undaunted, when the shooting was over, Harry went down to the turret and picked up the bits, a cogwheel here, a piece of spring there, and placed them in a match box. He then forwarded this to the Admiralty Chronometer Depot with a covering letter stating that as the watch now exceeded a rate of one second per day, it was requested that it be replaced. Someone must have had a sense of humour, for that is precisely what was done and he heard no more.

He claimed that his final demise from active service before the war was due to the fact that he was at sea and it had been overcast for days, and having been unable to take any sights, he was decidedly uncertain as to the ship's position. Between the ship and its destination there was only one underwater hazard, and as Navigation, particularly after no sights, is an inexact science, he considered that the safest way of missing this danger was to steer for where he thought it was. Alas, he scored a bulls-eye. There may just possibly be a touch of the Apocrypha in his tale, but nothing was impossible with Harry. His great instructional skills and his delightful company could not keep indefinitely at bay the ravages of his thirst and he died about as the war ended.

We then paid him one last tribute; in the hall of H. M. S. Dryad is a glass case in which are displayed some of the school's navigational treasures, such as Captain Cook's sextant and into this case we inserted complete with nicely printed label 'The gin glass used by the late Lieutenant Commander Harry Still 1939-1945'. Higher authority was not amused, and it was removed.

It was now the beginning of April 1944 and I was appointed as Navigating Officer of the cruiser H. M. S Arethusa finishing her refit at Chatham and destined for a very interesting year. Arethusa had been torpedoed in the Mediterranean in the autumn of the previous year and gone to Charleston, South Carolina to be repaired, and was now in Chatham being fitted with various bits of British equipment.

12
H.M.S. Arethusa

I N LATE MARCH 1944, I joined Arethusa at Chatham where she was finishing her refit. She was the first 'Big Ship' to which I was appointed as Navigator and was a Cruiser with three twin 6' Turrets.

I was interested to find, as I was a relatively late joiner, what a large proportion of the wardroom was from the R. N. V. R. In fact of the executive officers there were only two of us who were not. Amongst the reserves was the Torpedo Officer who was an executive of the Gas Light and Coke Company and two Lieutenants who were respectively straight from Eton and a Covent Garden stall holder. Also among the reserves were two who were to become great friends and with whom took place most of my recreational activities. They were both, like me, keen on games, but they were also good at them.

One was Jack Simpson, an Australian, who was the Surgeon Lieutenant-Commander, and an excellent cricket and tennis player. Large of girth and with a quiet but dry sense of humour, his communal social requirements were modest, amounting to an insistence, when he was tanked after a guest night, on being allowed to sing as a solo, the only song he knew which was 'I can't give you anything but love baby' in a ghastly off key voice for which he always received rapturous applause. He came to stay with us after the war before going back to Australia and alas we heard no more.

The other was Gerry Eaves, in peacetime Manager of a Martins Bank branch in Liverpool. He played for Cheshire at golf, cricket and bridge and was very good company to boot. He had not been married long and it was reputed that when they sat at breakfast on the first morning of their honeymoon, his wife leant forward to him and said 'What a coincidence Gerry, isn't that the other three members of your Saturday foursome sitting at the next table?' We kept in touch until 1951 and then later I saw in the paper that he was a hockey umpire in the Tokyo Olympics and some years later sadly saw his premature obituary.

This was the first ship I had been in that had been refitted with a modern type operations room which was part of the Navigator's responsibilities, and Gerry had been appointed as a trained Aircraft Direction Officer to run it and generally be my assistant. And finally, for the first time I had a 'Navigator's Yeoman' who were trained at Dryad to do the delicate work of chart correcting and generally keeping up to date all the records on minefields and so on. I do not know how they picked them, but this one, though a quiet and pleasant enough chap, was quite incapable of putting delicate corrections on charts, or keeping accurate records of anything.

However, I was soon to see another side to his character. I do not know what he did in peacetime, but he approached me one day confidentially to ask if there was a chance of going on leave the following week-end even though it was not his turn. I asked what the trouble was, and he informed me without batting an eyelid that the gang he was part of in Clerkenwell were expecting a visit from their deadly rivals in Shoreditch, and were a bit down on numbers and he would like to go and give them a hand! One thing for sure was that I was not going to miss his professional services and so told him to be on his way. Somewhat to my surprise he returned unscathed on the Sunday night and informed me that it was as well he had gone because it had just tipped the scales!

And so in late April we sailed for the Clyde where various unattached Battleships and Cruisers were collecting to form, as we knew later, what was to be the bombardment force for the opening hours and days of the Invasion of Europe, which was clearly imminent. So well had secrecy been preserved that there was still no inkling as to what was to be the landing area.

There was a bombardment practice area near Arran, and each ship took on board the Royal Artillery Forward Bombardment Officer, who on the day would be forward with the troops, and calling for our fire and subsequently spotting and correcting the fall of shot. We used to land him at the range and carry out practice firing until on about 1st June each ship received a large mail bag which carried all the invasion orders, and from that moment each and every ship was sealed with no connection with the shore in any form.

All the orders were opened in my charthouse, and the work began of abstracting from this mountain of tomes, the information that was relevant to us. In brief this was initial formations with other ships, times routes, communication channels and initial targets and functions. Our opening task after proceeding in company with the other bombarding ships was to arrive prior to H hour on D day on our extreme left flank of the invasion area to give bombardment support to the airborne forces dropped prior to H hour to capture the Merville Heavy battery, which otherwise would have enfiladed the invasion beaches with devastating effect, and also to capture the vital bridge intact.

In the event their attack was so successful that only limited support was required from us, although I have a photograph taken forty years on, taken on a holiday visit, still showing the pock marks from our shells on the face of the battery.

The bombardment fleet sailed from Clyde on 3rd June, ready for invasion on the fifth and as we moved into mid channel the following day saw a horizon full of small ships and craft of every kind. Then came the famous storm, and everyone turned round and came back twenty four hours later.

It is no intention here to talk about the invasion as an operation, much ink has already been spent on the subject, but only to make comments where odd items of interest fell within my vision. It speaks volumes for the Royal Air Force that through all this time, with the channel looking like a maritime Piccadilly, no enemy reconnaissance plane flew over, detected the armada and blew the gaff.

And so finally on the nights of the 5th/6th, we steamed across the channel with a positively eerie feeling in radio silence with all radar switched off, knowing that all round us and beyond the horizon were myriad small craft, full of soldiers, and in many cases about to have their first taste of battle, and overhead immediately before dawn was the drone of aircraft, some carrying the parachutists and others taking the glider borne troops.

The sheer scale of the whole operation, far exceeding anything before in history, and the consequences of victory or defeat so vast was in itself awe inspiring and emotionally the sort of situation where one tended quite pointlessly to talk in whispers. The huge special chart was ready on the bridge, in which all the sea was a Naval chart and all the land was an Army map. All the specially laid marker buoys were plotted together with our first anchorage, all ready once we were there to receive our first grid reference from our F. B. O. to open our bombardment. For short term security, both he and we had a coding machine, which was set with a fresh letter every four hours which was obtained from a rhyming couplet unique to him and us.

I remember the couplet to this day:-
'Little Susie had her beat
On the sunny side of Jermyn street'
and every four hours, starting from the beginning, we moved on one letter.

We all arrived at our anchorages on time, and it was still not H hour, and then as the sun rose, a sight impossible to describe unfolded. Waves of landing craft and support ships delivering their troops: warships opening up their bombardments, aircraft bombing, enemy fire returning; the whole panorama an anthill of boats and people and the whole picture unfolding to a carefully preconceived detailed plan.

There was relatively little enemy aircraft interdiction partly because, almost unbelievably they were caught completely by surprise, and as the airborne drop had been so speedily successful we had little bombardment to do and so for a brief while there was little to do except drink cocoa and gaze on this astonishing scene, and to realise that we were on the extreme left flank as viewed from seaward facing Sword Beach so stretching for miles along the channel the same scenes were being enacted at the British Juno and Gold Beaches and then on to the American beaches beyond. However, as soon as it was clear that our services were no longer required by the airborne drop, our F. B. O. was transferred to the main Army Artillery H. Q. and we were soon busy answering his requirements.

The system was that one plotted the grid reference of his target on the land part of the map, then fixed the position of the ship on the chart part, and measured off the range and bearing of the target and informed the Gunnery Officer. He then loosed off the guns, and the F. B. O. who was observing the target, radioed back corrections to bring the shells on to the target.

Most of our targets were on the southern edge of Caen at a distance of some nine or ten nautical miles and so the problems of getting accurately on to the relatively pin-point targets were considerable without correction from the F. B. O. After moving anchorage as required to cover various targets for four days we had virtually shot off all our ammunition. One repeated target was a factory chimney in Caen over ten miles away, the top of which held a few Germans, who in turn were spotting for their Artillery. Such a pin-point proved too much for us and we never did knock it down. The only real opposition was from a battery of 85 millimetre on the hills above Le Havre who could just reach us on maximum range if we anchored on the eastern end of our pitch.

We returned to Portsmouth, quickly ammunitioned and were soon back on beat. Before many days we were in the same situation with our ammunition and so back to Portsmouth once again. But this time there was a difference. After securing alongside, I was talking to the Captain on the quarter-deck when a motor cycle despatch rider came up the gangway, asked for the Captain, and handed him a small bag with a draw string. He opened it and inside was just a Royal Standard. I did not get the significance, but he did – We were to be taking the King to Normandy for a visit to the troops and the invasion area.

Next morning His Majesty came on board together with the three Service Chiefs of Staff and we steamed out of Portsmouth with the Royal Standard fluttering proudly at the mast head. Once there, and having shed our load into the safe arms of Montgomery and Vian, we just hung around until tea time, when we picked them all up and returned to Portsmouth.

As we steamed up Spithead just before arriving, we saw an interesting sight a few hundred yards away on the port side. We were attracted to the sound of a loud engine

Taking the King and General staff to Normandy

noise that was decreasing and spluttering and it turned out to be one of the new German VI pilotless aircraft bombs just reaching the end of its range and slowing right down, which gave us a very good view of it until it fell into the sea nearby. We ammunitioned again whilst at Portsmouth, and returned to our usual beat but not for long.

The German bombers, for whom the skies were not safe by day, had developed the practice of coming over by night and parachuting down oyster mines into our anchorage area. These were mines which sank to the bottom and rested there in the relatively shallow water, and were triggered by the change of pressure on a diaphragm when a ship passed over, thus firing the mine. A couple of nights after we had returned, there was just such a raid, and standing on the bridge in the moonlight, we were able to see two such mines parachuting down in our direction. One entered the water close to our bow and the other just missed our stern.

Whilst we were pondering whether to go slowly ahead by weighing anchor to get further away from the stern mine, or let out cable to distance ourselves from the forward one, the aft one made up our mind for us by exploding! Luckily it was indeed a little bit aft of the stern, and so there was very little structural damage but very considerable whip which distorted the stern and put two of our four propeller shafts out of line. Furthermore, the whip broke the suspensions of both our gyro compasses, which effectively put out of use our radar and gunnery controls, not to mention seriously handicapping our ability to navigate and steer. As the quarter-master at the wheel down below had no compass, he had to be conned continuously from the bridge.

It was clear that we were no use any longer as a bombardment unit, and so we were ordered back to Portsmouth to de-ammunition and then to proceed to the Clyde to be repaired at Stephens yard in Glasgow. This was to be a much longer break from active service than was expected, because it was thought that the business of re-aligning the propellers would not take long, and so we did not de-commission but virtually kept our full complement. It was in the end to be six months before we went to sea again.

It was during this time that the Admiralty conscious of the fact that many Army and Air Force regular officers were being given higher acting war-time ranks, which reflected unfairly on their Naval counterparts, introduced a new rank called quasi-permanent Lieutenant Commander, open by selection to all Lieutenants of over five years seniority, based on reports from their Captains, and promulgated half-yearly like the more senior conventional promotions.

I had just got five years in when the first list came out and was delighted to find that my name was thereon. The normal length of time for a Lieutenant was eight years, so it meant one was going to get three years benefit in the higher rank. One immediate effect it had, apart from pay, was travel. We were allowed one free rail voucher per month for a long week-end for going home, which was much appreciated, as it can be guessed that a return fare from Glasgow to Sussex was very expensive, but if one was a Lieutenant Commander then one got a free first class sleeper thrown in as well!

Apart from the joys of going home for a long week-end once a month, even though it was a long way for quite a short time, life was clearly going to be tedious for some months with little to do apart from taking one's turn as Duty Officer, and in my case trying as Ships Sports Officer to organise various pastimes for the Ships Company with somewhat limited facilities.

I heard through one of the dockyard workers that Benny Lynch who had been a famous World Flyweight boxing champion lived nearby in Gorbals and could always be found in a certain pub, and Jack Simpson, Gerry Eaves and I started visiting him and hearing fascinating tales of his past career. However it was really very sad because he was in the advanced stages of a drink problem that finally killed him, and even then it needed both hands to get his pint to his mouth. However, his career gave me ideas, and I put up a notice for the Ships Company, who were nearly all conscripts, asking if any of them had boxed professionally in civilian life, because it occurred to me that one way of passing the time would be to manage a boxer in the local halls.

Somewhat to my surprise, I got two applicants. The first one informed me that he had ninety eight fights, and had won one, drawn one and lost ninety six and so was put on the discard pile. The other had a reasonable record in four and six rounders in minor halls and it was thought worth while having a go, and so rather tickled by the whole thing he went into training.

The local hall was called the Grove Stadium, of modest size and heavily smoke laden atmosphere, round which every other Saturday sat rows of pretty tough looking characters, mostly ship-yard workers, with bottles of Red Hackle whiskey either in their coat pockets or in their mouths, and with currency notes in their hands, betting feverishly on what was happening in the ring.

Into this environment I brought my tyro for a preliminary six rounder against a well known up and coming local lad. On went the pound notes on the local lad and down the throats went the Red Hackle in anticipation of a financial killing. However to their amazement and mine, my lad had far the better of the first two rounds and was getting rapidly on top. In the subsequent interval the opponent's seconds complained about his gloves and they were changed, and shortly after coming out of the third he hit my lad on the chin and he stretched out cold. Was it my imagination that I thought I heard a metallic clink as the blow struck?! Suffice to say that my protégé and I both felt we had had enough, and my career as a professional boxing manager was over!

To help pass the time, every Saturday evening the officers asked to supper a different contingent of the opposite sex. They included Ambulance, Fire Service our Women's Services, American Women's services and later the choruses of various London shows which had left the Metropolis and were performing in tie big provincial cities in order to avoid the bombing.

Then another commission came our way. One of our young Lieutenants wanted to marry a local Wren Officer and his mother who was the widow of a Canon and lived in a grace and favour house at Lincoln Cathedral totally disapproved and would have no part of it.

Once more into the breach . . . . ! Jack, Gerry and I formed a committee at the ship end and liaised with three Wren Officer friends of the bride at the shore end. They made the wedding cake and all the food, whilst we slowly smuggled ashore all the booze. Three weeks later there was a splendid wedding in Glasgow Cathedral and an excellent reception thereafter in the Wren Officers mess; amongst the last minute arrivals needless to say was the tearful and grateful Bridegroom's mother. I reckoned arranging three quasi-elopements before the age of thirty was quite enough and have not offered my services further since.

And so 1944 drew to a close, and so did our enforced idleness, and with repairs completed, we moved down to the Clyde for trials, and on New Years day 1945 at nine in the evening we sailed to join a Cruiser squadron in the Mediterranean, but not before a last moment of drama.

Having celebrated New Years Eve customarily and let it free wheel a bit the following day, we were not all tuned to the minute on sailing that evening. Some mistake was made by those arranging for the narrow gate in the boom to be opened, for as we approached the gate, the Queen Mary, all 80, 000 ton of her reached the same point inward bound with a load of American troops. We must have passed through the gate together with a gap of no more than fifty yards and with a sigh of relief.

Next morning, still not feeling absolutely factory fresh, I found that during the refit I had managed to lose the key of my sextant case and had to get the shipwright to remove the lid before I could take a sun sight! However, that was the last of our immediate misfortunes, and after six months we were on our way once more to help fight the war, this time in the Eastern Mediterranean.

And so a few days later we were once more back in Alexandria, with the political scene much changed since I was last there. The Mediterranean basin had been freed from the enemy and Alex. was all bright lights and fun. Greece and Crete had been liberated, but in its wake the country was in a state of semi-civil war, with ELAS, the Greek Communist party trying to take over the country from the Government which was supported by the Allies. Palestine was in ferment, with the Palestinians trying to throw off the British yoke and resist the level of Jewish immigration, and Syria and Lebanon were sharing determination, as the tide of war receded that they would not any more fall under French rule.

The three other cruisers in our Squadron, Orion, Ajax and Aurora, together with ourselves, stationed basically on Alexandria, scuttled round these areas of ferment holding the ring as and where the need was greatest. From our point of view, although in each centre of trouble there were many problems, it was a gentle war, comfortable on board whilst in the main at arms length from the trouble centres.

Our first major sojourn was sharing our time between Haifa and Tel Aviv checking that there was no illegal immigration into the country by sea and having a liaison, more sporting than military, with the Army units bearing the brunt of all the discontent, although we did send guards and cab protection on some of the trains. We then moved to Beirut, and hoisted the flag of Admiral Tennant for what looked like the possibility of an ugly situation.

The French had decided that they should re-enter Syria and Lebanon to assert once again their authority over this area, and to that end had sailed a task force from Toulon. The British had decided to resist this invasion at the wish of those countries, who having received their independence, naturally wished to retain it.

It was clear that much diplomatic activity was going on, and we then heard that the French force, which had expected to be unopposed, had turned in to Bizerta. In the event it stayed there for a while and then returned to France and dispersed. Meanwhile we had nearly three months of bliss. Beirut had everything, lovely beaches, smart hotels, excellent French cuisine, good sports facilities including a very attractive race course, and a forty minute drive straight up into the hills at Alle where one was into winter sports. A paradise indeed, now reduced to rubble and seemingly unlikely ever to regain its former peaceful charm.

I mention the race course particularly because on our first visit we noticed that amongst all the professional Lebanese jockeys was a sole Englishman who turned out to be a Corporal in the Royal Army Veterinary Corps and had been a minor U. K. jockey before the war. It was but the work of a moment to invite him on board for drinks in plain clothes and establish a close laison. Thereafter, when we went to the races, which was quite often, we leant by the rails amongst the cedars between the paddock and the course. If he rode by as if not seeing us our money stayed in our wallets, but if as he went past he whispered a number, which may sometimes have been his own, on went the wager, nearly always with the most pleasing results.

Into this temporary Levantine idyll arrived a bomb in the form of our new Captain. Our Captain since first commissioning had been a pleasant, efficient and somewhat colourless officer by the name of Dalrymple-Smith, well suited by his nickname of 'Dimple'. To replace him came Casper Swinley, a dashing Destroyer Officer all his life and well known in the Navy as one of its characters. He was as eccentric and unpredictable as he was dynamic and in many ways resembled old Herival from my minesweeping days. He quickly acquired very positive likes and dislikes amongst his officers on a totally illogical basis. I fell within the first category which was limited in size but had compensating disadvantages.

The Captain's cabin was on the upper deck and the only person who had to pass it to get to his cabin at night from the wardroom was me. Casper was very gregarious and liked sitting up late reminiscing and consuming inordinate quantities of whiskey. If he saw me passing to my cabin from his square port, he would give a stentorian roar of 'Pilot' and I would be incarcerated until the small hours to the grave detriment to my health. I soon took to crawling past his cabin on all fours so that he did not see me, until one evening he emerged from his cabin door to have a stroll on deck only to see his Navigator shuffling along like an orang-utan which took some explaining in a way that was economical with the truth!

He also had a habit of emerging on deck in the morning, and quite irrespective of what the routine was for the day, suddenly ordering some evolution such as "Away all boats under sail' or 'Land all wire hawsers on the jetty'. He claimed that these evolutions kept every one up to mark, but whatever else it achieved it nearly sent the Commander, who was trying to run the ship, up the walls. Casper was in many ways as endearing as he was unpredictable, and he could be very savage to those to whom he took a dislike, but one thing was for sure, that life would never again be dull!

Our Levantine idyll ended when we went to Alexandria to pick up a contingent of Indian troops and then deposit them in small numbers through odd Greek Islands recently liberated from the Germans and to ensure that the inhabitants did not support the mainland Communists. The end of the run was a small port by the name of Kavalla in North Greece which then became our home for some while in liaison with the 4th Indian Division stationed nearby almost on the Bulgarian border and again with the purpose of dissuading the Northern Greeks from supporting the Communist movement in the South. I recall that in a large house on the edge of Kavalla lived a Dutch husband and wife and their grown up son and daughter in some opulence complete with tennis court and swimming pool, and they offered much hospitality to our officers. One was left with the very uneasy feeling however that they could only have come through the war virtually unscathed by a very considerable collaboration with the enemy.

There was also in contrast a fine example of Ghurka loyalty. The liaison with the 4th Indian Division, which included a Ghurka battalion, included having their officers to a formal guest night dinner to which they arrived in Jeeps with Ghurka drivers.

Such was the evening that they decided to sleep on board, and it was only after breakfast the next morning when they were to return to their camp that they remembered their drivers, who having brought them there the previous night, were still parked in a row at the bottom of the gangway, patiently waiting to take them home!

Shortly before what was to be V. E. day we moved down to Piraeus, which was the port for Athens, and by now there had been installed a full-time Naval officer in charge of the base, complete with Naval and Victualling stores, wanting for almost nothing. However, some of the staff were locally recruited Greeks who were wanting for almost everything and this situation led to some fairly bizarre transactions. Naval officers Burberries were quite expensive items, but the Royal Marine who looked after me was up to all the tricks. He drew two bars of Pussers soap ostensibly for cabin cleaning purposes, and flogged them to the Greek storekeeper in exchange for a Burberry. He in turn flogged them on the Black Market for drachma, put the value of the Burberry back into the stores cash and kept the change, to the satisfaction of all the contracting parties!

One astonishing fiscal feature of our early days at Piraeus was the manipulation of the rate of exchange. The official rate for the drachma was 40 to the Pound Sterling and the unofficial rate ashore was 140. Unbelievably the Ship's Company were paid in Sterling, and almost at once Jolly Jack cottoned on to the simple fact that he could take his pounds ashore and swap them at 140 to the pound and then come back on board and change them back into Sterling at 40 to the pound, before taking his increased poundage ashore and repeating the transaction. It was only when the Ajax ship's company were reputed between them to have banked £25, 000 in their Post Office savings on board during a week's stay that the gaffe was blown and the ship's companies were only paid in drachma to start with.

Then at last after five and a half long years, on the 8th May 1945 came V. E. day, and at noon Piraeus time all hostilities in the West ceased. I suppose the first reaction for most of us was the sobering realisation that we had survived when many of our friends and term mates from Dartmouth had not, and that slowly our lives and the life of the country would return to normal.

Nonetheless, it was a time for celebration and it was noon! much liquid flowed, and after a brief afternoon lull it continued to do so. It so happened that fairly close to the ship there was a Greek fair that evening and at about nine p. m. a few of us, still of course in our uniforms, as that rule had not yet been relaxed, decided to pay the fair a visit, all of us with a considerable quantity of assorted calories swilling around inside us.

My first, and what was to be my last, port of call was a rifle range where for a few drachma one got three darts to fire at a target. The prizes were fairly revolting packets of ten Greek cigarettes, built up like a triangle in front of and below the targets. Owing to a certain instability of control, I released my first dart prematurely and accidentally, and it hit the triangle of cigarettes amidships causing the prizes to collapse in a heap.

It was at that moment that the enormous and greasy Greek woman who was running the booth, made the biggest mistake of her life. She turned round and bent over to pick up the prizes and I had two darts left! Even I could not miss that target from that range, and pausing only to let out a piercing yell the giant lady broke the world's ladies standing high jump record.

Three things then happened in quick succession; my friends melted silently away, a menacing Greek crowd began to form, and a posse of British Red Caps clapped hands on my shoulder, and one rapidly sobering up Lieutenant Commander was led away to the dungeon.

To give them their due, they saw the funny side of it, and when the tumult and the shouting had died I was released to wend my way back in board, much to the relief of my chums who had deserted. And the morning and the evening was V. E. day!

Shortly afterwards, we were back to Alexandria and joined the rest of our squadron, and took it in turns with them to patrol off the Palestine coast to deter illegal Jewish immigrants.

A strong underground Jewish movement was fighting ruthlessly for the formation of the promised state of Israel, not unnaturally resisted by the Palestinians living in a country that was still called Palestine, and also by the British troops who were trying to maintain the status quo, until someone told them to do something different. These forays were interspersed with occasional trips to Famagusta in Cyprus for no obvious reason apart from playing the local Army contingents at every known sort of game.

Then, after a few months, in the autumn, we were sent up to Trieste, and as we steamed into harbour we saw the splendid sight of the New Zealand Division steaming out back home at the end of their well fought war, in two huge transports with what appeared to be every sort of loot all the way up to grand pianos hanging on the sides of the ships. There was no apparent military reason for our visit, and it transpired that it was so that everyone in the ship could be given a week's leave.

The choice was either to go to Klagenfurt in Austria where the Army had set up a leave centre or to Venice, some ninety miles away. Our usual gang of three chose Venice.

All the famous top Canal Hotels were reserved for officers, and we were booked in to the Royal Danieli for the princely sum of seven shillings and sixpence a day inclusive of all meals. All the big Lido Hotels had been taken over for other ranks and one visualised the lovely picture of Jack sitting back after breakfast in a large marble dining room, rolling his own cigarette, and having it lit for him by the until recently very prestigious head waiter. We were in the fortunate position of having an introduction to the Town Major of Venice, an officer of great influence who virtually ruled Venice by decree, and thereby hangs a tale.

As enemy territory was captured, so it fell under the jurisdiction of the Allied Military Government Occupied Territories with the short title of AMGOT, until someone found out that this was the Turkish for Horseshit, when the two last letters were dropped. As the Allies advanced up Italy and were nearing the top, it was clear that not only would the Venice area fall within the British sphere of influence but that they would need to find a suitable officer to be seconded to A. M. G. to be the Town Major.

We asked the lucky incumbent how he got this gem of an appointment, and he said that they looked through the records of all the suitably ranked officers and had come to the conclusion that as in peace-time he worked in the olive oil department of Crosse and Blackwells Pickles he must know something about Italy and therefore was most suitable for the job.

We had a very interesting week's stay in Venice, which was just as it had always been if a little more tawdry and scruffy as a result of no tourism for a few years.

It was when we were at Trieste that Casper Swinley, whilst being at his most pompous, nearly got hoisted by his own petard. It was nine o'clock on a pleasant morning and I was Duty Lieutenant Commander on deck when two motor launches (M. Ls) entered harbour in line ahead, each commanded by an RNVR Lieutenant with a Sub-Lieutenant to assist him. Casper came out on deck and saw them, and pausing only to ask why he had not been informed that we were now in company with other vessels of the Royal Navy, ordered the 'Senior Naval Officer Afloat's' pendant to be hoisted at the masthead. He now assumed that the Commanding Officers of the M. Ls would immediately signal a request to call on the Senior Officer Afloat.

It was understandably crystal clear that these two officers had not the slightest knowledge of this etiquette and could be seen through the telescope sitting on top of their boats in nothing but a pair of shorts chatting to their subordinates. At 10 a. m. Casper could wait no longer and made a signal to both Commanding Officers that the Senior Naval Officer Afloat would like the Captains to wait upon him at noon; dress No. 10s. Immediately pandemonium could be seen breaking out on both vessels as the Captains' one and only white uniforms were broken out from below, and all hands were turned to in order to try and lick the uniforms into shape.

I surreptitiously sent my Royal Marine attendant over with an iron, and precisely at noon two reasonably smart, if a little coy, young Commanding Officers arrived at the bottom of the gangway. They were ceremonially piped on board and Casper complete with telescope, graciously bent forward and shook them by the hand saying 'Welcome, to my fellow Commanding Officers' and led them to his cabin. And then came the snag – Not only did the two young officers not know about calling, but having been ordered to do so, they had equal ignorance about when to leave.

The customary time before taking one's leave on these occasions is about twenty minutes but as noon turned to 12. 30 and then to one and was moving towards 1. 30. whilst we all waited on the gangway ready to pipe them ashore, it was clear that a crisis had arisen. I diagnosed correctly that Casper, having ordered them on board rather pompously, felt obliged to play host until they asked to depart, and they in turn felt that having been summoned by such an august personage to attend, they could not leave until he gave the signal. Accordingly I barged into the Captain's cabin and said that there was a message from one of the ships asking for the Captain's presence, and with an audible sigh of relief all round the party broke up.

It was clear that our Captain had not spared his hospitality either to his guests or himself as the latter lurched down the gangway seen off by a Captain with a severe list to port. However, he was a sucker for punishment, because I was then summoned to his cabin to be thanked for extricating him from his predicament, and the party started all over again.

Then we returned to Alexandria once more; the war was long over, and apart from taking it in turns on Palestine patrol, life had reverted to sport and flesh pots. Finally, in late 1945, with demobilisation starting in England and a surfeit of ships in the Mediterranean, we were ordered home back to Chatham, stopping for fuel at Gibraltar and Malta, but not before Casper's final fling.

He was very conscious, because of his age, that these would be his last days at sea in the Royal Navy after nearly forty years, and soon after leaving Gibraltar, he went into an almost permanent state of maudlin intoxication. This did not matter until the last hours before arriving at Sheerness at 8 a. m.

Steaming up the Channel at almost ten the previous evening with lighthouses flashing all round us, and a need from time to time to alter course to avoid other ships, an action never normally taken without the Captain's permission, I deemed it essential that the Captain should be asked to come to the bridge and sent a messenger to convey this wish to him. After a lengthy absence the messenger returned to the bridge and informed me that he had at last found the Captain, but as he was in the galley playing Nap with the Petty Officer Cook he did not like to disturb him. Back went the messenger to tell him from the Navigator that a lot was happening around us and he would appreciate it if the Captain could come to the bridge.

He arrived, clearly enraged, wanting to know why all these lights and ships had not been reported to him, and stating that he was staying on the bridge and wanting every new sighting reported to him at once. Ten minutes later he went to his sea cabin and fell asleep and we called him next morning half an hour before reaching Sheerness, having had a busy night on the bridge, ship dodging up through the Straits of Dover and on through the Downs and approach shoals to Sheerness. It was not to be that I could sneak into my cabin and try to get some sleep after arrival, for Casper desired my presence to celebrate our safe arrival home! Next day we moved up into the basin at Chatham Dockyard, whence we had started nearly two years before.

It had been a happy and eventful two years, with a delightful wardroom and a good ship's company, in both cases comprising more National Servicemen than Regulars. In that time we had trained for and helped execute the invasion of Normandy; been mined and then mended, and then had spent nearly a year contending with minor brush fires in the Eastern Mediterranean in Palestine, Greece, Lebanon and Northern Italy. It was the gentlest of wars and always full of Human Interest. Now it was time to move on.

One last act of family interest took place. At the beginning of the Commission, I had, at the request of the Wardroom Mess Committee purchased a picture on their behalf, which hung on the bulkhead above the fireplace. I was very fond of it. Before decommissioning, the officers sold off all they had bought, to be shared out amongst ourselves, and at the auction, knowing I wanted the picture, they bid me up but I went on until I got it, and it has always hung in our sitting room from that day to this. And so, all packed up I headed for home, another of life's chapters behind us, yearning to see Peggy again and wondering after all this time how she had progressed.

It was now four years since we were married and her letters had seemed to indicate some improvement, and certainly not regression. She had spent the whole time that I had been away with her mother, and had clearly made a slow but steady advance, since she could go on quite long walks on the flat and navigate upstairs slowly but steadily. The time had now come to assess whether we could now move to total independence with an establishment of our own, and that in turn depended on where I was to be appointed to next.

13
H.M.S. Dryad I

A FTER A COUPLE OF DAYS at home I went up to Dryad, the Navigation School, which was my Alma Mater and did all Navigator's appointments, to see what was next in store for me, hoping against hope that I might for the first time since before the war have a reasonably secure shore appointment for a sufficiently long period to get our personal affairs secured and settled. And then all the breaks started coming our way.

I was to be appointed to Dryad, not as in the past as a temporary supernumerary, but in a permanent appointment likely to last a year, and my duties, together with one other Navigator, were to take all the subjects in turn, numbering about a dozen, which were taught to Sub-Lieutenants in their compulsory course, and re-write each syllabus, updating them in the light of advances in technique and method, that had taken place since 1939, not least the introduction of radar.

So far so good but now other slices of good fortune came our way. Friends who had a small bungalow near Chichester, rented it to us, at a low rent for one year, whilst the husband was appointed away, and we moved in to be independent and on our own for the first time since we were married.

Such was the boost to Peggy's morale, that she soon found ways of pacing herself so that she could catch the bus into Chichester, do the shopping and come back, and keep the house clean and do the cooking and so on without overtaxing herself. The whole secret was that everything was on the flat, including the bungalow. At the same time as we moved in, Peggy's mother was offered a delightful small cottage on a small private estate on the edge of Chichester at Birdham, by friends, at a low fixed rent for life. Next door was a very nice building plot of a third of an acre belonging to other friends of ours, and as their post-war plans had changed, they let us have it for the price they paid for it.

Now came the last and biggest hurdle. Post-war building had started, but three in every four had to be Government or local council built to replace war-time damage and there was much scrambling for the remaining twenty five percent. I accordingly made an application to the council, clearly stating that I had a building plot next to my mother-in-law. , and as my wife was partially disabled, and in order to preserve our independence, so

that I could follow my regular Naval career, it was imperative that I receive permission to build a house on this plot. I received almost by return of post, to our great joy and almost disbelief, permission to build.

It might be interesting to note, on historical grounds, that the limits imposed on all private building were £1, 300 in price and 930 square feet for a bungalow, or 1000 square feet for two storeys, adding both storeys together, excluding the cost of the plot.

My uncle and godfather kindly guaranteed the loan from the bank whilst the house was being built, when it would provide its own security, and Peggy and I got to work by the hour on graph paper and finally designed precisely the bungalow we wanted. We were recommended to a builder, and the project was started. One great advantage was that builders fell over themselves to get private work, so as to give decent work to their craft trades, instead of the endless mass production and prefabrication. Naturally we were highly elated, but of course completion was still many months away, and the next problem was transport.

In no way, on top of all this could we afford the immediate post-war price of a car. We had all been given a post-war gratuity, based on rank and length of service and I seem to remember that mine came to about £200, which all went on buying the building plot. So I scraped together £40 and bought a pedal assisted for starting Auto-cycle second hand which we christened 'Dorcas' because we hoped that, like the lady in the Acts of the Apostles, it would be full of good works!

It took me to and from the station each day to get to work, , and Peggy having become a skillful pillion rider, it took us on weekly trips to watch the house being built, in shopping, down to the sea in summer and even to Fontwell races, where they were so amazed that they let us in for nothing!

For a whole year we made great demands on the poor machine, and she performed unfailingly, never once letting us down in a whole year, winter and summer. Meanwhile, after a few week's leave I started work at Dryad, auto-biking to the station, travelling to Havant on a workman's ticket, and being picked up by a Dryad car along with a few other staff officers who lived along the route.

The other officer working with me, was none other than Colin Shand, who was to be my near neighbour many years later in retirement, and our task was slow and painstaking, going through a syllabus paragraph by paragraph, adding, amending and purifying. At the end of each finished syllabus, the new work was then supposedly vetted by the Training Commander and, if necessary, returned for further amendment, before becoming part of the new Navigational Bible.

It was finally part of our function as we completed each section, to set some specimen examination papers, the test of their suitability being that yet another Navigator had to sit down under examination conditions and finish the paper in half the allowed time, and his answers became the standard for marking.

After several weeks of work I raised my suspicions to Colin that once the work left our hands, nobody further bothered to read it, and to put it to the test I persuaded him in the next paragraph he was writing, to insert inconsequentially and totally out of context ... 'and that is why the compass points North'. My suspicions were quite unfounded. A. short time later Colin was sent for by the Training Commander and asked for an explanation and got soundly roasted. However his revenge was not very long in the coming.

Up to the outbreak of war, some three years after qualifying, Navigators returned to carry out the First Class Ship course, which not only carried a bigger allowance, but one was not allowed to be appointed to Cruisers or larger until the course had been completed. At the outbreak of war this course was suspended, and indeed a number of us had been Navigators of Cruisers without doing the course. However, it was suddenly decided to re-introduce the course again, and irrespective of one's previous experience, a seniority line was arbitrarily decided, and Colin fell just on the safe side of the line and I on the other. And so it came about shortly afterwards, that the first post-war course started with me as a pupil and Colin as my Instructor.

The syllabus was not arduous as most of us had done it all before in practice, but then came the all important practical test in ship-handling where we went to sea and each in turn carried out a stiff test on which we were marked by Colin and the ship's Captain, himself a Navigator. When it came to my turn, I was given the particularly difficult manoeuvre of passing another ship on opposite courses and calculating the moment to put the wheel over so that one's ship turned through 180 degrees and finished up in station astern of the one going the same way. All calculations having been made I took over the ship, set her on course and at the precise calculated moment said 'Port 20' down the voice-pipe to the quarter-master and absolutely nothing happened at all and the ship went serenely on!

It transpired that when I was working on my calculations, Colin had stuffed a pair of rolled up sea-boat stockings down the voice-pipe, thereby ensuring that the helmsman was never going to hear any of my orders! Anyway, it at least ensured that in the circumstances I could hardly be failed, and so the course drew to its close.

Meanwhile, the house was progressing well, and it was the subject of much interest, as it was the only house which our friends had seen which had been built privately since the war.

During this time my parents retired from tea and rubber planting in Ceylon, and first went to South Africa with the idea of retiring there. However, after about three months they decided that having spent nearly forty years in Ceylon, they had no wish permanently to settle where they already sensed years of coloured problems. They accordingly returned to U. K. , as in the event nearly all the British ex-pats seem to have done, notwithstanding the climate, and came to stay with us in our rented bungalow.

My Father had gone out in 1910 and my Mother in 1913, and had endless servants all their lives, and of course it only dawned on Peggy and me when they came to stay that my mother could not even boil an egg or make toast! However, she surreptitiously went off to W. H. Smith and bought an elementary cooking book, and with Peggy's help, announced after three months that she was ready to fly solo.

Accordingly they bought a house in nearby Selsey called 'Wayside'. As, on the very highest tides, the waters of Pagham Harbour almost reached the bottom of the garden, I went off to the ironmongers and purchased a 'T', and with a slight re- arrangement, turned it into 'Tideways'!

As the house progressed and it was in the shape of an E with the middle prong missing, in consultation with the builder, we kept gilding the lily, innocently assuming it would still come out within the statutory limit of £1, 300. In went central heating in every room, hardwood block floors throughout, a Devon brick fire-place with oak mantle, oak front door, York stone paving in the courtyard outside the front door and so on.

In December 1946 we very proudly moved in. Seven years earlier Peggy's life had been despaired of and five years ago we had married in the teeth of medical opinion, and here we were, moving into our own house, fully independent, and with only very few constraining limits, Peggy managing to do everything on her own. The heating was by an 'Ideal' coke stove, oil not yet having come into vogue post-war, and even this was mastered by bringing in half buckets at a time if I was not there.

In January 1947, with still three months to go before I abandoned the 'quasi' and became a real Lieutenant Commander, I was summoned to be given my next appointment. , and could scarcely believe my ears when told I was to go as Navigating Officer of the East Indies Flagship H. M. S Glasgow and as Squadron Navigating Officer, leaving by troop ship from Liverpool in early February. And so drew to a close an eventful year ashore in which all the breaks came our way and changed our lives.

14
H.M.S. Glasgow

O NE DAY IN FEBRUARY 1947, with snow thick upon the ground in one of the hardest winters for years, and with Emmanuel Shinwell, the Minister for Power announcing a fuel crisis and power cuts, we once more said goodbye, but this time there was a difference. Sorrow at separation, but also the knowledge that I was leaving behind a wife fully established in her own home and totally capable of looking after herself with always her mother nearby in the likelihood of a crisis.

The troop ship which I joined was the 'Worcestershire', bound for Port Said, Colombo and Rangoon and like all troop ships then, run by the Army and dry! The vast majority of the passengers were indeed Army or wives going out to join their husbands stationed in Burma, and a sprinkling of planters and their wives returning to Ceylon, one of which couples knew my father well. Amidst all this motley crowd there were precisely four Naval officers; two for the base at Trincomalee and two of us for the Glasgow, and the four of us naturally teamed up for the journey out.

The journey out was eventful only for its dryness, until it was announced that there would be a fancy dress ball shortly before arriving at Colombo, and the four of us directed our attention to showing what the Navy could do. We found a small hold not being used on a lower deck and enlisted the help of the ship's Boatswain. Long canes for cleaning bilges and some canvas were forthcoming and soon the framework of canvas and canes produced a splendid cow which began to emerge with horns made out of short lengths of masking tape and canes. The fingers off a glove were sewn to the udder, and down each teat went an enema tube purloined from the sick bay, the other end of which went into a bottle of blanco. We drew lots for jobs and my fellow officer going to join Glasgow got the back legs and I got the front half.

His was far more the responsible job, for getting ever more ambitious, we fitted a three way switch on the cow's rump marked ' Off – Fresh – Tinned' . If the switch was put to 'Fresh' he had to pump away at the enema tubes to deliver the blanco out through the glove fingers from the bottle slung around his neck, and if it was put to 'Tinned' he bunged a lot of tinned milk cans out through the cow's posterior.

Mine was a simple job up front; one hand was covered in a long pink sock which I could protrude out through the cow's mouth as a tongue for licking purposes, the saliva content being maintained via a bottle of washing up liquid sling round my neck.

We had incorporated one Army officer's wife into our team, sworn to secrecy, as wardrobe mistress and make-up artist and attention was turned to the third member of our team who was to be the Land Girl in charge of the cow. Breeches and a green jersey, together with two half coconuts mysteriously appeared and a splendid wig was made topped by a typical Land Girl's hat, and by the time our make- up artist had finished, he looked truly glamourous. We had tremendous fun during all the waking hours for four days preparing the project and now the evening of the gala had arrived.

Everyone sat down to dinner in fancy dress of varying degrees of originality and just as the first course was being served, all eyes suddenly turned to the top of the stairs leading to the saloon, where the cow and Land Girl arrived, whereupon she sat on her stool and milked it. After the brief initial silence of disbelief, there was a rapturous applause and laughter, and then came the first problem. We had not practised walking up and down stairs! That did not prove to be too difficult if done slowly, but the next problem proved somewhat more difficult, and that was how the two of us inside the cow were to eat and drink. In the end, we both sat in the same chair, the back legs sitting behind me, and he got his food through a ventilation slit at round about the cow's navel, and I took mine in through the mouth aperture.

Next day, having said goodbye to our cow, we arrived at Colombo and disembarked to the Grand Oriental Hotel where nine years earlier my father had met me when I had come out as a Sub-Lieutenant. It was also the first time for three weeks that alcohol had crossed our lips!

The Glasgow was not due in from an Indian cruise for another four days, so I telephoned Hapugastenne where Neville Marquis was Superintendent, having taken over from my father, and asked if I could come and stay for a few days until the ship arrived, and returned to our old home for the first time since early 1939. I then joined Glasgow in Colombo Harbour and met Peter Halliday from whom I was going to take over, who was a senior Lieutenant-Commander of bucolic visage and great charm who was not destined to go further in his career.

He remained as Navigator for the journey via the south coast round to Trincomalee and I noted that he had a habit of drawing all his course lines on the chart double, rather like very close together tram lines, and I asked him why he did this, to which he replied, I would have thought in comfortable earshot of the Captain 'One line is to navigate on, and the other is for the Captain to bugger about with'. So, having reached Trincomalee, Peter seemed in no hurry to arrange his onward passage to England, until the Captain sent for us and said that he did not mind which of us was his Navigator but he was not going to have two any longer, so would one please go?!

So that night at short notice, the wardroom had a formal dinner to dine Peter out and me in, and it was only after this fairly extended function that I realised why he had been reluctant to leave. He informed me that he wished to take his farewell of the Commodore's daughter, with whom he had been having a mild liaison, and as it was now midnight, she would be in bed in her bungalow. It was his proposal that I should row him ashore in the dinghy to their private jetty when he would stealthily climb through her window and take his leave, prior to returning to the dinghy to be rowed back. We could hardly have been more conspicuous, still in our full mess kit.

The dinghy was ordered alongside and off we set, looking a couple of right Charlies with Peter at the helm and myself at the oars, but all went well and we were soon at the jetty, whence he set off on his mission, whilst I turned the dinghy round and prepared for a longish vigil in the pleasant night air. However, it was not to be, for within a couple of minutes I observed Peter approaching at as brisk a double as his portly figure would allow, and jumping into the stern, he gave a gasped instruction for me to row as hard as I could whilst he lay puffing in the stern like a beached whale. When we were approaching safe haven at the ship, Peter got enough breath back to divulge that all had initially gone well and he had silently climbed through the window and had approached the sleeping figure in bed.

It was only then that the plan went seriously awry for as he bent down to implant a kiss on the unsuspecting young lady, he spotted in the nick of time that he had entered the wrong window, and he was gazing on a sleeping Commodore, his large and hairy naked chest, rising and falling rhythmically. He had enough sense to depart as silently as he had come, but once clear, did not stand upon his going. It seemed to me to be a cross between a typical Wodehouse plot and a Whitehall farce, but with a happy ending where the consequences could have been disastrous. Next morning Peter was ferried across to a homeward bound supply ship, and I was, like the Captain, not totally sorry that dual control had come to an end!

This was my first staff and also Ship's Officer appointment, and the staff office was ashore under the charge of the Staff Officer (Operations) who was based permanently ashore. My main staff function was arranging and checking the timetables of ships moving to, from or within the station and helping planning exercises. The main problem seemed to be that frequently, if I was ashore in the office, the Captain would want to see me on board, and vice versa, and I seemed to spend a lot of my time running from one to the other.

Not long after joining, for a reason which I can not now recall, collected in Trincomalee were our two station cruisers and also two aircraft carriers and a large depot ship. The Commander-in-Chief ordered first a period of a few days intense exercises and then our first post-war fleet regatta.

A fleet regatta was the Navy's answer to Ascot week. There was intense training in all ships with crews from Officers, Midshipmen, Petty Officers, sailors, stokers, Marines, Artisans, Boys and so on, even unto the Commanding Officers skiff race, all being over a straight mile, rowed in cutters or whalers, except the last mentioned. Racing went on at half hour intervals for two days and there was much fraternising between ships. However, the big thing was the betting, with much dark horse information being bandied between the different stables, and historically each ship ran its own Tote, which was not really satisfactory because every ship had different odds.

As a keen student of racing, this seemed to me to be a poor system, and as the modern Ship's Action Information Systems had improved so much through the war and were all linked by countless V. H. F. channels I devised a simple system that linked all ships to a common Tote. Each ship was an individual selling unit and in each race as soon as the 'Off' had happened, each ship in turn reported in how many tickets it had sold on each ship. By the time the race had been finished and the winner 'weighed in' we had added up all the tickets sold, knocked off 5% for Naval Charities, divided the remainder by the number of winning tickets and told each ship what odds to pay out. To our surprise and delight the system worked very well and was subsequently published in the Navigation and Direction Bulletin as the standard work. The only catch was that some ships were accumulating money through its clients having a surfeit of losers, and other ships were short of money, having had a disproportionate number of winners to pay out. Accordingly at the end of each day's racing, I went round each ship, giving or taking money and getting more and more waterlogged in the process!

I remember the Glasgow won the 'Cock' for highest overall points, including the Captain's skiff, the Officer's whaler which I stroked, backing us perhaps illegally, with a heavy wager on the Tote and the Midshipmen's whaler, which in my extra-mural capacity as 'Snotties Nurse' I had trained.

The only difficulty in these early weeks of exercises was that the Navigators of the other ships, particularly the aircraft carriers, were years senior to me and rather resented being ordered around by a dogsbody many years younger. However there was nothing that a little gin could not soon assuage.

In June our first major trip away, we were to take our Commander-in-Chief, Admiral Sir Arthur Palliser to Singapore to meet the Commander-in-Chief Far East, Admiral Sir Denis Boyd. The latter had, as in the Mediterranean Fleet, a frigate fitted as the Admirals yacht in which Lady Boyd accompanied him when the Fleet cruised, but the East Indies Squadron was not big enough for such luxuries and so Lady Palliser travelled in the Admiral's quarters with us.

We sailed from Trincomalee at 8. 00 a. m. heading for the Malacca Strait, and I was standing on the bridge on this beautiful tropical morning with nothing much happening, feeling slightly elated at my new status in the Flagship. Suddenly, the Admiral who was a charming, gentle and kindly man, stormed up the bridge ladder in a towering rage. As it could hardly have anything to do with the way the ship was pointing, I retired to the back of the bridge to avoid any mis-directed flak. The Engineer Commander was sent for and there was clearly a crisis of the greatest magnitude. And then, through careful eavesdropping, I cottoned on to the facts.

Round the ship goes a salt water fire main at the high pressure of 250lbs to the square inch, primarily for the purpose of coping with action damage. However, one of the subsidiary purposes is to flush the lavatory, each individual pan having a spring reducing valve at the lever, so that when it is depressed, the flushing takes place at only 5lbs per square inch. Apparently, the Admiral's wife retired to the loo after breakfast, in due course depressing the lever. Alas, the spring in the reducing valve had snapped and she received the full pressure straight up her posterior! The imagination boggled at the thought of the poor lady being suspended between deck and ceiling rather like a ping-pong ball on a jet of water at a fair.

Normal service was resumed during the course of the forenoon, and the rest of the cruise passed uneventfully, although I particularly remember, when going down the Straits of Malacca at sunrise with a gentle off-shore breeze, that one really could smell the spices wafted from Sumatra some distance away.

Back in Trincomalee, five of us formed the 'Trincomalee Curry Club' and those who were not on duty, having got flying speed on board, would proceed ashore at about one o'clock each Sunday, to one rest-house or another and have a giant and genuine curry, after which we rested off on a row of beds, before returning on board.

One Sunday we decided to write a letter to the Times, asking what was the right drink to have with curry? We made some stupid suggestions ourselves to set the ball rolling and signed ourselves 'Trincomalee Curry Club'. In those days, and indeed right up until the late fifties, every ship abroad was sent an air-mail copy of the Times, printed on very thin paper, daily, and so we were able to follow the correspondence. A few desultory letters came in from the odd retired Colonel in Budleigh Salterton or Cheltenham and then it petered out.

In late July H. M. S. Norfolk arrived to join the squadron, and shortly afterwards severe economy cuts were imposed on the Navy particularly on fuel and it was decided to cut the East Indies squadron to only two cruisers. And so suddenly in August we found ourselves homeward bound, but before leaving each watch and half the officers at a time were given two weeks leave up at the rest camp in the hills of Diyatalawa.

Apart from all doing our compulsory rifle-firing on the ranges, it was a delightful relaxing holiday, with a nine-hole golf course, tennis and various other activities. Each wardroom officer had a cabin to himself with a private native boy allocated. I was somewhat surprised on reaching my cabin and seeing my somewhat aged boy, when he took one look at me, fell to his knees, put his arms round my legs and kissed them. I had never thought I was that glamourous, and then he rose, tears shining in his eyes, fished a battered old wallet out of his garments, opened it and took out what transpired to be a bundle of references. From amongst them he pulled out a sere and yellow piece of paper and showed it to me. There clearly in my mother's hand-writing was his reference for being my donkey and fishing boy when I was six years old on Maddagadera Estate. There was no way in advance that the Lieutenant Commander Hoare to whom he had been allocated was the boy he had looked after twenty four years earlier. He could only have looked and recognised, and I gazed at him in almost stunned disbelief! As far as he was concerned, I could thereafter do no wrong, and I rewarded him well for his past services when I left!

In August we sailed for England, saying goodbye to my much loved island, not to return again for thirty five years when I was an old age pensioner. All our Goanese cooks and stewards came back to England in the ship with us and so The Trincomalee Curry Club arranged a giant farewell curry for all the officers and wives and families the day after we arrived, at lunch time. There was every considerable kind of curry, from very hot to mild, several different kinds of rice and every kind of sambal we could think of. A truly splendid spread.

Peggy had come over to see us entering harbour with our paying off pendant proudly flying, together with my father and mother, the first time any of the three had seen a ship returning at the end of a commission, with the whole quay lined with waving relatives. Next day she returned for the great curry lunch and returned home afterwards, to get up nearly a week later; apparently this was true of many other relatives. Perhaps we overdid it a bit!

The ship then de-commissioned and payed off into dockyard hands, and as there was no immediate Navigational appointment for me, I remained in the ship in a virtual general service job as First Lieutenant for a couple of months preparing the ship for refit. It suited me very well because I lived at home and commuted to Portsmouth daily and life was very pleasant. I was delighted to find that Peggy had managed to run our new home very easily including walking half a mile to the bus stop and back when shopping in Chichester. She had found an old jobbing gardener to give a few hours, and new beds had been planted and everything was looking very ship shape.

Then in October I received the summons to the Appointments Officer at Dryad and duly reported, wondering what I would hear. To my great delight I was to be appointed back to Dryad to carry out a specific task and in addition would instruct any odd course that did not fall into normal training pattern, and in October I was once more back at the Alma Mater, to Peggy's great joy no less than mine.

15
Back to Dryad Again

M Y SPECIAL TASK, not to be technical, was that 'Relative Velocity' pays a considerable part of the Navy's manoeuvring, tactics and the like, and was based on the other ship being made to be apparently stationery and one's movement relative to that ship to achieve one's purpose, then calculated.

With the advent of radar, the presentation became precisely the reverse. One's own ship put in the middle of the screen and everybody else moves relative to oneself across the radar screen. Accordingly it was necessary to take every text book, instructional manual, syllabus and the like, from the simplest to the most advanced and re-write it as it were back to front and re-draw all the diagrams.

Such was the task, which at first seemed Herculean, but it was really only a case of knowing where to start, and then plodding doggedly on. Interspersed with this, I took three special courses, widely differing, and all worth a mention.

The first was a course of six National Service Instructor Lieutenants, all with high powered degrees. I remember that one was a Nuclear Physicist and another spent all his spare time developing three dimensional chess, with eight boards, one above the other. In addition to being able to move conventionally on any one floor, pieces could move up and down within their normal constrictions. For instance a knight could go vertically up two decks and then horizontally along one square, or always providing of course that there was not a piece in the way, a rook could go vertically straight up any number of floors.

Teaching them was exhausting work, and in the examination I set them a pretty difficult relative velocity question, which one particularity clever Dick answered entirely correctly, but then went on to write that this was of course the Navigation school answer but in fact was wrong because, as every one knows, Einsteinian theories show the real answer differs by an amount equal to I/The Speed of Light. I gave him zero for trying to be too clever.

The next course was the opposite extreme. It comprised four very ancient and barnacled very retired Lieutenant Commanders, who had been called up to command four wreck dispersal vessels which were getting rid of all the myriad wrecks disposed in the waters round the British Isles. All their uniforms had that wonderful patina of age, and one even turned up wearing a stiff butterfly collar. Another was the father of one of the Lieutenants who at that time was doing his specialist Navigation course. They treated their young instructor with the utmost charm and old world courtesy, and I in turn enjoyed leading them back to all the first principles of getting from A to B upon the sea and then gradually to the new fangled electronic aids such as radar and Decca upon which they gazed with starry eyed amazement.

My final course was the most bizarre of the three. I was sent for and informed that two young Sub Lieutenants had failed the Navigation course and it was expedient that they should pass. They were kept back from leave and I was given the inside of a week to cram them so that at the end of that time they could sit and pass a re-take in their failed subjects and join up with the rest of their group for the subsequent course and be in step again. Their names were Lord Conynghame and the Honourable Massingbird–Mundy, known to his contemporaries as Washingday Wednesday and a right couple they were.

No gentle courtesies for them, but a hard slog. On one of the days they asked if they could polish up their Radio Aids and we adjourned to the Radio room when I quickly found out their real motive. They soon asked if I would mind if we tuned for a few minutes to the running commentary on the Caesarawich at Newmarket, and when I enquired why, was informed by Massingbird–Mundy that he had a horse running in it which he had heavily backed each way. I remember the name to this day; it was Geoffrey's Lady and it came in second at 50-1 enabling the young lad to clean up a tidy sum. How they passed their exams at the end of the week I shall never know. Perhaps Dryad decided it was easier to pass them and get them off their backs than keep failing them.

Meanwhile, the main project had been progressing, when in April I was sent for and told that Pat Morgan and I had been selected to take the Navigation specialist course for the year as the two Instructors. Pat Morgan was the senior of the two of us and came from the Astronomic Navigation Department and so took all the subjects such as Spherical Trigonometry, Astronomical Navigation, General Navigation, Gyro and Magnetic Compass and such like, whilst I was to take Action Information, Relative Velocity, Tides, Radio Aids, Meteorology and similar subjects.

Passing out Course, H.M.S. Dryad, 1948

Like most top examinations and syllabi in any profession, much of what had to be taught was of an abstruse and theoretical nature, which once learned and passed for examination purposes, was hardly used again. The only trouble was that we, the Instructors, had to re-learn it and then quickly teach it before we again consigned it to oblivion in our minds.

We had a pleasant interlude in the middle for two weeks, at least pleasant for the Instructors, when in two frigates we took the whole course for their Navigation practical and their surveying, up to the west cost of Scotland, and in and out of all the most tricky lochs and sounds, whilst each pupil in turn took the ship for half a day.

Finally came the exams and the successful passing out and the Royal Navy now had six more qualified Navigators, the Canadian Navy had two, and the Indian Navy one, and a very strenuous but rewarding few months came to an end. New pastures were beckoning and I was back seeing the Appointments Officer after nearly a year back at Dryad.

I was offered H. M. S. Dido, a cruiser in the Mediterranean, which it was assumed I would accept, as it would be good for my career, or almost as an afterthought the cruiser H. M. S. Jamaica on the America and West Indies station, reckoned to be fun but a backwater. I instantly, to their astonishment, opted for Jamaica, realising that she would be based on

Bermuda, where Peggy's sister lived and was married and that with any luck Peggy could come and stay there.

In the event, the Commission in H. M. S. Jamaica was to take a very different path to that enjoyably planned and was to lead to a very big step forward in my career.

16
H.M.S. Jamaica ~
America and West Indies Station

IT WAS IN LATE OCTOBER 1948, that on an evening pouring with rain I joined H. M. S. Jamaica in a dry dock in Devonport. With me came the the luxury of a second Navigating Officer.

When the course we had been taking had finished, I was told that I could pick one of them to come with me as my Assistant, and to be in charge of the operations room, and was undecided whether to pick the one likely to pass out top or the one likely to be the best mess-mate. I chose the latter, who also in the event, was also the former, and who after one or two brushes with authority in his subsequent early career, was to rise to be Flag Officer Royal Yachts and a Knighthood.

The wardroom indeed was not only to be a very happy one, but was to establish a reputation wherever the ship went for hospitality mingled with a certain eccentricity. As I entered the mess for the first time on the evening of joining, the Surgeon Commander, who had already somewhat unusually joined, moved forward from the bar and said 'How do you do; my name is Robarts but my friends call me 'Ropey'; have a drink'!

Ropey, who was already well known in the Navy, was without a doubt the finest mess-mate with whom I have ever served. He really needs a chapter to himself, but two stories of his early career will suffice. He went to a medical school in London, an Irish orphan with a great love of horses, and an aunt who said that she would pay for his training. After eight years during which he tended to miss his examinations because they coincided with Ascot, his aunt asked him how long the course went on for. Fearing that she might call his bluff he obtained a L. M. S. S. A. and joined the Navy. Soon after the outbreak of war he was the 'Doc' of a sloop stationed in the Red Sea which, with nothing better to do, escorted two British Merchant ships from Aden to Port Sudan.

On arrival there both ships invited the officers on board for a drink and Ropey went to one, and the remainder to the other which had meanwhile sent two sheep to the sloop to help with their fresh meat supplies. Ropey got back before the others only to find the two sheep standing on the quarter-deck. He enquired of the quartermaster if they were guests who replied that he supposed in a manner of speaking that they were. Then show them down to the wardroom' said Ropey, who accompanied them thence.

When the rest of the officers returned to the wardroom, they found Ropey with his back to the mantle piece on which were rows of empty glasses, he having repeatedly ordered three whiskies, one for himself and one for each sheep, and drunk all three, solicitously enquiring of the sheep whether they didn't feel dashed hot in the Red Sea wearing duffel coats!

Later on in the war in 1944, Ropey, who seemed to have the knack of getting mixed up in any odd thing that was going, was attached to the Army in Italy for some special operation. One day, when travelling in a jeep, they got blown up on a land mine and his intestine was ruptured. After on the spot repairs, he was flown home to the Masonic Hospital where he was for about four months. On completion, he hired a large private room in the 'Goat' just off Piccadilly and asked a number of friends of both sexes to a party.

During the function he was repeatedly taxed by his guests as to what the party was in aid of and was very non-committal until the end, when he climbed on a chair and said 'You have all been asking why I have invited you here today, and now I will tell you. It is to celebrate the fact that this week for the first time for four months I have used my fundamental orifice for the purpose that it was intended'. After the war Ropey threatened to write his autobiography which was to be called 'Ropey remembers', and many a senior officer both serving and retired worried as to what Ropey would remember!

Ropey died, still a bachelor in his early seventies in Frenchay Hospital, leaving all his money to the Disabled Steeple Chase Jockey's fund. He was one of a very few people I have ever met of whom it can be truly said 'He had no enemies'.

Returning to the Jamaica, his first brush with authority was also his last. The normal rule is that an officer's wine bill is limited to £5 per month, which with duty free gin at 2 pence (old money) a glass represents a reasonable sum. At the end of the first month Ropey's bill was £23 and he was sent for by the Captain. It should be mentioned that although he had a good thirst, most of this was spent on hospitality to the many callers on board.

He went away promising to do better and the next month his bill was £18 and the Captain sent for him again, whereupon he pointed out to the Captain that he was sure he was the only officer the Captain had ever met, who had reduced his wine bill by £5 in one month! The Captain gave a sigh and said 'Go away Ropey, you are a law unto yourself' and Ropey went out and pursued his normal ways, unmolested thereafter. Shortly afterwards the other half of the medical team joined, and it was clear from the start that he was to be an able assistant. A bachelor straight from qualifying, except for a brief period of training in the ways of Navy, he started going ashore every evening and coming back at about eleven.

Finally we asked him what he found to do, and it transpired that on the first evening he went into a pub, and announced that he was light house keeper from Eddystone on his first night ashore after being stranded for three months and he was plied with free beer, the next night it would be another pub and say Longships, the one after that Bishops Rock and so on. However he concluded that he was now running out of pubs and lighthouses and it was time to think of some other alternative means of obtaining free beer!

The First lieutenant was 'Eric' who had turned over from the Merchant Navy during the war, and he and his wife had rented a cottage at Saltash on the other side of the harbour. He was delightful but somewhat absent minded, and one week-end, when he was off duty, he came back on board to collect something just before the bar opened on Saturday and somehow never did make it back home before work started on Monday, which caused the rest of us to have to institute very considerable matrimonial repairs before normal service was again resumed.

The Gunnery Officer 'Peter', a very friendly character, had bumped his skull badly on the roof of the Director Tower when the Saumerez got mined and had a large silver plate in the top of his head, which did not affect him in any way other than to acutely accentuate his strongly held view that the world was made up of two sexes.

'David', our Torpedo Officer, had come up the hard way from the lower deck and somewhere along the line had married an ex-senior prefect from Roedean. Peggy became Godmother to their new born son and a few years later David sadly fell down dead coming out of Gieves leaving us to act as his trustee for a great number of years.

The Lieutenants included 'Jimmy' who at a young age had been engaged in cloak and dagger operations in Norway and as sometimes happened when thrown close together in such operations, married a co-conspirator, a relationship which had not lasted long, but which had left him pretty insecure; the son of the chairman of B. O. A. C. , 'Mike', a splendid young officer of great good looks, who was to be married before the commission concluded, and of course 'Hugh' the second navigator who mixed high competence, charm and irresponsibility in an exciting mixture.

There were a number of other officers who had lived life richly and who contributed to life in what was to be a very happy mess, and over this lot ruled the Commander, a singularly colourless character, which virtually meant in practice that we ran our daily lives without his assistance.

One or two officers and their wives were staying at a very nice little hotel on the edge of the moor and just before Christmas approached, so the hotel filled up with the leading members of the cast of the Plymouth pantomime; these included Tommy Fields, the brother of Gracie, who was the leading comedian, and his wife, The Fairy Queen, the witch, and the principal boy who was very young, demure, monosyllabic and with beautiful legs.

It was not long before they were all regular visitors to the wardroom, and it was only a few days after Christmas when they kindly agreed to giving a show on board for the benefit of the ship's company.

In early December we were informed that on sailing for our new station in January, our first duty would be to make a formal visit to the colony of Jamaica in recognition of the fact that the ship had been paid for by the colony as their contribution to the war effort. Their Lordships said that we were to commission a portrait of the ship which would be presented to the legislative council and hang above the speakers chair. They omitted however to inform us that the officers would be left to pay for the major part of the cost. It being assumed, being in dry dock, that the Navigator had less to do than some, I was detailed off to secure the services of a good artist at a reasonable price, and after much searching I found a well known marine artist, who had been in the R. N. V. R. during the war, who painted an excellent picture at a reasonable price.

The time soon came to sail, and we bid our farewells at home, but this time not with miseries of long separation, because their Lordships had introduced a scheme by which wives could now follow their husbands to their overseas base, once suitable accommodation had been found, and we were sitting pretty as Peggy's sister lived in Bermuda, and so it was that she would sail out in March.

Mid January saw our much heralded approach to the colony and two days out, we received an invitation by radio from the regiment stationed in Jamaica, which were the Gloucesters, to a fancy dress ball on the Saturday which was our day of arrival. This was a tall order in the time, but the ships resources managed to turn out 24 officers each hidden in a large rum bottle, driven to the ball on a lorry as a load of 24 bottles, and out of each one stepped an officer dressed as a calypso dancer.

The whole thing went over with our hosts like a lead balloon. They were all dressed in fairly staid fancy dress and all had their wives with them in organised parties, and we of course did not know a soul and there seemed no great wish to introduce us to their parties. Fairly soon a lot of us started drifting off, and the whole thing was really rather a flop.

The next morning we had the Gloucester's officers mess on board for customary Sunday drinks before lunch, and awaiting their arrival I was talking to Instructor Lieutenant Seaman. When they arrived I detached a Major to entertain, and he shook hands and said 'How do you, my name's Cock, and without thinking I replied 'How do you do, my names Hoare and this is Seaman'. Our guest almost exploded with anger at thinking he was hearing the mickey taken out of him on such short acquaintance, until he suddenly realised all names were for real at the same time as we realised the double-entendre and normal service was resumed.

The next day was the big ceremony at the Parliament when the great picture was handed over amid much delight, and in the evening we gave our official formal cocktail party which was attended by the Governor, the Prime Minister who was Mr Bustamante, all the local high dignitaries and of course the other services.

After all the other guests had left, Bustamante who, amongst his other qualities, had a magnificent thirst, insisted on staying on, and between rendering local songs whilst standing on the after capstan, reminisced about his unusual past. This included discussing with him the time in 1936 when he was a fugitive from justice and I was in charge of one of the platoons from Ajax trying to find him. It transpired that we had combed a large garden area, whilst he was successfully hiding in a nearby water butt.

As normally happens on such Naval occasions, we got to know various Jamaican families during the course of the evening who asked us to come on ashore to one function or another which we were only too pleased to do, and then realised the look of horror on the faces of our Army opposite numbers and their wives, who still operated an inviolate colour bar in their quarters, their private lives and possibly even in their mess. It was clearly implied that we ought to have known better, but I fear we took no notice and went on happily cementing the entente cordiale between H. M. S. Jamaica and the Jamaicans!

From Kingston, the capital, we went round to Port Antonio on the North East coast, where the harbour is almost land locked, rather like a flooded volcanic crater with a hole knocked in the side. It also had a large hotel, and not much else, and it was here that another formal ball in full mess-kit was held in our honour, and there also in some mysterious way also arrived a number of the girls some of the officers had met at Kingston!

The ball could perhaps have started sedately, but grew ever less so, until long before the end, Peter, our Gunnery Officer could be seen parachuting off the roof of the hotel into the swimming pool in his full mess-kit with one of the garden umbrellas as his only visible means of support. We then moved on to Montego Bay and in turn gave a reception ourselves, before, after nine fairly busy days and sleepless nights we sailed for the Panama Canal and a brief cruise down the Pacific coast of South America.

This was to be my third transit of the canal and my first as a Navigator, a journey that never ceased to enthral, but an interesting insight into the Administrative ways of the Navy was to happen first. The Paymaster gets a fixed sum per head for feeding the ship's company and to get over the problem of price fluctuation, certain items are allowed for at a fixed price, irrespective of the actual price that has to be paid in practice. For vegetables, cabbage, carrots, and onions were recorded at a fixed low price, and so a considerable quantity were ordered forward by signal to the British Consul at Colon before traversing the canal.

On arrival, the Consul came on board practically tearing his hair out, asking what the hell we were ordering cabbages for? They hardly grew in the Canal Zone, were very expensive and considered a luxury, and by combing the area he had got just enough to fill our orders, but at a very considerable expense to the crown. If we had ordered asparagus or courgettes in the same quantity, he could readily have filled the order at a low price, and invoiced us for cabbages!

It was now February 1949, as we emerged into the Pacific Ocean, always a thrill, and headed once more, the last time having been as a midshipman, for Buenaventura in

Columbia. It had not changed; still a low featureless coast with a wide very muddy river with bits of jungle coming down in it flowing out to sea and still to be navigated upon by a chart surveyed in 1830 by Captain Fitzroy of H. M. S. Beagle assisted by 'Mr Darwin Gentleman'! Having found the seaward channel buoy, I was not really quite sure from the chart depths, whether our draft was equal to the challenge. I had my Yeoman calling up the depth under the keel and when the echo sounder was showing four feet I told him to desist in case the Captain heard and took fright!

I never did know if we touched the soft mud going over the bar, and if so, it could only have been a very light graze! My enjoyment of Buenaventura which had always been minimal was even more dimmed by wondering throughout our stay whether, having entered, just, there was any certainty that we would get out again. However, all went well, and we set out on our very long leg all the way down to Valparaiso; shades again of our Midshipman's visit some thirteen years earlier.

I casually mentioned to the Chilean pilot who boarded us at the entrance to the harbour, a girl's name which I recalled from those earlier days, and to my amazement he not only knew her, but said that she was now married to Chile's leading race-horse trainer and lived in Vina-del-Mar, the upmarket sea-side suburb of Valparaiso.

I got in touch with her, and even more to my amazement, she remembered me. I got hold of Ropey, who being Irish was mad about horses and we struck up a liaison with Carmen and her husband which resulted in being taken all over the stables, and then being invited as guests in their box to the big race meeting on the following Saturday, at which was being run one of their major classics, and in which her husband had a runner.

His horse duly won, and a terrific celebration started up with all their Chilean friends with Ropey and I feeling rather like fish out of water in the middle of it all, until liberal intake of Pisco sours by all and sundry broke down the barriers, and the pair of us were poured back on board at a late hour, tired but happy!

We left Valparaiso for Lima, and I persuaded the Captain that it would be a good idea, as it was fairly straight forward, if I turned over the whole of the trip to Hugh, the second Navigator, for training and experience.

The first evening at sea, I wandered up to the bridge for some fresh air and to check that all was well just in time to hear the Captain ask Hugh what time moonrise was going to be. I feared that he may have forgotten to calculate this in advance, but no – there was a brief pause before he answered 1. 42 a. m. sir, and in due course the moon obliged within a few minutes of forecast.

I mentioned to him afterwards that I had mistakenly thought that he had forgotten to work it out to which he replied that I was absolutely right, but he had remembered quickly that the previous night at the Vina-del-Mar casino with a young lady on his lap, he had remarked to her how pretty the moon was which was just rising and had looked at his watch and remembered that it was just 1 a. m. he also knew that each night moonrise was about 40 minutes later than the previous night, and the whole of the above flashed through his mind, and rightly believing that round numbers bred suspicion had quickly told the Captain 1. 42 a. m. In such a way did romance come to the aid of science!

Between Valparaiso and Lima was one of the more remarkable ornithological sights to be witnessed. The Humboldt current comes up cold from the Antarctic and meets the equatorial current about thirty miles off the coast. There is a popple on the water in an absolutely straight line, almost as if drawn on a chart where the two currents meet, and on this boundary must exist an almost inexhaustible food supply.

For mile after mile on this boundary line, marine birds of every size and hue from pelicans to little petrels dived and

Peggy, eight years down the road to recovery

fluttered and hovered and splashed, presumably subsequently to drop their guano on the rocks of the Peruvian coastline to build up even more fertiliser.

Lima came and went without anything untoward. We carried out the time honoured ceremony of laying a small wreath on the statue of General O'Higgins to commemorate his victory over Captain Pratt of Chile in the war between the two countries, having at Valparaiso earlier laid a wreath on the memorial to Captain Pratt for his famous victory over O'Higgins.

And so we set sail back through the Panama Canal to Bermuda, stopping only briefly at Jamaica to fuel. This was a brief unannounced operational stop, but that did not prevent all the young ladies that had been met during the official visit, appearing as it were out of the woodwork and lining up on the jetty for the ship's arrival.

Meanwhile in late March, the first officer's wives including Peggy, had sailed from England and arrived in Bermuda, under the new Admiralty allowance that made it possible.

They were booked on a maiden voyage of the new Cunard liner Caronia, albeit second class and two to a cabin, and Peggy had bought a new evening dress and so on for the big occasion. Alas, it was a fairly rough crossing, and not being a good sailor at the best of times, she retired on leaving Southampton, and rose again in Bermuda, the evening dress still in its tissue paper. However, the big triumph was that she had made the journey at all, which was far the biggest step forward since her illness, and her sister Joan whisked her home on arrival and she was soon back to normal.

In early April we finally arrived at Bermuda, which was our base, with all the excitement of our wives and families all lined up on the jetty, and with our flagship the Glasgow already moored alongside. Peggy was staying with her sister and brother-in-law, Foster, who was a good friend of mine, and a small waterside cottage had been ear-marked for us to move into. It transpired that this was a cover plan in case Joan and Foster quite reasonably felt that they did not want us being with them in their house for a long period, In the event it was deemed by all parties 'to be a good idea' and we settled in to make our home with them at Bayswater cottage.

Easter came shortly afterwards, and once again, after a gap of twelve years, I found myself in the Bermuda rugby side for the annual Easter Rose Bowl match between the Island and the combined touring rugby side of Harvard, Yale and Princeton. But this time I was older! About three quarters of the way through the game, I saw a huge all-American boy with close cropped hair and thighs like oak trees bearing down on our line and foolishly tackled him. He failed to get his try and I came back to duty two weeks later having very badly torn a thigh muscle!

I had bought yet again an auto-cycle in order to get to and from work, as this was in the days before cars were allowed on the streets of Bermuda, and shortly after my injury I was due to take my test, which was a demonstration of one's ability to drive whilst watched by an examiner on the steps of the Civic Hall. As my leg was bound round with heavy duty plaster and could not be bent, the people of Hamilton were treated to the remarkable sight of my going round the block with one leg stuck out rigidly at right angles to the bike like a circus turn. The astonished examiner passed me, not having seen the like before and then disaster struck.

We had three idyllic weeks at home in Bermuda, and a very attractive cruise had been arranged for us for May and June up to some of the smaller New England resorts and then on to Nova Scotia and Prince Edward Island. Then came news that Chinese Communist forces had reached the banks of the Yangtze river at Shanghai and had shelled H. M. S. Liverpool lying in the harbour, killing the Navigator seriously wounding the Captain and damaging the upper works. In addition the frigate Amethyst was locked in up stream and could not escape to sea.

Within a couple of days our Commander-in-Chief sent for the Captain, who in turn, on returning on board, sent for the Engineer Commander and myself. He informed us that Jamaica would be sailing in three days time to Hong Kong to replace Liverpool and we three were the only ones to know until twenty four hours before sailing.

We needed to know in order that I could work out which would be the better bet. Either we could go east about, which although it would be longer, would be quicker because we could go faster, re-fuelling at Gibraltar, Aden and Singapore, and would also of course use much more fuel, or go west about, across the Pacific, which although shorter, would take longer, as we could only manage the two legs of Panama to Hawaii and Hawaii to Hong Kong at our most economical speed and trailing two of our four shafts. It was decided to adopt the latter course.

Then ensured a very depressed forty eight hours, behaving both on board and at home as if nothing untoward was due to happen. Twenty four hours before sailing the Captain made the announcement, and all our wonderful plans for the next two years on station lay in ruins.

Peggy and the other wives took it very well; they could do little else; and I think in those early days a number of people, but not I, thought perhaps we might return after a couple of months.

The Admiralty are sometimes criticised for their inhumanity, but they behaved excellently. They left all wives on full allowances for up to two months during which time, they could opt to be repatriated at any time suitable to themselves. In the case of Peggy they were more flexible, stopping her allowances after two months, but allowing her to stay on with her sister for a further three months before arranging her passage home. Furthermore, knowing her position, they sent her home by Queen of Bermuda to New York and then by Queen Elizabeth home, so that at no time would she be in a ship without lifts, my respect for their Lordships rose very considerably.

And so one early May day, we sailed out of Bermuda, somewhat shattered to start our long six week journey on a slow boat to China.

17
The Far East

So ONCE AGAIN, a few weeks after traversing the Panama Canal on the way to Bermuda, looking forward to our long sojourn in the Americas, we were back passing through the canal the other way to a very different destination and outlook. The problem immediately facing everyone was how for several weeks, with only a brief stop at Pearl Harbour to fuel, to keep everyone's interest up when apart from the watchkeepers there was little to do.

A newspaper was started, and a daily amateur radio show devised, and in addition an inter-divisional indoor games competition was arranged to back up the usual evening tombola. The weather was consistently clement and life just flowed from one day to the next with an increasing desire to get to Hong Kong and get on with it to allay the disappointment of our transfer. Of course the one person who was consistently employed was the Navigator which suited him very well! At last in early June we steamed through the narrow entrance and in to the harbour of Hong Kong for in my case my first visit.

The war had only been over for four years, but to a new arrival the place was already looking like a teeming anthill. The naval exchange of official and social visits followed, and we settled down to our new environment as a private cruiser under our Flagship H. M. S Belfast and in the company of a Destroyer Flotilla and sundry Frigates. One of these Frigates of course was H. M. S. Amethyst moored up the Yangtze river, and the partial cause of our presence in Hong Kong.

Belfast left for England to refit and recommission not long after our arrival and the Flag Officer Second in Commander Far East, Rear Admiral Alex Madden moved ashore. However. not long after that he moved to Jamaica and hoisted his flag and it was clear that something was in the wind.

It transpired that using the five figure groups from the logarithmic tables of Inmans Nautical Tables which were the standard tables used for Navigation in the Royal Navy, as a cypher, Amethyst had succeeded in sending a coded message that she prepared to try and break out, and we sailed with Admiral Madden on board to rendezvous with her to seaward of the Yangtze river.

The saga of the Amethyst has been well recorded, and suffice to say here that we had on board the officers who had earlier been flown out from the Amethyst when she was first marooned, as they had been wounded, and as we arrived at night to seaward, so it was known that the Frigate had started her dash for freedom.

A tense night ensued, and then in the first light, there she was, safely at sea and under our protection and escort. The young Sub Lieutenant and Navigator Stewart Hett was later to specialise in the subject and become my navigator when I was commanding H. M. S. Burghead Bay, and I am certain from all I heard that the escape was to a great degree due to his skill, for which he perhaps at the time got insufficient recognition. And so, after this heady interlude, we returned for a brief quiet period in Hong Kong and then in the late summer of 1949 we once again hoisted the flag of Admiral Madden for a formal cruise to Japan. Admiral Madden combined obvious efficiency with great charm and courtesy and we were all delighted to have him as our boss.

Japan was of course still very much an American sphere of influence, but an area round Kure was overseen by the Australians, and it was to there that we first headed. It was my first visit to Japan, and although, not uniquely, I had and still have a deep prejudice against the Japanese as a race, I was very happy to enjoy the scenery and there could have been no more attractive introduction than the long journey up through the Inland Sea to Kure with scenery very similar to the mind picture built up from various illustrations.

Whilst the Admiral was in discussion with the Australian Military, the rest of us were engaged in the usual sporting and social liaison with the lower echelons. Having returned on board latish from an Army dinner, I found that the mail had arrived and retired to my bunk with some letters from Peggy.

Hardly had I settled down when there was a most odd feeling of instability and could scarce believe it was some by-product of over indulgence. Then I heard movement from the deck above, and suddenly realised that for the second time in my travels I had felt the effects of a minor earth tremor, but luckily nothing worse.

We then moved on to Yokosuka, the main American Naval base on the edge of Tokyo bay for further military discussions and for most on board it was their first experience of the U. S. Navy en masse. Since, as is well known, all U. S. Navy ships are dry, so our Wardroom was even more crowded than usual, with a quid pro quo at the Navy luxurious American Club ashore. They are always fascinated by pageantry in any form at which their experience and capacity are limited, and so the performance of 'Beat retreat' by our Royal Marines and band at sunset each evening was a great attraction. And so once again back to Hong Kong but not for long.

During our short stay our somewhat quiet and ineffectual Commander departed to be replaced by a very different and dynamic character in the form of an ex-destroyer Commanding Officer Bill Beloe, soon to be known as Uncle Bill who having teamed up with Uncle Ropey, were to become a formidable pair in the ships and particularly the Wardroom life.

It was a time of change for not long afterwards we also changed Commanding Officers. Our Captain to date had been pleasant enough and also efficient enough in a rather dull way and had always been very civil to me, partly because he knew nothing of Navigation and ship handling and partly because like me he was very keen on sport and we played a lot of tennis together. In fact his only minor vice was that he liked the particular brand of cigarette that I smoked, and used always to come up on the bridge with one cigarette in his spectacle case and then help himself from my tin on the chart table. His successor, Jocelyn Salter was a tall relatively elderly courteous tee totaller to whom we were devoted and with whom I got on extremely well: indeed he was a pleasure to serve.

Christmas 1949 came and went and early in 1950 we took on board our new boss, Admiral Andrews and sailed to meet the American fleet based on Subic Bay in the Philippines and had several days of exercises at sea; the first major Anglo-American co-operation for most of us since the end of the war. We all then returned to Subic where we hosted a reception on the Flight Deck of our Aircraft Carrier for our American friends, complete with the band of the Argyll and Sutherland Highlanders for a display of marching and Beat Retreat in their full regalia.

Our ships then all separated to various areas for brief relaxation and our first stop was Jesselton, the capital of North Borneo which gave a chance for our new Admiral to meet the Governor, and for us to meet the members of this somewhat remote community, which had a strong Australian flavour.

Here again was the typical British outpost. A Governor with a small supporting cast, a Chief of Police, a Parson, a few small commercial units mainly in oil and export/import, and the inevitable club with its two tennis courts. Again, as has been mentioned before in these somewhat isolated pockets of Empire, there was a splendid spirit of enjoyment, built up within the limited population and resources. We then went on to the Naval base at Singapore so that our Admiral could meet the C-in-C who also took the opportunity to visit our ship and its company.

The Staff Officer Operations to the C-in-C was a member of my term at Dartmouth, Peter Dickens, who was much decorated and got early promotion as a result of his deeds of daring with coastal forces in the war. He also seemed to have become rather lugubrious. He was in his early thirties and was not sure whether he was in love with the daughter of the C-in-C, Daddy Brind. He accordingly came on board and consulted our Commander Bill Beloe on the subject. Bill informed me of the consultation afterwards and said that he had given him a simple piece of advice. If you feel you can share her toothbrush, marry her: if you can't, don't. He did and they lived happily ever after!

We returned to Hong Kong in the early spring, and official thoughts were moving towards the fact that, apart from the continued domination of the Chinese mainland by the Communists, the area was getting very settled. Before the war the China station had a recreational base at Wei-hai-Wei, an island off the coast of North China whence they moved during the hottest time at Hong Kong for the annual regatta and other sporting activities. It was now thought that a similar base would again be a good idea, although for political reasons it clearly could not be off the coast of China. The place that came under the microscope was Ominato, a large sheltered harbour in the island of Hokkaido in Japan and we sailed thence in May to reconnoitre the place, and I had the job, for which I had little experience, apart from learning the subject in my specialist course, of surveying the harbour. Little did we know then, that far from our work being the harbinger of a new era of peace, it was shortly to herald another period of strife.

Our work was completed after a couple of weeks and we then sailed back up through the Inland Sea, with the hinterland covered in the most lovely blossom, to visit Kure once again.

By now Belfast had returned from England, and with the Admiral on board met us at Kure. There on 25th June 1950 came the news that North Korean troops had crossed the border and invaded South Korea. Both ships then left Kure and we were ordered to the east coast of Korea whilst the flagship sailed on south to Hong Kong. Perhaps it was a measure of how minor a skirmish that this was presumed to be at the time, that the Flagship steamed south and we were despatched to the scene. And so it came about that we became the first British military force to reach Korea, and off the coast met the American cruiser U. S. S. Juneau which had been at Sasebo and was the first United States force on the scene.

Before moving to the Korean war, the departure of Peggy from Bermuda back to England should be brought up to date, particularly as large organisations such as the Admiralty are often accused of having cold hearts. Peggy was allowed to stay on in Bermuda for many months after I departed, but of course with no extra allowances, and when she felt it was time to go home, (partly because the money was running out!) she informed the Commander-in-Chief's staff.

All the other wives had already departed on small liners or banana boats, but the staff, knowing that Peggy, for all practical purposes could not do stairs, got permission from their Lordships to book her on the Queen of Bermuda to New York and then Queen Mary to Southampton, a kindness which I much appreciated. I ordered some flowers to be delivered to her cabin in the Queen Mary all the way from Hong Kong and wondered if they would ever arrive. They indeed did so, because I got a letter from Peggy after she had arrived safely home to say that she had found these lovely red roses waiting for her in the cabin, and could not think who could have been so kind and thoughtful and assumed it must be my father!

Ah well! You can't win em all!

18
The Korean War ~ The Early Days

ON 27TH JUNE the Security Council endorsed military assistance to South Korea and here we were back at war. By the 2nd July we had been joined by one of our Frigates the Black Swan and by day with no specific orders, we would steam along the coast looking for North Korean military movement along the coast road and then start bombardment. It was difficult to measure what degree of success was achieved.

That night we all made rendezvous with the Juneau and during the hours of darkness we were attacked by a number of North Korean E Boats, a number of which were sunk and which were of course the first North Korean maritime casualties of the war. A few days later we paid the penalty of our increasing impudence at going ever closer inshore with our bombardments when an enemy shore battery suddenly returned our fire, hitting the mast and causing a few fatal casualties and some wounded. We were recalled to Sasebo which was established as the Allied Naval Base for the war, and which as usual, almost in the instant acquired the inevitable U. S. Officers club, enlisted men's club and P. X. store. The internationally famous Miki Moto cultured pearl farm was already there!

Allied ships were gradually collecting there, but as the founder members, Juneau and ourselves had set up a particular liaison, which led to the odd skirmish in the enlisted men's club where the two lots of sailors combined forces to take on any newly arriving upstarts.

It was now decided that American forces would cover the East Coast, and the remainder the West coast, and as the only Cruiser for that side, we found ourselves working with our own Destroyers and Frigates and also Dutch and Canadian ships. Our function was to patrol the coast to prevent any enemy seaborne operations and to bombard them should the opportunity arise, and it proved to be the most exhausting time of my whole career. Our time for any one patrol varied from two to three weeks and a lot of it was close inshore and with no lights. I was of course the only Navigator and although the Officers of the Watch were perfectly competent, there was never a long stretch for rest. I reckoned at most on getting a broken four hours sleep in each twenty four hours which equated about a hundred and forty hour week. Three or four days in harbour and then back for another stint.

Our pay was of course miniscule compared with our American counterparts, and to add insult to injury we were allowed a ration of precisely two 'scrip' dollars a month out of our pay. These were special dollars which could be used locally but were not generally legal tender.

I was far too weary to go ashore during our few days in harbour between patrols, but those with less arduous duties at sea naturally wanted to go ashore to the U. S. Officers Club. The problem however was that two scrip dollars was not going to get them very far. And then one of our officers made the magnificent discovery that a Hong Kong 5 cent piece which was almost worthless fitted the club 25 cent fruit machine.

The Jamaica Is Now Known As "The Ship That Did Everything First"

FRANK GOLDSWORTHY ON H.M.S. JAMAICA

Tuesday.

The Royal Navy men in the Korean campaign are calling the cruiser Jamaica "the ship that did everything first".

Here is the Jamaica's record in the first three months of the Korean war.

June 30th. The first British ship to enter Korean waters.

July 2nd. With U.S.S. Juneau and the frigate Black Swan in the first surface action of the war. Six E boats attacked and five were sunk, three being credited to the Jamaica's guns.

The Jamaica took the first North Korean prisoners of war.

The same day with the Juneau took part in the first bombardment of South Korea at Chumonjin.

July 2nd. The first ship of any nation to penetrate the Bamboo Curtain by firing in Communist North Korea. 138 six-inch shells fired at Yangyang.

When the American flagship was withdrawn, the Jamaica became the first British ship to command a mixed British and United States force.

July 8th. The first ship of any nation to suffer war casualties when a shore battery shell burst on the mast killing six and wounding nine.

September 7th. With the destroyer, Charity, was the first ship to sight and sink enemy mines off Korea.

September 13th to 19th. Was in the Inchon bombardment force preparing for and supporting the first big opposed landing of the war.

September 17th. At Inchon was the first ship of any nationality to shoot down enemy aircraft, suffering one fatal and two minor casualties.

Big mileage

In this period the Jamaica has steamed 18,000 miles and fired 2,500 six-inch shells and 1,000 four-inch.

Her Captain is tall, quiet-voiced Captain Jocelyn Stuart Salter, D.S.O., O.B.E., of Weybridge, Surrey. He is 48, has a son and daughter in their teens and has enhanced the Jamaica's long-held reputation for being one of the "happiest" ships in the Fleet.

The Jamaican men have one wry comment on their Korean campaign record. Their's is a ship that should not be here at all. It was due to spend a two-year commission in the pleasant waters and ports of the West Indies Station.

Then H.M.S. London was damaged in the Yangtse Battle and the Jamaica was hurriedly ordered to the Far East, leaving its West Indies base three days before 30 wives were due to join their husbands there.

Being briefed by the Americandmiral, befor ethe invasion of Inchon

This proved a ready source of provender fodder until one evening a somewhat inebriated Lieutenant Commander of the U. S. Navy tottered in to the club inserted his 'two bits', got, to his great delight the jackpot and to his alcoholic astonishment, received as his reward a large pile of Hong Kong five cent pieces. That was the end of that racket.

I did go ashore on one occasion, to the Miki Moto pearl farm and bought Peggy a very nice graded pearl necklace for the princely sum of £10 which was to give her great pleasure. During this time we had been topped up to war complement which included getting a third medical officer.

Our first potential casualty was on our next patrol when one of the ships company was diagnosed as having appendicitis. Normally, in peace time we would have returned to harbour and dropped the casualty at hospital, but being on war patrol, action had to be taken in situ. Accordingly the three doctors adjourned to the wardroom and collected a set of liar dice. The result of the play was that the newly arrived doctor who was an experienced surgeon got the knife, the young doctor got the anaesthetic and Uncle Ropey got the bucket! Suffice to say that the operation was entirely successful and the patient had a speedy recovery.

By the end of August, the military situation was getting more serious, and indeed what at first had seemed to be not much more than a border incident had now reached a point where most of South Korea was in the North's hands and only a fairly small area in the South East was still under the South's rule.

The United States therefore decided that a major invasion should be planned and executed as soon as possible at Inchon in order to outflank the enemy, give access to a major port and open the way to re-entering Seoul the South Korean Capital. The plan was made and the Forces assembled, with great rapidity, and whilst the initial assault was entirely with American and Korean troops, we, and other allied Naval units were a key part of the bombardment support. We were accordingly briefed by Rear Admiral Higgins of the U. S. Navy on 11th September and shortly thereafter were ready at dawn off Inchon supporting the invasion force. Shades of Normandy, just six years earlier.

We had considerable success on the very first day, when our bombardment was directed to a large North Korean ammunition dump which was on our maximum range. To our surprise and delight, we succeeded in hitting it and witnessed, almost over ten miles away, the single biggest explosion which I had ever seen. Thereafter it was the mixture as before; bombarding targets out of our sight to order, an invasion land battle continuing on the horizon, and only occasional awareness of what was happening, over and above the general realisation that the operation was going successfully.

At night we anchored in near by anchorages with our American boss ship, and were stood to at dawn daily 'Just in case'. Sure enough, early on the 17th, three North Korean, old fashioned propeller driven monoplanes dived out of the breaking dawn and strafed our two ships with machine gun fire and dropped a bomb each. Being already at dawn action stations we shot one of them into the sea, whereas our American friends were not so prepared, and the bombs all fell clear.

To rub salt into the wound, our Operations Room Officer reported in to our boss on the radio 'Splash – one bogey – out' in a very laid back voice as if it was the sort of thing we did before breakfast every morning, but it was rather wasted because their ops room was not manned either, so they never heard it.

After the successful invasion, we went back to rather desultory patrolling for a short time, but more and more ships were coming out to strengthen our forces including two carriers and two cruisers, and we had now not had a major refit since leaving England over eighteen months earlier. Accordingly in October we bade farewell to Korea and returned joyfully to Hong Kong and a brief period of relaxation, which included opening the bar at 9. 30 on Sunday mornings so that Bill Beloe and Ropey could have a stiff drink in order to ensure being able to hold their hymn books steady in church afterwards!

Which reminds me that I have said nothing of our Chaplain Raymond, who fitted in well with the many eccentricities of our somewhat unusual wardroom. We all at first thought he was a bit of a nanny, but he managed with no little skill to combine a powerful upholding of the faith with a considerable tolerance of the sins of us lesser mortals, and was not above trying a drop of sinning himself occasionally. His wife was the perfect 'Chaplain's Lady' and did a tremendous job in Bermuda keeping up the wives morale and helping to sort out all their problems, when we sailed away and left them all stranded.

Raymond was much in demand to preach in the Anglican church at some of the odd little places we visited, but did not get many brownie points at one place I recall, where at the cocktail party on board on the previous Saturday to one of his visitations, a local lady came up to him gushing, and said 'Dear Vicar, how wonderful that you are preaching to us tomorrow, and what is going to be your text for your sermon?' . . to which he replied in turn 'Dear lady, as one worm said to another in the churchyard, lets go and make love in dead Ernest'.

Unlike the ordinary peacetime commission, Raymond had to deal with unexpected separations, both war time and peacetime problems that flowed from these changes, wounded and fatal casualties, and a somewhat unusual collection of mess-mates. He did a fine job!

In November 1950 we sailed to Singapore and entered dry dock to start a major refit and effectively to end the active part of our commission. The refit was to take at least two months and we would be returning to England to pay off thereafter.

This should have been a quiet time for the Navigator, but I was also the Ships Sports Officer. The ships company had relatively little professional work to do, and it was essential to keep them occupied and so an enormous games programme was arranged daily, with up to twelve teams out on some days, mainly in soccer, rugby and hockey.

I had a considerable running battle with the Base Chief P. T. I. who was in charge of grounds, because he had a habit of drinking an excess of rum at lunch time, waiting for the first shower, putting up all the 'All grounds unfit for play today' notices and returning to bed. This so infuriated me, because usually the grounds were perfectly fit, that I took to taking down the notices and putting our teams out to play. This in turn, not surprisingly enraged the P. T. I. and the running battle was finally resolved in my favour by higher authority.

I started playing rugger myself and was asked to captain the Navy team in the coming annual five cornered contest between the three services, the French Air Force, which flew down from Saigon, and the Singapore civilian side. This placed me in a bit of a quandary, as at the age of 33, I was not in the mood to go into serious training, so I approached the Navy's sole selector, the base R. C. Chaplain, a splendid fellow called Father Briscoe, who not surprisingly was neither wedded nor a tee-totaller, and explained to him that I would not be training and would at Saturday lunch time have my regular couple of gins and a good curry, but if he nevertheless deemed me worthy of my place in the afternoon I would be happy to participate, but equally I would not be the slightest bit offended if wiser counsels prevailed.

In the event I led the side, and in our first match which was against the French Air Force, we won 3-0 (tries being worth three points then) and I was lucky enough to score the only try in the closing minutes. We then beat the R. A. F. and civilians by the same amount, and came to the final match against the Army who were also unbeaten. All the Navy had to pick from were the base personnel, four minesweepers and Jamaica and always traditionally been the wooden spoonists whilst the Army with large forces all over Malaya deployed in the battle against the Communists were considered to be automatic cup winners, particularly as they could fly all their best players down from where ever.

The battle was to take place on the Army ground at Nee Soon, and all the morning it pelted down like a monsoon. However the sun came out just before the match but there were large areas of standing water on the pitch. I got our side together and told the three quarters they would not see the ball, but I would buy them plenty of beer afterwards, and the forwards, supported by the halves were to kick and run, or dribble at every opportunity.

For 35 minutes each way we hacked and splashed through the water to an eighteen points to three victory, every point being scored by the forwards, and sustained by the sounds of myriad Brigadiers and Colonels screaming 'Bloody soccer' through their moustaches! The cup was ours for the first time ever, and I honoured my promise to the three quarters with interest and conducted other alcoholic Exchange and Mart before finally arriving on board and dropping my rugger boots out of my cabin port hole, never to play rugger again.

New Year's Eve, 1950. Promoted, and then . . .

It was now approaching New Years Eve, and some of the Lieutenants who had struck up quite a liaison with the girls, set about planning a fancy dress party to go to the Tanglin club on that occasion, and with the help of the girls, produced a set of very effective costumes for Nelsonian sailors and their molls, and included me in the party. However, somewhat of a personal drama was to come first, for on New Years Eve the half yearly promotions come out at 10. 00 G. M. T which was 6. 00 pm Singapore time, and to my great thrill I found that I had been promoted to Commander at the tender age of thirty three. I immediately played host to the wardroom, it having just become bar opening time and then our mates gathered as can be seen from the photograph opposite in the mess to start the party, having acquired as props, a Carley raft, hand cuff, a cat-o-nine-tails and a caged parrot.

Our arrival at the club caused quite a stir amongst the more staidly arrayed members of the club and not a little merriment, but later in the evening, unfortunately, one of our young officers overstepped the mark by letting off a thunderflash, quite overlooking the delicate military situation then reigning in the area. Instantly all the members were diving under the tables or taking similar avoiding action, thinking some insurgent attack was taking place, and were not amused when they found out the facts.

Having acquired my brass hat, I was no longer doing any of my previous ships duties, except for navigating because there was no one else to do that so I was not sorry when with the refit completed, and our duties in the Far East completed, we sailed for England in late January, arriving at Devonport in early February, a little over two years after leaving and having circumnavigated the globe and taken part in a number of activities far removed from what we had in mind when we sailed for Bermuda late in 1948.

Our Commander, Bill Beloe's wife very kindly brought Peggy down to Devonport to meet us when we came in, and indeed most officers wives all met together at the Grand Hotel amid much celebration. There was little to retain me any longer in the ship so we were on our way home within a few days for much needed leave.

I presumed, now I was a Commander that I would go down some other avenue than Dryad to seek my next employment, but I soon got a summons from the old Alma Mater and was delighted to find that I was to return there as the Trials and Development Commander for all matters connected with Navigation and Aircraft Direction, and was to join in early April which would give me a nice spell of leave.

19
Trials and Development Commander ~ H.M.S. Dryad and Staff Course

I N APRIL 1951 I was very happily back at the Alma Mater once more, but this time in one of the three Commander's appointments, the other, and more senior, being the Commander of the Establishment and the Training Commander. My function was to be in charge of all trials and development of all future equipment and design for both the Navigational Specialisation, but also Aircraft Direction, the chain being that the Admiralty decided the policy in these fields, the Admiralty Radar Establishment on Portsdown Hill where all the Naval Scientists worked, as it were, invented the hardware to meet the policy requirements, and then we carried out the trials to prove the design and then made plans to fit the end product into the ships.

I had two sub-departments, one dealing with the trials, and the other with designing the future ship's operations rooms, within the space allowed by the ship designers to accommodate the new equipment. We were totally divorced from the rest of the establishment, whilst being part of it, as they were, as we had been in previous incarnations, totally concerned in instruction, and we were the odd bodies who were only seen at meals!

Amongst my assistants were a couple of long-in-the-tooth Lieutenant Commanders, who were never to be destined for the higher ranks, but who possessed the particular type of egg headed brains which particularly fitted our trials requirements. One, Vernon by name, had been there six years, and claimed that he had eaten cold pork pie in the mess every week for those six years, and was now deeply concerned whether the trials he was conducting should cover investigations on whether his diet had changed his metabolism to the point where he was becoming part pig!

All of our work was overshadowed by the very large project which was being developed by our scientists at Portsdown, and which was leading the world to change aircraft interception and the display of action information from chinagraph pencils and plastic screens to entirely electronic display. This was called the comprehensive display system, and it is interesting to look back and realise that the system took up a very large amount of space and contained many thousand old fashioned valves, and much experimentation went into finding a way of producing writing on the display screens as this had never yet been achieved.

There were indeed so many valves that, with their average life, one was expected to blow every half hour or so, and so there was a monitoring system so that a special chap could rush round replacing the valves as they blew. It is indeed a far cry from modern computerisation, miniaturisation, microchips and all the rest.

The genius behind the whole concept, which was then far ahead of its time was a brilliant scientist called Doctor Benjamin of considerable quiet humour and modesty, who was a Naval Scientist at Portsdown and C. D. S. was his special brain child. I remember well when his American counter-parts came over for a visit to see how development was going and one of them said 'Benji, I am sure if you only go on developing your project for another year you will have a much better final answer', to which he replied that when one feels that if one was to go on for just a little longer the answer would be much better, that is the moment to freeze for production, or one just goes on developing for ever without achieving anything. However, C. D. S. , although fitted in a few snips, was not to last long. So rapid was the development of miniaturisation and the like that soon it gave way to replacements of much smaller size and much greater reliability.

On a more domestic note, as I had been abroad for the few years before the war, and with parents living abroad and no private income of my own, I not only never owned a car but had reached this point without even being able to drive one. There were of course practically no new cars available, and such as there were had long waiting lists. In addition, as no cars had been built in the war, the second hand market comprised cars that were over ten years old and costing roughly double their pre-war price when new. I purchased an ancient Morris Eight, had a set of driving lessons, and took my test, straight from work, complete with brass hat, and promptly knocked a cyclist off his bike! A second test four weeks later was successfully negotiated and the increased mobility greatly helped our lives. It was now six years after the end of the war in Europe and it is interesting to think back and realise that food rationing was not to end for another two years.

One of the functions of this appointment was to be on the Naval Sub-Committee of the operational Sub-Committee of the Medical Research Council and many and varied were the subjects investigated and it may be of interest to mention some. One test showed that if a Radar Operator was watching a screen when on watch continually for, say, four hours, his capacity for spotting a blip as soon as it appeared diminished considerably after the first 30 minutes! This meant that large financial resources went into increasing Radar Detection range all to no avail because the operator might not spot the blip until the range had considerably decreased. The obvious answer was to have two operators on watch and change them round every thirty minutes.

From this the natural extension was to Captains on the Bridge in wartime. Their natural inclination was to stay on the bridge round the clock if there was any chance of anything happening and thereby placing themselves in a position that when something eventually did suddenly happen, they might well be too tired to make the right decision.

Other subjects I recall varied from sea-sick cures for assault troops that would not also make them feel drowsy to the best way of arranging a bank of gauges, so that it would most easily become apparent if one was indicating a fault.

However the equipment that intrigued me most, which was investigated by Professor Broadbent of the Applied Psychology unit at Cambridge University, who was a member of our committee was how best to present a mass of information on screens such as aircraft readiness or the like so that, if one single discreet piece of information was changed, the user who required that information change would notice.

In the past all Action Information was written up on plastic screens with chinagraph pencil and attention drawn by the writer simply tapping the screen with the pencil, but now C. D. S. was going to generate masses more information which would change more quickly and chinagraph was out. It was then that I had one of my few bright ideas, perhaps because of a misspent youth, and recalled the greyhound racing tote, keeping continuous betting information up to date.

Even service experimentation has its demarcation disputes, and because this was electric and not electronic, I had to trot off to the Director of Electric Engineering at Bath to chase down this avenue. We jointly found that these totes were made by Standard Telephones at Foots Cray and from this starting point the information tote for the C. D. S. progressed to fruition. My associate at Bath warned me that we had need to proceed with extreme economy because his bosses professional parsimony stemmed from his private life where he was reputed when driving his car in the rain to switch off his windscreen wipers when passing under a bridge in order to save his battery!

Not long after I joined, Lord Mountbatten, then first Sea Lord, paid a formal visit to Dryad and came to our Department during his tour. He was intrigued at our models and drawings of the operations rooms for ships being built incorporating all the latest equipment. He then turned away, gave a grunt, and said 'Just like a London night club, more and more tables, and less and less room to dance'! I then asked him whether he had often used the Mountbatten station keeper which he had invented before the war and which was fitted on the bridge of every destroyer. 'Once only', he said, 'and that was when I stood on the top of it to dive into the sea when the Kelly was sunk'!

All specialisations ran an occasional trade magazine in order to keep the Fleet in touch with latest development and thinking, and ours was called the N. D. Bulletin to which, as previously mentioned, I had contributed an article on how to use the Action Information to run a Regatta Tote. The contents were usually pretty turgid stuff, so I leavened it a little by contributing an article on how navigational skills could contribute to domestic harmony. When sitting in my sister-in-law's kitchen in Bermuda, she had put an egg on to boil and found she did not have a watch. Luckily I noticed through the window the flashing of Gibbs Hill Lighthouse which I knew flashed once every thirty seconds. After counting off eight flashes, the egg was removed done to a turn!

On the Dryad staff was an officer of each of the other specialisations, mainly in an Instructional role, but also for working with us, and they were in general hand-picked and of considerable talent if occasionally eccentric personality. I remember particularly the dining-out of one 'Peter', and although he only lived a few miles away at Wickham, we decided it advisable that a cabin be arranged so that he need not have to drive home at the end of the festivities.

It was a splendid evening, as he was a particularly popular officer, and in due course in the early hours he returned to his cabin. However, having failed to bring in any sheets, he woke up at about 5 a. m. between hairy blankets, got up in disgust, half dressed, got in his car and drove home to Wickham. Having arrived, instead of going to bed, he pulled the sheets out from under his protesting wife, and drove all the way back to Dryad, made his bed and went back to sleep!

Meanwhile, at home, there were considerable developments, and since they were of a somewhat personal nature, I have thought long whether to commit the events to paper. However, since the results that were to evolve over the ensuing years were so remarkable and might just possibly be of help to someone who might read this, that I have felt it right to record the events, without wishing or being able to record all the emotions involved.

Ever since we were married, and even before, I had always been clear in my mind that we would never be able to have children, but I had reckoned without Peggy's determination. By mid 1951 we had been married nearly ten years and it had been twelve since Peggy had fallen ill. She had steadily improved in what she had been able to do and of course was encouraged by having her own home, but she still had the same two damaged heart valves and there was clear medical opinion that the strains of childbirth were out of the question.

However, she was now determined that whatever medical opinion might be, she was going to take the risks involved in the final fulfilment of her embattled life to have children. Accordingly, and with some reluctance, I took her up to London to see Claud Elman, the same specialist who had attended her in September 1939 in her initial battle for survival. Needless to say, he made it very clear that her intentions were not to be countenanced, but had not reckoned with her determination, and finally agreed, but said that for the last months of pregnancy she would have to come up to London and stay in the London Clinic under his personal attention. We could hardly afford to buy an aspirin at London Clinic prices let alone a sojourn, but decided to face that problem when it came!

Early in 1952 Peggy was confirmed as being pregnant and was of course extremely jubilant, but the fates had a lot more in store. A month later she was found to have an ectopic and was rushed in the middle of the night to hospital in Chichester for an emergency operation which was happily successful. She was still determined and undaunted as she sat up in bed in a room with just one other patient.

Her room mate turned out to be a girl of eighteen who had been a novitiate in the local Carmelite nunnery for the previous two years. This is a very strict order where the members were not in general allowed to talk, and when she had to leave the order in order to go into hospital for an appendicitis operation, this appears to have been taken as a sign that she was not suitable to remain in the order.

Within the few days out, in her new found freedom, that I had met her, she seemed to be rehabilitating very quickly and already enjoying her new life. Peggy had long talks with her and I finished the cure on the following Sunday by bringing her in a large selection of the fruitier Sunday papers! We kept in touch with her for a little and lost track of her after she had settled back quite easily into normal life.

Peggy staged a good recovery and by the Autumn of 1952, we were back in London seeing Claude Elman and also his associate Gynaecological specialist, and then came fate's cruellest blow of all. She was informed categorically and without question that with damage from her original illness together with the ectopic, it was now physically impossible for her to ever have children, and for the first time through all her travails she was absolutely shattered and beaten. She lost all will to battle on, for the ultimate goal of motherhood had been the great motivation in keeping her going, and it was a long autumn.

Then help came from an unexpected source. My brother-in-law in Tanganyika and his wife separated, she returning to America, so their eldest daughter Alison was flown home for Peggy to give a new home to. I met her off the plane at Heathrow and one tall skinny and unkempt five year old was borne home to provide very therapeutic company for her aunt.

Meanwhile life went on at work without undue incident until the date for the Coronation of Queen Elizabeth approached on 2nd June 1953 to be followed by the customary Naval review at Spithead. Most of the major Naval powers sent large ships and I was detailed to be the liaison officer to board the Russian cruiser 'Sverdlov' and help pilot her in and moor in Spithead.

However I was soon to find that that was not all of it, when I was sent for to the Directorate of Naval Intelligence and found I was to be an amateur snooper as well as assistant Navigator. I was also supplied with a Navigator's Yeoman who was an Able Seaman who could view the scenery amongst the other ranks, and at 4. a. m. we set off in a boat for Spithead and boarded the Sverdlov some hour and half later. We were also accompanied by a Spithead pilot because some odd rule apparently said that no ships other than those of the Royal Navy could enter these waters without taking a pilot. However we did not see him again until it was time to leave.

I was introduced to Captain Rudakov who was extremely pleasant and they then just got on with it, having clearly rehearsed the whole evolution repeatedly, and needed little help from me, causing little inconvenience to my efforts at memorising everything that I could see. Their clearly great pleasure at being the first Russian naval vessel to visit Great Britain since the war was further heightened by watching the American cruiser which was mooring in the next berth, make a complete mess of the operation and having to go round and have a second shot at it.

When mooring was completed I was taken down to the officers mess for a caviar breakfast by the Navigator who was as seedy looking as his Captain was impressive and we were then joined by other officers and I found myself at nine in the morning and very tired entering into a typical Russian 'Bottoms up' vodka session celebrating and toasting practically everything they could think of! The boat to take me ashore finally called some hour later and I was poured into it along with the other two, who had not been subject to the same treatment.

I took the opportunity on the hours journey home to Portsmouth to de-brief my Yeoman on his espionage, but his only contribution was that he was sure that Russian sailors normally always went about bare-footed, because they walked in a very ungainly fashion and all their boots looked brand new! I doubted if his theory had any validity and even if it did would be unlikely to swing the balance of military power. My own overall impression was of a smart ship captained by a very competent Commanding Officer. Other observations which I was to make later to their Lordships have no place here.

On landing we found a number of the national press waiting which I was able to dodge, but they clearly found willing co-operation from the pilot who had accompanied us, for the tabloids the next morning had screaming headlines of how the Russian cruiser had wonderful automatic means of navigating, communicating and steering which had been very impressive!

On landing, I was taken back by car to my office at Dryad, with what seemed like a quart of vodka swilling around inside me, and hardly had I arrived at my desk to collect my thoughts when the phone rang, and it was some senior officer from the Admiralty saying that Sir Winston Churchill, who was then Prime Minister again was asking for a report on the Sverdlov. I gave him a potted version on the phone, and returned home at the end of a somewhat dramatic day. A couple of days later, the review itself took place and the Training and Trials and Development Commanders of Dryad were each allocated to one of the Government guest liners as Liaison Officer and I got the Strathmore.

I was allowed to take Peggy and we joined the ship the evening before all the official guests were to arrive at Southampton. Although our total sea voyage was from Southampton to Spithead in a 20, 000 ton liner, she took the precaution of having dramamine anti seasick tablets, which were then unobtainable in England, flown in from the United States! All the guests arrived alongside in special trains on the morning of the review and were shown to their cabins where a copy of the main London daily papers awaited them. All the ships bars were open for free drink from when they arrived on board until they left the following morning. For the Review in the afternoon the two guest liners took station behind the Royal Yacht and steamed up and down the lines and then anchored in their allotted berths for the formal dinner in the evening followed by the fireworks display.

Peggy and I sat at a corner table with the young Admiralty civil servant whose job it had been to arrange the dinner. This had been no easy task for he had to ensure in every one of the courses that there was some dish compatible with the religious or traditional rules for all the many nationalities on board. It certainly gave a wide choice for us gastronomic Philistines. After the firework display guests did as they pleased, and I was impressed that both that evening, and next morning, before we sailed back to Southampton, boats plied out from Portsmouth delivering evening papers and then the morning papers for every cabin on board. Next morning the passengers all went and so did we, back to reality after a remarkable two nights the sum total of which fell just within Peggy's survival capacity and which was put right by a couple of days complete rest.

And so in the summer of 1953 my sojourn at Dryad was coming to a close and in advance I had applied to do the staff course, for which I had long wished and thence I was posted starting in the Autumn. I had long had an urge to return to fishing for the first time since a boy, and so I borrowed a fly rod and we went on holiday to the Tynycornel Hotel on Lake Tal-y-Llyn at the foot of Cader Idris I with my rod and Peggy with her paint box, and from this small beginning stemmed joint hobbies which were to sustain us for the rest of time.

And so to our six month staff course at the Royal Naval College Greenwich, and what a place, so attractively situated, so architecturally splendid, and so steeped in history in which to have the course. It is hard to describe the course in detail or in headline. The Admiralty Fleet order described it as 'to give certain selected officers a higher education' but it was more than that. There was a hard core of training in logical thinking through writing appreciation and operation orders, and these were interspersed with lectures by experts from all leading nations and organisations from the U. S. A. and Russia to a Bishop and a T. U. C. high official.

A number of outside organisations were also visited, varying from the Houses of Parliament, to seeing a newspaper printed, to a day with the London Fire Brigade. I remember striking particularly unlucky with my two Parliamentary days getting 'The closing of the Liverpool Cotton Exchange' in the Commons and 'Amendments to the Nigerian Independence Bill' in the Lords.

I drew the Daily Telegraph for my 'putting a newspaper to bed' evening and during the initial drinks and question time in the boardroom, one of our team asked the inevitable question as to how many Peterborough's there were and was told with some indignation that of course there was only one. As we were going round the printing processes, another of our team saw an old school friend and asked him what he did 'Ah! I am one of the Peterborough's'!

Our lecturer on Russia, wishing to point up the style of East European humour, described the Boundary Commission at the end of the war, drawing the boundaries between Russia and Poland and reaching a farm in the middle of nowhere. They asked the farmer whether he would rather be on the Polish or Russian side of the border. 'Oh! Polish of course' he replied at once, and when asked why, he replied 'because I can't stand those

Russian winters'!

I recall also Vic Feather giving the T. U. C. lecture and having great difficulty in making numbers of our course hoist in the simple truth that Union Leaders were not elected to help Government or even the nation, but were elected by their union for the sole initial purpose of obtaining for their members the highest possible living standards, and any other actions they might pursue were subservient to this prime purpose. It was certainly an extremely interesting and very intense course from Monday to Friday, but there was the great compensation that we went home every Friday evening and did not return until early Monday morning.

Near the end of the course I was suddenly sent for to the second Sea Lords office at the Admiralty, and went up to London wondering what on earth I was wanted for and I was soon to find out. On entering the Naval Assistant's office I was asked if I would like the appointment of Commander of the Royal Yacht. I was absolutely flabbergasted, and naturally quickly said yes and then paused briefly before deciding that it was only fair, in view of the nature of the appointment, to mention Peggy's health in case it might affect their decision.

There was in turn a brief pause and it was suggested I went on leave at the end of the course and waited whilst they discussed the matter with those most concerned, and so I did. It was to be another six weeks before I was sent for again to be told in the circumstances it was decided not to offer me the appointment, but to alleviate my disappointment I was to be given a very attractive command. I will never know whether I ought to have kept my mouth shut!

The frigate H. M. S. Burghead Bay had returned from a somewhat unsatisfactory commission on the West Indies Station where they had made few friends, and after a refit in Devonport I was to take her back to the West Indies to try and restore a few good names and then go down via South America to be Falklands and Antarctic guard ship. The base would be Bermuda where of course Peggy's sister lived and where I had many friends, and although there would be none of the kudos of serving in the Royal Yacht, there would be all the fun and challenge of one's own independent command with some fascinating tasks ahead.

Meanwhile, with the aid of acting as foster mother to Alison, Peggy had anyway outwardly stabilised and come to terms with her sad personal news, but somehow I knew that underneath it all she was still shattered, and could not accept the inevitability or the absolute finality of the medical news.

And then came Maurice Elliot. He was a chubby septuagenarian cheerful retired Parson who came to our village as a temporary locum until a permanent incumbent arrived, but in fact he was to be there for several months. He was on the Church of England commission on Psychical Research and had written a book on the subject. He was very far from being a crank in any way and was a great supporter of the church's mission on healing and doctors working together in the healing field.

He and Peggy were to have many a talk together and there the matter rested as I went off to Devonport in September 1954 to take up my first command as Captain of H. M. S. Burghead Bay, rusty and in bits at the bottom of a dry dock.

20
Outward and Southward Bound ~ H.M.S. Burghead Bay in Command

I N THE AUTUMN OF 1954 I journeyed to Devonport to take over my first command, I suppose the ultimate aim of all young cadets when they entered Dartmouth at the tender age of thirteen. It was not much to look at on first sight; a rusty looking vessel much of it in bits, sitting disconsolately in the bottom of a dry dock. But it was mine own . . .

Most of the officers of the previous apparently somewhat inauspicious commission were still there, and were to remain for a short while, and it was soon easy to tell that all had not been well. However, that was now water under the bridge and looking forward was the name of the game.

My own quarters were, to say the least, somewhat more spacious than to what I had so far been used. They comprised a spacious day cabin with a bathroom and lavatory leading off and a separate sleeping cabin, and when in full commission there would be a Petty Officer steward, an assistant and a cook to attend to my needs when showing the flag on station.

Then came the time for the remains of the old order to go and the new to take over. In this respect we are somewhat different to the other services, because all on one day the ship is commissioned with a new crew, most of whom will not previously have met each other and none will have before seen the ship.

A few key officers and assistants will have joined a little in advance, and with a scheme of complement, will have set up the administrative framework into which the new crew would fit. And so came the afternoon, when with the Bluejacket band at our head, the new crew with myself and the officers in front, marched from the barracks to the ship. I was somewhat puzzled that in the heart of Devon we marched to the strain of 'Sussex by the sea' and when I asked why afterwards, was told that it was in my honour as it was known that I came from Sussex, a nice compliment which I am afraid had missed me by.

On arrival on board, everyone was given time to find their mess-deck and stow their kit and hammocks and then 'Lower deck' was cleared and after a welcoming address by me, the Chaplain of the barracks conducted a commissioning service, and the new commission of H. M. S. Burghead Bay had begun.

It may be interesting to remember that this was 1954 and National Service was in full swing and National Servicemen comprised over half of the ships company below N. C. O. level and also some of the officers. The officers were a wide assortment, the First Lieutenant was ex. Royal Indian Navy; one watchkeeper was a short service Fleet Air Arm observer and another was on his first commission after being promoted from the lower deck. The Engineer Officer, who was to be a tower of strength, was an officer of high intellect who had come from nuclear research at the Royal Naval College Greenwich to our little frigate, powered by a good old fashioned set of reciprocating engines!

Perhaps our two most unusual young officers were our two young National Service Midshipmen. I was telephoned by the Third Sea Lord to say that he had a young godson who was an R. N. V. R. Midshipman and could I find room to take him and his similarly placed young friend for the commission. I of course answered yes and so joined Julian, his godson an old Etonian of some wealth and a scion of one of the country's leading Merchant Banks and his friend Brian, straight from Marlborough and the son of a Film Director.

They were to be the cause of much interest and amusement as we cruised through South America. At each port Julian would flush out all the most attractive young ladies soon after arrival and then Brian, with all his considerable natural charm, would steal the best of them, leaving his friend the small change. Then. , on each occasion of leaving harbour they could be seen gazing back down the wake, their hearts broken, wondering if life could ever be the same again until it started all over again at the next port!

I decorated my day cabin with old maps and prints of the American coasts and the West Indies and over the mantle piece had a fine old print of New Amsterdam, which caused a lot of puzzled interest among the many Americans who came on board who were told it was the picture of a port in one of our old colonies to whom we gave self government too early, and then the truth gradually dawned that its modern name was New York! By the end of November, our refit had come to an end, stores had been taken on board, the ship had been painted, and the maximum amount of training, both ashore and afloat undergone.

And here I should make mention of Navigator Stuart, who I mentioned earlier as having been playing a leading part in bringing the Amethyst down the Yangtze River in 1949. He had since gone to Dryad and qualified as a Navigator and had now joined us in his first subsequent appointment. A quiet, self effacing and competent colleague he proved to be.

No sooner were we ready to sail than it blew a succession of howling gales, delaying our sailing day by day, which if nothing else, represented an emotional strain, as having said all one's good-byes, one had to keep ringing up and doing it all over again. Peggy had not been able to come down to Devonport during the refit because she was busy at home looking after Alison, but I had been able to get home most week-ends. We finally sailed for

Bermuda on Ist December 1954 into the teeth of a moderate gale and to what was to be a year of absorbing interest.

I wonder how many National Servicemen of any service were to have the opportunity to spend their time cruising through the Caribbean, down through South America to the Antarctic and back again, although they were not at the time to know what lay ahead. Perhaps it was no wonder that Burghead Bay berths were much sought after in the barracks, and the great majority of the Ship's Company were volunteers.

Progress across the Atlantic was slow because of the very bad weather and we finally arrived at the dockyard in Ireland Island just ten days before Christmas to berth whence we left in Jamaica in such dramatic circumstances in 1949. The first few days were taken up in the customary formal calls, and cleaning the ship up for the weeks ahead, and I of course re-established contacts with all our relatives.

It was always the custom for one of the ships of the squadron to go up harbour and berth on Front Street in the heart of Hamilton the capital, and I dropped the hint that we would be very delighted to fulfil that task, the more so because of my island connections. I was even more delighted when it was agreed and on 23rd December we went up harbour and berthed right on Front Street outside Cooper's Stores, a gin and tonic's throw from my brother-in-law's office.

Christmas Day followed the usual routine except in one respect. I conducted a brief service in the morning and then went the rounds of all the mess-decks, being given a drop of rum here and another drop there and finished up with Christmas dinner in the wardroom. Then came the difference!

Bermuda families all tend to congregate in one place with anything upwards of thirty or forty present and sit down to Roast Turkey followed by Cassava Pie at about three in the afternoon. I just had time to get to the family party by about two thirty, pretending I had not yet eaten, and had to do the whole thing all over again!

We were given our future programme at Christmas and very exciting reading it made. We were to sail on 7th January to Trinidad for a few days, mainly to oil and then to progress down the Brazilian coast to spend Mardi Gras carnival at Punta-del-Este, the resort for Montevideo, before going to the Falklands as Guardship for the second half of the southern summer. As my brother-in-law, Forster Cooper had been in the R. N. V. R. during the war, I got permission for him to come as a passenger in the ship as far as Punta-del-Este, and being a keen carpenter, he was appointed Shipwright's Mate!

It was of course the first time most of the Ship's Company had seen anywhere outside Great Britain, and we anchored for a day and a night in the Grenadines to put final touches to the ship's appearance before arriving at Point-a-Pierre in Trinidad on the 13th. This is the oil terminal for Trinidad Leaseholds oil fields and the last time I had been here was as Midshipman in charge of a platoon in the oilfield riots in 1937. There was little to do apart from formalised entertaining, both home and away, but I did have one moment of unusual enjoyment.

Before leaving England, I had started off two bowls of crocus bulbs to see what would happen, and by the time we reached Trinidad the bulbs had shot a tremendous amount of foliage up, but only a few buds and I don't think they were really used to trying to flower in a temperature in the mid-eighties Fahrenheit. However, I found on arrival that they were about to have their annual flower show, so I entered the somewhat seedy looking crocuses of which only two had struggled to the point of trying to bloom. Nothing like this had ever been seen at a flower show on Trinidad, so I was given an honorary award which took the form of two pots of orchids to see if I could later make them flower in the Antarctic! It proved to be a highly unsuccessful experiment!

We found that Leary Constantine the famous cricketer was in the Legal Department of Leaseholds and so I asked him on board, and very much to my surprise and delight not only did he accept, but we took him round the mess-decks to the delight of the cricket enthusiasts amongst the Ship's Company.

We moved on to Georgetown in British Guiana, as it then was, Georgetown being the very cosmopolitan capital comprised

Leary Constantine

of Afro-Carribeans, Indians and Chinese in almost equal proportions and with a fair amount of inter-marriage, leading amongst other things to extremely attractive young ladies!

One has to take a pilot a long way out from the mouth of the river owing to the alluvial deposits coming out to sea and causing ever changing shoals, and then the course is up river and alongside the wharf in the somewhat steamy jungle surrounded town. Much of the commercial, sporting and social activities were controlled by Booker Brothers, who seemed to have a finger in every pie, rather like Jardines and Butterfields were once to Hong-Kong. This was our first 'Showing the Flag' call and was a good baptism for what lay ahead, for the six day stay was an almost continuous non-stop session of soccer, rugger, cricket, formal lunch parties, various evening parties including our official reception on board, evening dances for the Ship's Company at which one was expected to put in an appearance, and a nightly increasing lack of sleep.

It was here that I discovered that at each port the Captain is very kindly asked to stay with the Governor or Ambassador as the case may be where applicable, and so half my stay was with Sir Alfred and Lady Savage who were kindness itself. However, it did make life more exhausting, because with the best will in the world Government House is never the most relaxing place in the world, however kind one's host and hostess and it would be by no means abnormal to come on board in tropical rig, change later into full white uniform for an official lunch time function, then back into sports rig for the afternoon. This might be followed by back into full white uniform for an evening reception, and then again into dinner jacket for an informal evening dinner, or any permutation of all the above.

No wonder one needed two stewards, who also of course had to be present for serving for all callers, either formal or casual and all the many meals one had to give. In this connection, it might be worth observing that my average drinks bill per month was about £35 which, with gin and whiskey at threepence a measure (old money), this represented a pretty liberal dosage, of which only a modest modicum went down my own throat. There was also a considerable expenditure on food for the many lunches and dinners one had to give. For this, a generous government gave me the princely entertainment allowance of four shillings and sixpence a day.

However, having said that, I was very conscious of the fact that here I was cruising through the Caribbean and south America, with two cabins, a private bathroom and two stewards in attendance, a scenario that perhaps many a rich American would be delighted to enjoy, and I was never to regret the privileged position in which I found myself.

We left Georgetown early in the morning of 25th January for Recife where we were to fuel and to depart again all in the day on 2nd February and looked forward to a few recuperative days at sea, but it was not to be as easy as that. After lunch on the first day, all being quiet I thought I would catch up on a little sleep and had hardly got my head down when the voice of the Officer of the Watch came down the voicepipe. 'Captain, we have got a stowaway on board'; I told him I was in no mood to have my leg pulled but he was insistent and. so I climbed reluctantly to the bridge to find it was only too true. The story got more and more bizarre as it unfolded. It appeared that the gentleman in question was none other than a Mr. Winslow Stoute, a coloured, legless acrobat, who feeling that his turn was getting stale in Guiana, was seeking fresh fields to conquer.

Although there were Guyanese police sentries on the jetty, it appears that a friend had helped him, both leglessly and acrobatically up the forward mooring rope and down a ladder through a sleeping messdeck, and down into the cable locker, where the anchor cable is stowed. It seems incredible that they achieved it without waking anyone up, but achieve it they did, and he was only detected when during the afternoon after we had sailed, he was heard by those on the deck above crying out for water.

It was clear that we could not take Mr. Stoute on to Brazil where he would not have been allowed to land, so there was no alternative but to return to Georgetown to arrive at dawn the following morning to drop the stowaway, and signal the C. in C. and Admiralty that we would be arriving a day late at Recife and the following port, and sheepishly giving the reason.

So, stopping only to make an embarrassed signal which I hoped would at least raise a smile as well as an eyebrow saying that I was returning Mr. Winslow Stoute, a legless acrobat, whence he came; we retraced our steps once more to the mouth of the Georgetown river, to arrive at dawn the following day. Meanwhile, the sailors, as only sailors can on these occasions made a complete pet of Mr. Stoute, and fed him on liberal portions of corned beef and rum and ensured he was never short of a smoke.

We had managed to get a radio message through to the Harbour Master and the boat was waiting on our arrival to remove our contraband, and Mr. Stoute was dumped in the boat, hugely grinning, surrounded by corned beef and cigarettes, and cheered on by the Ship's Company, but not before I had my only contact with him and that was to get him to sign my official visitors book. It had occurred to me that 'Winslow Stoute – Legless acrobat' would look good on the line below 'Sir Alfred Savage – Governor'!

So, once more we turned for Recife, but this time enjoyed a rest at sea before arriving at Recife on February 3rd, where we were met by our Naval Attaché Captain Cockburn who stayed on board for the rest of our time in Brazil and was of great help. In fact his assistance was required almost at once because although we were only in for oiling, and out again after lunch, out Attaché had arranged that I should address the weekly lunch of the Recife Rotary and furthermore do it in Spanish. It took but the length of a glass of gin to disabuse him of this plan, and so I made a one liner in Spanish, having been briefed by Cockburn on this task and then he took over the oratory.

That afternoon we sailed for Maceio to arrive there the following day on the 3rd February. This was a visit of a very different nature, for Maceio is a small coastal port in North Eastern Brazil and capital of Brazil's smallest state. There were only a handful of British residents and no British warship had visited there since before the war. There was a tremendous patriotic fervour amongst the small British community at our visit and they put themselves out to the absolute limit with their very limited resources to do what they could for everyone in the ship and we in turn did all we could to give them a piece of home.

Whilst here Captain Cockburn arranged a little four seater aircraft from the Brazilian Air Force to fly him and myself inland at not much more than tree top level over the jungle to the huge new hydro-electric power scheme that would bring much needed power to the then under populated North Eastern region. It was very impressive and we were informed that there was only one problem. Distribution had been planned and was being constructed, mainly for costs reason, above ground, but unfortunately the young bloods who lived along the distribution route found that their most enjoyable spare time hobby was to shoot out the insulators as target practice!

We sailed from Maceio on 7th February for Victoria at seven in the morning, having really felt that this was one of those worth-while visits where we had contributed something to the lives of these somewhat lonely but very loyal British ex- pats.

The final act was perhaps the most emotional. At that early hour, with dawn having only just broken, and we having just cast off and begun to move off the jetty, there on the quay in a row was every single member of the British colony, standing to attention and singing the National Anthem.

This was not to be the end of our association, because we had one absentee who missed the boat on sailing and so was due for dire punishment.

When we got to Victoria, there was the culprit waiting for us on the jetty! Apparently the small colony at Maceio had had a whip round to pay for his air fare down to Victoria, and he returned aboard with a letter to me from the doyen of the community asking me to treat him leniently! The plea went in vain!

There is little to be said about Victoria that differed from other flag showing sojourns. It is a medium sized town built at the foot of a hill comprised of very high copper bearing ore which was shipped out in large bulk carriers. It also had the terminal of the underwater cable from Britain run by Cable and Wireless Limited. The usual functions having been completed, and the Midshipmen's hearts having been as usual broken once more, we sailed south once more, stopping for a few hours at Santos, to arrive at Punta del Este on 19th February and a remarkable four day's stay it was to be. We arrived on the Sunday before lent in time for the Mardi Gras carnival which was to occupy the next three days.

Punta del Este is the out of town sea-side resort for the rich of Uruguay in general and Montevideo in particular and I heard it described as a 'concentration camp for millionaires'. Most of the Montevideo embassies including the British had residences here for use in the summer, and there was a fair sized British Colony and an English newspaper. The Uruguayans were very pro-British, and apparently had grand-stand seats along the sea front here for the Battle of the River Plate, and when they saw the Graf Spee turn and run for Montevideo, rushed up and down the front shouting 'We've won! We've won' as if it had been a football match.

Our Naval Attaché met us on arrival and was of somewhat sterner mien than the representative at Brazil, and our first day was devoted to the usual official calls. The following day as a limber up for the main festivities that were to follow the Honorary British Consul gave a fancy dress cocktail party for the local bigwigs and our officers followed by a dance at the home of one of the leading lights.

Once again cropped up the problem of fancy dress, not only for myself, but also for our Attaché. I then remembered that I had purchased two identical very gaudy calypso shirts in Trinidad and suggested to him that we could wear one each and go as 'The Urinal Twins – as like as two peas' which got a fairly frosty response. However, whilst not adopting the title, he agreed to the costume, there being no alternative. A return in the early hours of the morning and a brief sleep led to the main carnival day, which was complicated further by the kind invitation from our Ambassador to spend the night at their residence.

The morning began with receiving calls on board and then giving a formal lunch party, followed by going ashore to watch the ship play the locals at soccer. Back on board in time to host the official reception by the ship for the local dignities, including the Ambassador with whom I then went ashore, with my precious calypso shirt packed ready for the evening carnival ball. His Excellency had me shown to my room and I was given a key and was told that he did not expect to see me until breakfast the following day; he was only just right!

A large table had been reserved for the Attaché and myself and our officers and various ladies and there we all congregated from our various previous engagements, the officers having brought ashore a valise containing a number of bottles of whiskey which ensured instant popularity, that commodity at the time being both very scarce and very expensive in the country.

Most of the music was of the South American Rumba type and each dance went on for a long time, but it mattered not for dancing went in and out of everywhere including the bars, and so one was able to pause during a circuit and order a drink as one passed through the bar and collected the drink the next time round!

I was whisked off during the course of the evening to meet the newly elected President of the country and felt a bit of a Charlie carrying out the formalities dressed in carnival regalia, but so was he, and was so relaxed that I even offered him a glass of our smuggled scotch, which he readily accepted. I then found that I had accepted an invitation to make up a tennis four for the following afternoon, but when I found out that the other three were to be the country's Davis Cup team and the Ladies singles champion I quickly pleaded a prior engagement. And so the long evening drew on, until I arrived back at the residence in time to have a bath, ruffle my bed clothes and change my clothes and appear at breakfast with the Ambassador, assuring him that I had a good night, before returning on board to start a new day.

The Ships Company were also very well looked after, with the ladies providing continuous sumptuous teas at the Yacht Club, the local Brewery providing free vouchers for two pints of beer for each sailor as he stepped ashore, and dances laid on every night to provide them with the carnival spirit.

On the following morning, which was the final day before leaving, I had to go to a quasi-formal open air carnival lunch, and it needed considerable calorific intake before and during the jollifications to stop my eyelids from sticking together irrevocably. In the afternoon the ship was open to visitors which seemed to include a large number of attractive young ladies clad in the briefest of carnival costume causing a number of cricked necks amongst our company!

One more final 'do' ashore that night, given by I can't remember whom, which went on until precisely midnight, at which moment the carnival stopped and Lent began, and at last one was able to get back on board and crawl into bed for a few brief hours before sailing on south the next morning. That was the carnival, that was. We knew before we started that it carried a Government health warning, but no matter, it was great fun whilst it lasted, and quite a relief when it ended.

At 8am on the 23rd February we sailed out and headed for a very different scene, of three months based on the Falkland Islands with forays into the Antarctic and activities of much absorbing interest.

We had embarked in England a detachment of Royal Marines under a Captain, who were to be the first regular military contingent to be permanently stationed in the Falklands, and indeed their successors were still in place when the Argentineans invaded in 1982.

We also had taken on board in England a National Service Midshipman, here after called 'Mac' who was born in Valparaiso in Chile where his parents still lived, and he was totally bi-lingual in both English and South American Spanish. He was also trained in Wireless Telegraphy. From now on he was to come into his own, for his raison-d-etre was to listen to all the Argentinean and Chilean radio traffic between the mainland and their, to us illegal, bases in the islands which they claimed were theirs, and which we claimed were part of the Falkland Island Dependencies.

Within two days we were to see a dramatic change both in weather and mood. Behind us was the sunshine, the gentle zephyrs, the calm blue seas and all the junketing, and around us, together with a large drop in temperature, were rough seas, lowering grey clouds and a feeling that there was rather more serious work to do, as magnificent albatrosses glided around the ship, and then at day-break on the twenty seventh, there was the low-lying wind swept island of East Falkland, last visited by me eighteen years ago and never yet seen by any other member of the crew.

21
Falklands Islands Guard Ship

WE STEAMED IN past the wreck of the 'Great Britain', later to be raised and returned to Bristol whence it started life, into the almost land-locked harbour of Stanley the port and capital of some fifteen hundred souls unchanged and one would think unchanging until 1982 came along. For me the island held a certain magic to this day, although no doubt not everybody's cup of tea.

Outside Stanley there were no roads, and if it comes to that, not many in either, and there were a handful of cars, travel between camps and generally around the island, being on horseback. There were no newspapers or cinemas and only one pub. This stocked a particularly potent brew from Youngers, and working on the principle that if it had to come all these thousands of miles, the recipient might as well know that he had had a drink, it was of near lethal density, causing a number of casualties amongst our crew until they got used to it. All the main activities were controlled by the Falkland Island Company who owned the only store and hotel and rather more that half the farms, the rest being privately owned. They also recently brought all the way out from England their first ever lady hairdresser, and hardly had she arrived than she got married to my predecessor as Captain of the guardship, Basil Ward.

The replacement had clearly been selected so as not to present the same problem, and when I met her not long afterwards, she informed me that she had already had three husbands shot from under her and did not intend to pursue the matter further. – They had chosen well!

Basil told me that prior to coming south his Frigate had been in Boston, where he and his officers had been invited to a very posh socialite dinner. His hostess had asked him what part of turkey he would like, and being British, he unthinkingly said 'A little breast, thank you' to which she replied in a somewhat haughty voice 'In Boston we call it white meat'. Next morning he sent her some flowers with a thank you note which said 'Please pin these on your white meat'!

The Falkland Company ran a ship, monthly between Montevideo and Stanley called the 'Fitzroy', and could not of course ply with Argentina because of the latter's dispute and claim to the Islas Mal Vinas as they called them. This was our only monthly source of mail, and the Captain and his wife became good friends. I was surprised and delighted to see not long after that he had been made an Elder Brother of Trinity House.

The day to day communication between people on the camps was by what was colloquially known as the Farmyard Radio by which stores could be ordered from the central shop, symptoms could be relayed to the doctor at the hospital or whatever; it sometimes proved pretty fruity listening. If something was urgent it would be flown out on 'The Early Beaver' which was a Beaver float plane which took off normally from Stanley at first light, which was usually the only time when it was calm enough, otherwise the Fitzroy went round monthly between its Uruguayan trips, dropping off supplies at the farm jetties which required no little navigational skills. These all had romantic names, resonant of the unspoiled nature of the islands, such as Teal Inlet, Goose Green, Fox Bay and so on.

The island seemed to be extremely crime-free and had one single prison. There was a young lady called Sealskin Mary who was no better than she ought to be, and she was simply taken in for a day or so a month on some minor charge to ensure that the place was scrubbed out and kept clean.

The folklore of the Falklands is extensive and I will here mention but three, all of whom could so easily be absolutely true. The previous Governor to the one in residence on

With the Governor and Colonial Secretary

our arrival was not universally popular, and a member of the Legislative Council went round in the Fitzroy on its monthly trip round the camps to collect signatures on a petition for his removal. It so happened that the Governor was also travelling in the Fitzroy and on arrival at Roy Cove took dinner with the owner, it being the custom, visitors being so rare, to dispense the utmost hospitality to any passer by. As dinner was drawing to a close, a maid came in and whispered in the ear of Syd Miller, the owner.

Syd turned to the Governor and said 'Excuse me a minute, but there is a man at the back door asking me to sign a petition for your removal; it won't take me long', and a short time later he was back to continue dispensing his hospitality as if it was the most natural thing in the world.

Then whilst we were out there, plans had been submitted to the Colonial Office for the new hospital that was to be built, and rumour sped round Stanley that they had been turned down because the Colonial Office said that with all the wards facing north, they would not get any sun!

Everything in the Falklands revolves round sheep and apparently a very well known young lady, who had taken over running their camp when her father died, was due to be married at Stanley Cathedral, a day or so's ride away. However on the morning of the wedding day, a message came in to Stanley to say that she would not be able to get there as she had not finished dipping the sheep!

However, back to our arrival – The Royal Marine detachment were landed to go to their new quarters, and then I went ashore to make my formal call on His Excellency. He was not only a tall handsome, delightful Old Etonian but ideal as Governor of these islands as he had a slight piratical streak. He was very fond of good food and drink, and we had brought all the way out from England, a large supply of excellent wines to replenish his stock.

Ray Arthur was a keen and efficient horseman who endeared himself to the locals, and kept a good stable, and to my initial great fear I was to play an increasing part in its use. Not only did H. E. feel slightly isolated in a relatively small community, but we found an increasing rapport and I was to spend a lot of time at Government House. His family had not joined him and as a housekeeper, who mothered him and saw that he wanted for nothing, was a splendid middle aged capitalist called Mrs Pollet, who was indeed the sister-in-law of Harry Pollet, England's leading Communist.

The extreme windiness of the Falklands is well known, and it was as well that the bottom of Stanley Harbour was deep in generations of deposited peat into which the anchor would sink, but even so, it was often an anxious time when ashore whether a particularly strong gale would suddenly blow up and prohibit returning on board. An example of the wind strength was that it was not all that unusual to come out of Stanley club leaning right forward against the wind, turn down to the road to the jetty out of the wind and nearly fall on your face, and not entirely due to the products of Mr Younger.

The immediate time after arrival was spent in getting to know the locals, since our liaison was obviously going to be more extended than elsewhere, and for recreation there were excellent natural history walks to see penguin rookeries and seal colonies. Ray Arthur was soon insisting that I get on board a horse, though the sum total of my previous experience was measured in terms of a few minutes aboard an Ecuadorian Cavalry charger, and frightening I found it. It seems absurd to say it, but apart from anything else, I suffer acutely from vertigo, which was even alerted by the height off the ground of sitting on a horse.

The Falklands horse differs in some ways from others in that, for example, normally if one pulls on the port tiller line a horse turns that way. Not so an Island pony where the reverse is true and it turns to starboard, in so far as they took any notice of anything I tried to make them do.

Having settled in, it was time to plan our first trip south which was very exciting, as it is not given to people every day to go cruising in the Antarctic. There was need as Captain to hoist in quite a lot of facets of this business, bearing in mind that the ship was thin skinned and not strengthened for ice. The problem was not so much large bergs which could be seen or detected on radar, but smaller stuff which of course only showed a little above the surface, but might be large enough to pierce a thin skinned hull. With care one could work through brash, which was thinly formed sea ice, and a scattering of bergy bits, but great care had to be taken all the time with double look-outs on the bridge, and two right up in the bows with long poles for pushing off any small stuff.

Our first stop was to be Deception Island on the edge of the South Shetland Islands, where not only was there one of our bases but also both Argentinean and Chilean bases. Entering harbour was a most impressive sight, because it is like a flooded volcanic crater and the entrance is rock strewn except on one side which is deep up to a towering cliff and one steams in so close to the cliff that one can almost reach out and touch it. The name of the entrance is picturesquely called Neptune's Bellows.

I had received much help before leaving from Captain Bill Johnston of the Royal Research ship John Biscoe who brought his ship down every year in the open season to service all the British Antarctic bases, and was very knowledgeable in the ways of the area. Over the ensuing months he was to take too much money off me at cards, but conclude by being of the greatest possible help, as will be seen.

Coming south, on this our first trip, we encountered the all too common rough grey seas and the occasional iceberg, and always the wheeling, swooping and soaring albatrosses which I never got tired of watching. As we steamed into Deception, there, in addition to the three national bases and the fairly considerable remains of a long gone whaling station, was a large Chilean transport, anchored in the harbour.

'Mac' had been beavering away on the radio listening in to all he could, without knowing that this great ship was going to be here, and it seemed to me that it behoved us to protest at her presence, and accordingly I sent for Mac in the middle of the morning, and told him that as our Spanish speaker he should go and deliver the protest to the Captain. To assuage his natural fear I gave him a large rum and sent him on his way, and we watched from the ship as he clambered up the long ladder of the towering transport and was shown forward to the Captain's cabin. Some hour later he returned and reported to me and I asked how he had got on, and he intimated that it was not exactly as he had expected.

It appears that on arrival at the cabin, the Captain rose from his chair, shook him by the hand and said 'Ah! you must be Mac; I met your father in Valparaiso the other day and he said I would probably run into you down here. ' Put the protest on the table over there and have a drink! So much for all the secrecy! We established contact with our base, who were naturally delighted to see us, and we were both able to give them some solid and liquid luxuries, but also a meal on board and a film show.

Whatever the Governments at home in their respective countries might think, short of direct military intervention to throw them off, which was not part of the inter-nation politics at that time there was really nothing much that could be done, because the weather was so inclement and the temperature so low, that there was no purpose in the bases simply raiding each other because it would only lead to death for all. Accordingly, as they were stuck there, not only in the open season when the odd supply ship came in, but

An Argentine shed in South Shetlands

A base in South Shetlands

The British base hut at Signy, South Orkneys

through the whole dark inclement months, they set up an inter-base social arrangement by which each Sunday one base played host to the other two.

Our base personnel warned us of the danger of crevasses, but it was to no avail. We gave leave to the Ship's Company in the afternoon, doubting if many would avail the opportunity, but we could not have been more wrong! We had more ashore in Deception than in any South American port. They streamed ashore in every known 'keep warm' rig, complete with all the mess tin trays as toboggans and had the most magnificent winter sports, varying from snowballing to hazardous home made Cresta runs, oblivious of the danger of crevasses or any other danger.

Not only was it very healthy exercise, but it cost nothing. In this connection it should be mentioned that as we were on the 'America and West Indies' station, we were paid a cost of living allowance that was constant for the whole station, irrespective of where one was and on a sliding scale depending on rank, and so with many weeks in regions where little money could be spent, the Ship's Company were able to save a considerable amount before finally arriving back in the United Kingdom.

We then went on to visit the other places in the Antarctic where the South Americans had bases in addition to ourselves, the three main being Signy in the South Orkneys, the Grahamland peninsula and the South Shetlands. At each base, we were able to give the personnel a bath, a good dinner, a night at the pictures and a change of faces, and ourselves never got tired of visiting the large penguin rookeries, seal colonies, sea elephant herds and, when at sea, the majestic icebergs and the large numbers of albatrosses, skuas, petrels and gulls.

On some trips, particularly that to Grahamland which was further south, actually on the Antarctic mainland, it was slightly nerve wracking, because one was going to the limit of the ice conditions which the ship could take whilst watching the weather constantly, because it only needed a sudden change of wind direction and speed to get one into possible serious trouble.

Each base had a leader and a number of researchers, some doing a university Ph. D. in say Biology or Geology, a motor boat and a team of huskies. They lived in very comfortable huts and sometimes stayed out for two seasons, being locked in for the winter in between. The main drawback must have been lack of privacy for all experience had shown that there are unacceptable psychological disadvantages in allowing people to have a room to themselves. Long Antarctic winters do funny things to people. And so after a couple of weeks in the south, we returned back to Stanley from my first trip.

There was from time to time more than usual activity in Stanley and in the south, because they were beginning to set up the base and the stores for the expedition led by Sir Vivyan Fuchs which was to cross the pole two years hence. They had set up a small office in Stanley, and I had become so entranced with the deep white south, even on such short acquaintance that I toyed with the idea of volunteering for the expedition. Accordingly I went into the office to make enquiries and was told without hesitation that there were one or two drawbacks, namely that I was too old, too fat and too inexperienced! The star dust dropped from my eyes and I returned back on board deciding that I would stick to what I was doing!

Our next trip was to take H. E. on board to visit a couple of camps, the first being Teal Inlet run by the son of the Manager, Mr Barton, of the Falkland Island Company. The inlet was only shown at not much more than a postage stamp size on the chart, but we had some advice from Captain White of the Fitzroy that the kelp grew to such terrific lengths off any rocks that it was really quite safe to go anywhere where there was no kelp. Using this as an aid but not our only means of navigation we eased our way in and then went ashore for a fascinating day's fishing. The rivers were only small, like say the River Meon in Hampshire and were full of 6"+ trout and even they were linked to sheep! They were fished for just like fly fishing except that instead of a fly, one inserted a small piece of mutton fat on the end of the hook. The Government Biologist when we were out there, imported brown trout from England and stocked these streams, and I heard later that within a couple of years they all became migratory and that there were now a nice run of small sea trout running up these streams.

We then moved on to Ajax Bay, made famous as the place where the British invasion took place in 1982, but then all peaceful with the farm on one side owned by an Old Etonian and that on the other by a Harrovian!

Standing on the hill was the empty Ajax Bay freezer, standing empty as mute testimony to yet another Colonial Development Corporation folly. The idea had been that as the

Falkland's economy was geared entirely to wool, it could be expanded to develop lamb and mutton exports from a freezer. The drawback was that sheep were not killed until a good age because the wool trade was so buoyant, and those which might have gone to the freezer could not be got there except on foot in which case, by the time they arrived there, they were not good for much. However, at the end of the day the freezer was to come in useful as the emergency Field Hospital for the 1982 invasion.

Then came a stunning blow from on high. The Queen's Birthday Parade in April was always a big event and a patriotic display of much fervour for which every conceivable kind of unit and contingent turned out. This year the ranks would be swelled by the presence of contingents from H. M. S Burghead Bay, and so I suggested to the Governor that, as it had never been done before and he was such a keen and good horseman, he should attend the Parade and inspect the troops on horseback!

'What a splendid idea' he said, and then came the totally unforeseen codicil, 'and furthermore you will also come on horseback and come as my Parade Officer'! No amount of remonstration would budge him, even though my first feeble attempts at learning had not passed the trotting stage and had certainly not reached the point of being in control of one's horse at all times.

None of the Falkland ponies had of course ever been on a parade or anything like it, let alone stood still whilst a twenty one gun salute was fired off around them, but H. E. was absolutely tickled with the whole idea, and most particularly at the thought of my accompanying him. He went out with me and put me into hard equestrian training on more days than not, but fears as to what would happen on the great day were not eased in any way.

Meanwhile the Governor decided that he would like to pay one of his rare visits to the Dependencies in late March and he came on board and moved into my quarters closely followed by Mrs Pollet. I think she was firmly of the impression that her master would starve unless he got his usual victuals, and so she deposited with my steward numbers of chicken, ducks, geese, joints of meat and bottles of wine in order to ensure that he would survive the ten days or so that he would be with us, and then having taken her departure we set sail south again. The weather was particularly foul and also very cold, and my bridge clothing used to be a shirt and four pullovers under an oilskin anorak. Ordinary duffel coats were of little use as the wind went straight through the wool. The wind had been blowing from the south for some time and so there were a particularly large number of big bergs which had calved off the main Antarctic ice barrier and blown northwards on the wind.

We made a long stop at Signy in the South Orkneys because H. E. was particularly keen on Natural History, and here were some of the largest and most accessible penguins rookeries, and also sizeable colonies of sea elephants as well as seals. Subsequent visits on the rounds to Grahamland, Deception and King George's Island in South Shetland were relatively uneventful until we arrived at Potters Cove in the latter island. It seemed as if a new Argentine base had been set up there, and we went ashore to investigate and indeed there were fairly new huts in place and a small amount of food therein, but there was no sign of life, and so we entered Potters Cove and anchored for the night not far from where a glacier came down to the sea.

The weather had calmed and the cove was potentially well sheltered, and apart from having look-outs in the bows all night poling off the small bergs that calved off the glacier and drifted out to sea, all seemed peaceful. However, the anchor holding ground was not very good and the lee shore not far away, and so we kept steam at thirty minutes notice, and I was soon to regret it had not been five minutes. Suddenly, early in the morning an almighty blizzard blew out of a still night and the ship immediately started to drag slowly towards the lee shore.

I ordered steam for immediate notice at once, but it would theoretically take thirty minutes to reach that desired state because the engines could only be warmed through at a given rate to ensure the correct rate of expansion of all the metal. It was difficult to know whether to let out more cable to provide more weight to help anchor the ship, but this meant that the ship would drop nearer the lee shore whilst the slack of the extra cable was being taken up, and the lee shore was getting horribly ever closer. I had a seaman stationed right in the stern with a lead line, calling out an even more frightening and ever lessening number of feet of water under the stern.

Meanwhile the Chief in the engine room was doing everything he dared risk in order to get ready to put steam on the engines, whilst on the bridge through my mind was flashing the vision of the nearest British ship thousands of miles away and the ignominy of a British warship complete with the Governor on board being rescued by an Argentine warship! Meanwhile it was blowing at a very high force, and the noise of the wind was interspersed with the occasional roar of bergs breaking off the glacier at the head of the cove, and the sea even in the cove was very rough.

By now, as viewed from the bridge, the shore astern appeared to be almost on our quarter-deck, and the leadsman was reporting depths of only three feet more than our draught, and I could wait no longer. Main engines had not yet been reported ready, but I rang on 'Slow ahead together', and the Chief in the engine room realised that the ultimate moment of crisis must have come. Accordingly, he cast all caution and the rule book to the winds and obeyed the order. As the screws began to turn so the dragging slowed down, and as the revolutions were increased, so the ship slowly moved into the wind and we started taking in cable and finally the anchor was weighed.

It still needed quite a lot of manoeuvring to turn the ship off the wind, in the confined water, whilst missing all the newly calved icebergs, and finally reaching the open sea. Here we met the full force of the blizzard with the wind luckily coming from the east, but all we could do was to batten down and turn head to wind with just enough speed to keep steerage way, whilst the ship pitched and tossed and the spray covered the ship and froze on the guns and the rigging. Throughout all this drama, his Excellency to his eternal credit never said a word other than of encouragement, and by now even that ceased, for he became acutely sea sick.

And so the day progressed until the afternoon, when the blizzard seemed to have eased a little and the wind was starting to shift round, and suspecting that we were going through the eye and that the wind was going to go on shifting, and since our next destination was in a westward and not a eastward direction, the ship was slowly eased round through a hundred and eighty degrees, executing one or two giant and quite frightening rolls in the process. This enabled us to get a few sailors with lifelines on deck with steam hoses to melt down a lot of the ice as there was the worry of getting top heavy with ice, particularly if we were to roll badly.

Sure enough, the wind soon shifted round to the west and increased again, and once again we were hove to, only this time going west! By now of course a great number of bergs, large and small had blown up from the south and were all round us, which was a little alarming as our manoeuvrability was limited to say the least. And then night fell and our alarm rose, because now our only eyes were our radar which was no good for small bergs close to, and they would be no good for us.

And so, hour after hour, Stuart, our navigator, and I sat in front of the radar plotting berg movements relative to ourselves, and periodically nipping out to the bridge to ease the ship a little bit one way or the other or to keep out of the way of the monsters. And then at almost midnight the most amazing transformation took place, almost unbelievable in its rapidity. One moment we were peering bleary eyed and exhausted at the radar whilst the blizzard raged all round us, and as it were the next moment the clouds had rolled away, the wind totally dropped, the sea went absolutely flat, and a bright full moon shone down on one of the most awe inspiring and beautiful sights I had ever seen.

There was our little ship, having been bobbing around like a cork, steaming serenely through an absolute mass of bergs, all blown up from the south, but now we could see them, no longer a threat, and all shining almost iridescently in the full moon. With a sigh of relief, we returned to normal routine and to bed, although the scene was so majestic one could barely bear to leave it.

We arrived at Deception Island one day late, and as we had his Excellency on board, we decided against a procedure which we had developed on other calls south, of negotiating through our own base a transfer with the local Argentine base of protest and vino for protest and Scotch!

And so after an adventurous trip south we conveyed the Governor back to the Falklands and, for in my case, an anticipatory fear almost outstripping that which had recently passed, namely being horse borne for the coming Queen's Birthday parade.

My horse and I were given light training and then forty eight hours before the great day, the three camp horses which were to be on parade had their oats ration cut to stop them being too frisky. When the great day dawned the prisoner ate a light breakfast, washed it down with a stiff gin and by 10 a. m. was on his way ashore to face what may, sensing a slight feeling amongst the Ships Company of amused intrigue tinged with pity that the idiot could have got himself in this predicament.

I reported to the Governor in plenty of time, and after some discussions we decided that my legs would not be tied underneath, as if I was to fall off, it would be better to go all the way down than hang suspended upside down below the horse!

The time had come to mount and H. E. led the way on to the field of play followed by the A. D. C. and myself. There was a very good turn out, perhaps partly because the news of the impending music hall turn had reached their ears, and we jogged past them to take up our positions for the 'off'. To reach there we had to pass all the assembled school children patriotically waving their Union Jacks and as I went past they called out 'Bumpity – Bumpity' in unison, causing me to reckon that King Herod had a good idea or two after all.

The parade was now all formed up and the moment arrived when we had to ride up and down the ranks of our officers and Ships Company. They managed to contain or stifle their sniggers to a man and so far I had to admit that these inexperienced horses had done remarkably well and I began to think that I was not doing too badly either. Next was to come the acid test. The Governor flanked by his two fellow horsemen would take station below the flagstaff whilst a twenty one gun salute was to be fired from near-by.

My worries were two-fold. Firstly the horses had never even heard one gun fired in their lives, although we had fired a few thunder flashes near them beforehand and if my vehicle was going suddenly to bolt this was going to be the moment. Secondly, only a short way behind the tail of my horse stood the Colonial Secretary in full morning coat. If the horse was to stay put, it might relieve its feelings in a different way with possible inconvenience to the Colonial Secretary's eye sight!

In the end neither fear was realised and before long we were in the sitting room of Government House having the nicest gin and tonic which I had ever tasted! The whole island rated it the best parade ever and all credit had to be given to the three camp horses who had never done anything except farm work before and who had faced the crowds and the music and the gunfire faultlessly, and in the case of one of them without a proper Officer of the Watch on its bridge.

In the birthday honours Mr. Barton, the head of the Falkland Island Company, had been made a C. B. E. and it was decided that this should be presented to him by H. E. at the first suitable opportunity. The only morning coats on the island were owned by the Governor and the Colonial Secretary who needed theirs for the ceremony. Then it was found that I too owned one and 'Bartie' and his wife arrived on board to have a look. He was considerably stouter even than me but his wife and I got to work on the problem.

With scissors, razor blade and a large piece of grey flannel cut from an old pair of my trousers, the problem was soon solved, by splitting the trousers down the back and inserting a large grey flannel gusset, and Bartie went ashore, almost properly attired for the presentation, which finally brought the Queen's birthday activities to a close. Shortly after this I was placed with a tricky administrative and disciplinary problem.

One morning a less than attractive Liverpool Irish National Serviceman whom I shall call O'Malley reported to the sick bay and the doctor told him that as usual he was just trying to avoid work and that there was nothing wrong with him. Presumably thinking that so far from officialdom, nothing much could happen to him, he proceeded to thump the doctor and was promptly put in the cells under close arrest. He was indeed right that there was only limited Naval authority that was on the spot, because my total authority with facilities I had on board was to give him fourteen days cells which was much too low for the crime that he had committed, all of which gave me furiously to think. The Ships Company, who had no particular use for O'Malley none the less were clearly intrigued to see how, if at all, the dilemma would be solved.

And then I had an idea. The season was coming to an end and the John Biscoe was due to sail for England in a couple of days. She was not of course one of Her Majesty's ships and our writ did not run thereon. However I went over and saw Bill Johnston, the somewhat wild and eccentric bachelor Irish Captain, reminded him of all the gambling money he had won off me and asked him what he thought of the idea of taking a prisoner, over whom he had no jurisdiction back to England and hand him over to the detention quarters at Portsmouth and I explained to him my predicament. He replied that he could not see the slightest problem, and that if the chap tried any rough stuff I could leave the solution to him!

Accordingly I sent a secret and personal signal to the C-in-C who was at the time at the opposite end of the earth at Vancouver, explaining the situation and my solution, and to my astonishment and delight he agreed to everything. Next morning lower deck was cleared and the prisoner brought on deck, and I arrived with my warrant to read it out. One could feel the tension amongst those present when I sentenced him to ninety day's detention to be served in H. M. Detention quarters Portsmouth and there was an air of puzzlement. However when O'Malley was immediately escorted to our boat and delivered to John Biscoe who sailed within the hour, they reckoned that honour had been satisfied.

There was an amusing sting in the tail for the following day our monthly mail arrived and in a Liverpool paper there was a letter from O'Malley, no less, saying that his friends might like to know that he was in the Antarctic upholding his Country's honour and they might like to know that his address was H. M. S. Burghead Bay c/o G. P. O. London. It was some weeks before, with the mails once more regular, we saw in the same paper another letter written by one of his mess-mates, saying that O'Malley's friends might like to know that his new address was now H. M. Detention quarters, Portsmouth, England!

In the mail, before leaving the Falklands, there was, amongst others from her a particularly long letter from Peggy. After more conversations, as mentioned earlier, with

Maurice Elliot, she had finally decided to visit Dorothy Keren at Groombridge in Kent. She had written books about her own apparently miraculous cure in her early life, and had set up Burrswood at Groombridge through private donations to combine a private nursing home with resident doctor with a private chapel for worship and divine healing by the laying of hands.

There was no 'up front' guarantee of miraculous healing to all who came, but there was a great record of the fact that nearly all who came would depart mentally and spiritually greatly refreshed and uplifted, and in addition numbers also departed considerably physically improved, although it was impossible to know to what proportion of these the improvement could be attributed to conventional psychosomatic reasons. Peggy had booked in to Burrswood for two weeks, but was initially unimpressed as Dorothy was away and so it was a week before she saw her.

But then the transformation was apparently magical, for Dorothy was a mixture of considerable personality and dynamism mixed with a gentle and compassionate manner. After she had listened to Peggy's story, she took her down to the chapel where she, very unusually, held a one to one healing service and declared thereafter that she was sure that Peggy had nothing to worry about, because she was absolutely certain that Peggy would have a son, whatever the medical profession might say to the contrary. Peggy left Burrswood totally buoyed up by this and in no doubt of the outcome and it was clear from her letter giving me all this information that her whole outlook and spirit were once more as they had been.

Our time for leaving was now getting close; the John Biscoe had sailed home. It was now May and the Antarctic winter was beginning to close in, and it was then that the Governor received an urgent message from the British base at Signy in the South Orkneys that their generator had a defect which they could not mend and unless repairs could be effected they would be without power for the winter.

I signalled the C-in-C for permission to attempt a repair, in view of what the ice conditions might be like and got a reluctant approval stressing that in no way should the ship be hazarded. Very luckily Murphy's Law operated. We went south in perfect weather and arrived at Signy only having to work through light brash where the sea was just beginning to freeze over for the last twelve hours or so.

Our splendid Chief and his assistants successfully mended the generator; we gave the whole base staff a splendid dinner, a film show and supplies of whiskey to help them through the long winter nights and sailed back to the Falkland Islands. The Governor was due for leave and consultations in England, and so a few days later he arrived on board officially in cocked hat and full regalia and took passage with us to Montevideo.

I was very saddened at leaving the Falklands and Southern Islands. I have not gone on about the ice and the bergs and the penguins and seals and the fascination of desolation because not only would it be boring but I do not know how to describe the feeling of being

Farewell to Falklands, June 1955

'where white man had never before trod'! Suffice to say I loved both the majesty of the south, and the simplicity of the Falklands and its people. I felt I would never tire of having too much.

22

H.M.S. Burghead Bay ~ Northward and Homeward Bound

IN JUNE WE STARTED NORTH, and within a few days, to my great sadness, the last albatross had been left behind, the seas had turned from grey to blue and we were back in the large bright outside world.

Our destination was Montevideo, where we were to stay informally for a few days in order to rehabilitate to the rough and tumble once more, and as we approached, still one day out, President Peron was ousted as President of Argentina. We did not know, as we passed the entrance to the River Plate, whether to expect the loyal remnants of the Argentine Navy to come steaming out to sea, or whatever. However, on entering Montevideo the following day, it was clear that the Uruguayan Navy, both ships, had gone to instant alert and everyone was confined on board in case their day of Trafalgar was to come, although I was not at all clear how or why.

However, this produced a charming knock-on effect, because that evening a reception had been arranged for us at the Naval club to meet the officers and their wives. Unfortunately the officers were all confined to their ships, but the wives none the less very sportingly, and very unusually for South America, still hosted the party, an arrangement which we found flawless, until half-way through, when the Navy had been stood down, and the husbands hastened to the party to ensure that normal service would be resumed forthwith!

Although this was on paper an unofficial visit, none the less the pattern soon followed all that had gone before on our journey south with the addition of a wreath laying ceremony at the statue of their national military hero, the occasion taking the form of a ship's guard of honour, in front of whom staggered two of our sailors carrying the biggest wreath I have ever seen, ridding themselves of their burden at the foot of the statue and making room for me to reach out and touch it and stand solemnly for a brief while, before we all trooped back on board again, with another job done.

We said farewell to our Governor from the Falklands Islands who had been such a kind friend to us all, at the main hotel in the evening before we departed to the strains of Roberto Ingles and his Rumba band who had become the stars of the country and acquiring considerable wealth. On talking to Roberto, I soon found that in fact his real name was Bob English lately of Edmondo Ross's band in London, who spotted a good thing and started a new life, a new band, and a new found wealth.

We departed north again, passing on the way out, as indeed we had on the way in, the wreck buoy marking the wreck of the Graf Spee whence she had settled herself sixteen years earlier.

Back to Brazil, and to Santos, where we had just stopped for oil on the way south. I suppose, of all the places we visited on the way, Santos had the most active and hospitable British Colony, which together with a very hospitable Brazilian Navy contingent, led to a pace of life that even exceeded British Guiana.

Considerable assistance was given by Mr Stoute, yes yet another one, the excellent British Consul and also once again Captain Cockburn our Naval Attaché, and one had learnt to cope with endless changes of uniform, and switching between the formal and informal, but what I found difficult to cope with was inserting a tennis match in between say a large and fairly liquid lunch and a formal reception on board.

At half time we made a major invasion of Sao Paulo, the relatively new and fastly becoming number one city of Brazil, some dozen miles inland from Santos, and linked by a multi-lane highway. There appeared to be only one snag; it was no road for the absent minded, for there was no feed-off. If one set off from Santos and after a mile, suddenly realised that unfortunately the spectacles say had been left behind, there was only one way to recover them, and that was to go all the way to Sao Paulo, down the other side and start again.

We were given a large official lunch by the Sao Paulo Chamber of Commerce, and I was grateful once again for our Attaché being able to reply on my behalf in Spanish! I was also yet again surprised that in this city of millions, a dozen miles from the port of Santos, the presence of a small British Frigate should give rise to formalised entertainment of this dimension. After lunch we were all taken to see the famous Sao Paulo snake farm which combined the provision of a sort of horrified fascination with the practical function of the extraction of considerable amounts of poison for the manufacture of serums.

The unconcerned strolling amongst these very large numbers of very lethal reptiles by those who operate in these pits, must establish some sort of record in apparent nonchalance, and it appears that with what appears to be no special precautions, they never get bitten, or if they are, presumably never twice! In practice, it is understood that the labour turnover is negligible.

Having given a giant children's party to a mixture of the young of the British Colony and local orphans, and played every known sport against the locals and attended or given a variety of social functions, it was time to move on. As far as children's parties were concerned, we were in some fear of providing disappointment after recent visits of one of our cruisers who had apparently laid on a party of tremendous dimensions, but we need not have worried. One of our lot thought up a simple counter; having had it is hoped a reasonably good party, every child, before departure, was given a tube of Smarties, and all that went before was forgotten in this moment of unalloyed rapture!

Departure from Santos was to mark the end of South American cruising on our own, for the next step was to be Recife, known to old South American hands as Permambuco, and where the new Captain in charge of our Squadron in H. M. S Mounts Bay, was to meet us for the purpose of inspection and a brief couple of days of exercises. After this brief excursion once more into the martial arts, we separated, they to make a brief cruise south, and we to journey north to Trinidad to a month's interim refit at the U. S. Navy base at Chagauramas, which was one of those leases to the United States for ninety nine years, negotiated by Winston Churchill in 1940 in exchange for the transfer to the Royal Navy of fifty old destroyers to help fight the war against German U Boats. Other bases were at Bermuda and the Bahamas.

On our way north, we again suddenly and totally unexpectedly ran into a gale of almost the intensity, but not the temperature, of our Antarctic blizzard. On this occasion however, the gale being off shore, and we being not very far off it, we were unable to turn into it, the ship not being suitably fitted for entering the Brazilian hinterland, and so had to find the best slow speed to cope with the sea almost on our beam. The degree of roll was very considerable, and at the end of twenty four hours, when the gale subsided as quickly as it had risen, the only damage of consequence was the destruction of both our weather-side boats.

And so six months after leaving Trinidad and having steamed many miles and carried out many and varied functions, the ship was back there once more, this time to be put out to rest for four weeks.

Holiday brochure weather reigned throughout and the ship went into tropical routine of starting work at 6 a. m. and knocking off the day after dinner at 1 p. m. Most of the work was maintenance and repair, whilst the U. S. Navy were under contract with local labour, to carry out most of the routine dockyard refit work. This meant that anyone who so wished could go ashore for swimming and laying on the beaches whenever they were not on watch.

I was asked to stay at Government House for quite a lot of the time and the Beathams were extremely kind. However it inevitably restricted the ability to do one's own thing and have a bit of a rest. One evening I was asked to dinner by the Colonial Secretary to meet a parliamentary delegation comprising two Tory and two Labour M. Ps who were touring the West Indies during the summer recess. It was the first time that I had meet this phenomenon and had naively assumed that there would be a strained atmosphere. Nothing of course could have been further from the truth, and they were all like a bunch of sailors on shore leave on pay day, with never a harsh or contradictory word spoken. I did just wonder with what vital information they were going to return to the House of Commons for the benefit of the tax-payer who had given them the trip.

Whilst we were there a tragedy took place in the sea just to the north of Trinidad. A bulk ore carrier full of bauxite was coming north on its way to the United States, having stopped at Trinidad and in full moonlight on an absolutely clear night, had collided, some hour or two after leaving port, with a Harrison line cargo ship, coming south to berth at Trinidad, sinking the latter with loss of life. This is no place to go into cause, although naturally there was suspicion directed at those on the bridge of the bulk carrier, having only left port that night a short time before.

After we completed our refit and trials, we were to proceed to cruise in the Caribbean whilst acting as Hurricane Guard Ship for that season was just beginning, but our first task, at the request of the Trinidad government was to try and use our sonar to locate the sunken Harrison ship, because there appeared to be considerable doubt as to where the sinking had actually taken place. Accordingly, we steamed up and down the approximate area and then just as we were beginning to despair, we suddenly got the all important 'ping' and slowly approaching the spot, were rewarded, even some two weeks after the accident, with the sight of bubbles and traces of oil, still coming to the surface. We were able to f ix the spot and report it to the Governor before going on our way.

It was to be nearly a year later before I was to be summoned out of the blue to a court of enquiry in London sitting to assess blame and the award of damages, as I was the only witness who could pin the position of the wreck. But even then there was much cross-examination by Lawyers whose expertise in navigation might well have been to get their yachts from Lymington to Cherbourg!

We then sailed on westward to the Central American mainland to the tiny British Colony of British Honduras (now Belize), and I never did find out how it became a colony. We had to anchor far out because of the accumulation of river silt close in, and the whole aspect from seaward was of a very low-lying flat strip of jungle on the edge of which sat the capital, Belize, following much the same pattern of scores of other such places across the empire of a Governor, tennis club, social club, a few expatriates, a contingent of the army and a failed Colonial Development Corporation project. The expatriate community was outnumbered by the local born white Honduras families who were in permanent residence.

The failed C. D. C. project was a banana plantation scheme which had apparently been started in a valley that promised every success, but unfortunately the only reason why there were not bananas already there was because the area had been abandoned by the locals for this purpose because there was some form of pest in the soil that killed all the plants off.

The army contingent was a company from the Duke of Cornwall's Light Infantry, hereafter called the D. C. L. I. One battalion was stationed in the general area, of which one company was stationed here, one at Bermuda, and the third together with the headquarters were at Jamaica, and it was this last team who were to play a big part in our lives for a short time. The brief visit followed the usual round of considerable hospitality from the local community, staying at Government House, Sunday church and having to read the lesson, tennis matches and so on, but with the added novelty of having together with the carnival queen to kick off ceremonially at the football match between Belize and the ship's team.

Our next stop was the Cayman Islands which then fell under the Governorship of Jamaica but had a local Administrator in charge. It was also then almost the last really unspoilt Caribbean chain of islands. This was not to last long, for an exquisite seven mile long unspoilt beach was about to be developed with large hotels for the delectation of the populace of Florida near-by. But first they had to solve one formidable problem, which I gather has been achieved. Grand Cayman had the greatest mosquito problem I had ever encountered, and when accepting an invitation ashore to dine; one leapt out of the boat into a car, and when arriving at the house, made a lightning flit through the front door which was quickly opened and shut, into sealed rooms where no predator could penetrate. I understand that now, the mosquitos have been banished, the hotels are all up and running, and Grand Cayman has taken its place alongside the many other 'resorts' spread across all these lovely Islands.

However, Grand Cayman already then had one notch on its holster, namely a very successful C. D. C. project which was a factory making real turtle soup, and excellent it was too, as I can testify having been given two cases. I believe it to be no more. Either ecological considerations may have dampened the demand or possibly Lord Mayor's Banquets have stopped having turtle soup, or perhaps they just ran out of turtles. In this connection, I wonder what has happened to mock-turtle soup which was always freely available on shop shelves, but which is never now seen.

Thence to Jamaica to start a visit to Dominica and St Lucia to celebrate the 150th anniversary of the liberation of these two islands from the French by the then D. C. L. I. To this end we took on board the Adjutant and one other officer, a contingent large enough to form a guard of honour and the whole Battalion band. How we squeezed them in I can not recall, but it was somehow achieved and we headed north to Dominica to the first round of celebrations.

Dominica was rather less attractive than many of her sister islands in that all her beaches were of grey volcanic ash, and this origin also produced another problem, in that the shore line was very steep-to, so that by the time one was close enough in to be shallow enough to anchor, one was unhealthily close to Dominica if an on shore gale was to spring up. The island was also the home of Rose's Lime Juice!

The very first parade was to reveal a small hitch which was subsequently repeated at other stops. Every arms movement of a Light Infantry has to be carried out only to or from the 'order arms' position, contrary to conventional practice, but that was no great problem; it simply but rather boringly meant giving every order twice; one to suit the D. C. L. I. and one to suit the sailors, so far, so good! However, whilst everyone else marches at 120 paces to the minute, the Light Infantry, and they alone march at 180 which means that they cover the ground at an appreciably higher velocity.

The Navy always marches in front, so all my navigational skill at relative velocity was called upon for each church parade to work out how much start we should give the sailors ahead of the D. C. L. I so that they all arrived at the church door together! Parades, and receptions to and from the local Legislative Council having been executed, we sailed to St Lucia to repeat the programme.

The passage to St Lucia was enlivened by two episodes. Diamond Rock off Martinique had been commissioned during Rodney's campaign against the French as a warship and guns hauled to the top of this very steep island and the White Ensign flown, for it was from this vantage point that it was possible to see if the French ships came out of Martinique. We continued the tradition, carried out to this day by any British warship if it is in the area, of going slightly out of our way, and steaming slowly past whilst we dipped our ensign, sounded 'the still' and saluted as we went close past H. M. S Diamond Rock.

The other occasion was the night before arriving at St Lucia. The ship cruised slowly through a calm sea with a warm breeze; overhead was a cloudless canopy of bright stars and there was the occasional shower of phosphorescence as either flying fish or dolphin broke the surface. Nearly all the ships company who were not on watch, found any pitch they could around the quarter-deck on chairs, cushions or just on the superstructure, and in the centre in the open air, the band of the D. C. L. I played semi-classical, operatic or nostalgic music for two whole hours, and everyone present was caught up in the pure magic of the occasion. I held this simple concert, as we steamed along through the night, as vividly in my memory to this day as many more dramatic moments.

Having returned our soldiers to Jamaica, we sailed to Bermuda, having supposedly completed our stint as Hurricane Guardship and to have a brief September respite after our nine months respite but Murphy was soon hard at work with his law. After a few days Hurricane Janet gave Barbados a glancing

HURRICANE TOLL MOUNTS IN W. INDIES

JAMAICA ALERT

MIAMI, Florida, Sunday.

Jamaica was placed on the alert to-day as the hurricane "Janet," centred 500 miles south-east of the island, built up new force over the Caribbean and headed in a westerly direction.

Winds of about 110 miles an hour were whipping up the sea as the storm increased in violence after losing much of its force when it devastated the British Windward Islands on Thursday. Fifty people are now known to have died on the island of Grenada, and many more deaths are feared.

Carriacou Island, in the Grenadines group, reported 25 deaths, with 30 injured. The hospital was demolished by winds of 120 m.p.h.

Mr. Deverell, Governor of the Windward Islands, has been holding daily meetings in Grenada to organise relief for the homeless. The few people who have braved the hazards of a journey over the landslides told harrowing stories of families buried alive under debris.

FRIGATE DUE TO-DAY

The problem of supplies may be partly resolved to-morrow by the arrival of the frigate Burghead Bay. 1,580 tons. A Red Cross statement said the whole island was damaged, and "in the Grenville-St. David's area three of every five houses are totally destroyed.

"Damage to crops, particularly bananas, breadfruit and cocoa, is immense," the report said. "Bridges round the island and its sole airfield have been destroyed, and it will be at least a fortnight before the debris can be cleared. The need for food is urgent."

In Barbados, which bore the full fury of the hurricane, publication of the first casualty list showed some of the communications were being restored. The list contained the names of 30 killed.—Reuter, B.U.P. and A.P.

blow and then drove across the island of Grenada causing very considerable damage, and we at once loaded up with Hurricane stores and were on our way.

We anchored off St George's harbour to watch a scene of desolation. A supply ship alongside the only pier had capsized, and there were only two barges and one small tug afloat for off-loading supplies from a ship anchored off-shore. I called upon the Governor on arrival and he at once made clear that the immediate problem was that none of the local merchants trusted each other, and as one owned the tug and another the barges and neither would co-operate with the other so there was no unloading in progress. He asked me to take charge of everything to do with the bringing in of supplies, and so I immediately called a meeting of the recalcitrant merchants and various other involved parties and read the Riot Act to them.

They all immediately offered to co-operate fully providing all the equipment to work for me, but they would lend nothing to each other, in case one party could manage to take advantage of the other! On this basis we soon had the off-shore ship unloading. Meanwhile the young local lads soon found out that the ship, capsized and under water alongside the smashed pier, was lying on its side with her hatch open and the hold with considerable supplies of tinned stuff which had come to no harm from sea water.

Accordingly they spent a happy day jumping off the pier, holding each time they jumped a couple of large stones, arriving in the hold and exchanging the stones for cans and returning to the surface! This pastime was then stopped by spoilsport authority who deemed correctly that a lot of these goods could be salvaged by more conventional means and in larger quantities to help solve the supply problem.

One of the big economic problems that came in the wake of the hurricane was that the island of Grenada was one of the worlds major suppliers of nutmeg and mace, and the nutmeg trees, being very shallow rooted, were destroyed en masse. Local government circles, no doubt apocryphally, said that the Colonial office had suggested to them that, with the nutmeg crop gone, perhaps they should concentrate on mace, which of course is nothing more that the husk which grows round the nutmeg! Poor Colonial office; the many stories told about them to their disadvantage can't all be true! Once the capital had got back on a basis, we loaded up stores and turned round to the outlying small islands and towns dropping off emergency supplies. Their plight was much worse than the capital and the structural damage greater, because the buildings were less robust.

There was an amusing piscine interlude at the particularly stricken isle of Carriacou, when, just as we were weighing anchor for our next stop, there was a shout on the intercom asking us to hold on as they had hooked a shark. As a keen fisherman, it was the first time that I had used a ship rod to play a shark. Within ten minutes it was safely landed and we proceeded on our way!

There was soon nothing more that we could do for the battered island, and so we called briefly at Antigua and Barbados both of which had a minor brush with the hurricane but who had not acquired any really serious damage, on our way back to Bermuda. However, first I took a brief part in a radio programme that launched a hurricane relief fund in the United Kingdom. Sadly, distant parts do not inspire, and although the damage and loss of life in Grenada was on a vastly greater scale than Lynton and Lynmouth, the appeal for the latter had recently netted some millions of pounds whilst that for Grenada reached just sixty thousand!

Having finally returned again to Bermuda, there now only remained a period of relaxation before returning to England in November at the end of our commission, and so the time seemed appropriate to take a few days leave with my sister-in-law Joan and her husband Forster who had accompanied me on the early part of our trip. She was determined that I should be shown all over the island during this time, but it was not to be.

Forster and I went fishing on the reefs with hand lines from dawn to dusk on every day bar one catching all sizes up to about fifteen pounds, and when we got back they were gutted and filleted and on the local hotel menus the same evening. This was very thirsty work and correcting this symptom occupied the rest of the evenings.

On the missing day from fishing I was grabbed to look round the island but only got as far as the Aquarium, and then Devils Hole, where a number of large fish are incarcerated in a natural sea inlet and one pays to fish for them with barbless hooks off which they quickly free themselves.

There was one last formal act to carry out in a scenario with which I thought I had dispensed. The new Governor was shortly to arrive and there was a parade on the jetty for his reception; once again I found myself in charge of a major piece of pageantry, and once again there was a Light Infantry contingent on parade necessitating every order being given twice; once again too I marvelled that, having specialised in navigation with the additional spin off advantage of not having to play many martial roles, I had seemed to spend the last few months being sucked in to the very acts I had look forward to avoiding.

And so at last came the final act. On 13th November 1955 we sailed for England and on the 22nd anchored in Plymouth Sound prior to going up harbour the following morning. This enabled the Customs to come on board and clear the ship, so that the following day, after the ships company had met their families, there would be no restriction in accompanying them ashore.

I was the last stop, and the customs officer related the false pride of one of his earlier clients. A sailor declared a very nice and quite valuable silk scarf, and the customs officer, to help him, mentioned that it was only artificial silk and that the sailor had been robbed, but nothing would shift the sailor from his insistence that it was the genuine article, which indeed it was, and so the customs officer was left with no alternative but to charge him the full amount.

He also mentioned that the previous week the Isle de France had come into the sound to drop some American tourists and he had gone on board to clear them through customs before they landed. He entered the cabin of an elderly blue-rinsed tough looking lady who had nothing to declare when he spotted a case of twelve bottles of gin tucked in a corner. He asked what they were and was assured that they were water, and so with a wry and weary smile he opened the first one and found that it did indeed contain just that. Being used to that old trick he went through all twelve bottles, and to his amazement they all really did contain water, and so he asked the lady what the game was; she replied with complete truth that her husband, back home, told her that the water in England was not fit to drink, and that she was to be sure to take her own supply with her.

And so next morning on the 23rd November, on the morning tide, we steamed up harbour with our paying off pendant flying and with mixed feelings. On the one hand we had completed a wonderful year of mixed fun and adventure that does not come many people's way, and on the other we were going to meet our families again after an absence of a year. I particularly thought of all the National Servicemen in our company who must have had a year's experience that transcended their wildest dreams.

Peggy had of course come to meet me and stayed locally whilst the usual end of commission obsequies took place. There was a final ships company dance, the clearing of the lower deck for the formal farewells and then the company, all but a skeleton crew who stayed to turn the ship over to dockyard control, marched back to barracks, and I got in my car, had a long backward look, and that was that.

In the beginning of December, we were once more back home, with much past news to catch up and a wondering what the future would have in store. We had a very good holiday break reaching until after Christmas, and then I was telephoned by the Admiralty to say that they were considering posting me to be Captain of H. M. S. Royal Arthur, the Petty Officer's Leadership School at Corsham in Wiltshire, but were concerned, as there was a high level of hosting and entertaining to be done, in view of the somewhat unique nature of the establishment, whether we could cope in the light of Peggy's health. I assured them that we could and would cope, and if it was essential, I would get additional living in help.

Royal Arthur was the only independent shore based Commander's command in the Navy and a plum appointment and to my delight the appointment was confirmed to start in March, so we had a continued and relaxed winter holiday, including visiting various relatives until it was time to join. On a personal basis, it was intriguing to be coming to Wiltshire in a Naval capacity, it being my family home, and where I was brought up periodically as a schoolboy, and where many of my family still lived.

The appointment included a Commanding officer's furnished married quarters, and so for the first time we let 'West Winds', packed all our belongings into our old banger and set forth to Wiltshire on a lovely early spring morning to start a new appointment, and to find changes in our lives which could not then be known, but which were to have a great influence on our future.

23
H.M.S. Royal Arthur

I T I S W O R T H M E N T I O N I N G how the Petty Officers Leadership School came to be in the middle of Wiltshire in the first place. At the start of the war, in order to cope with the large influx and basic training of Naval conscripts, Butlins Holiday Camp at Skegness was commandeered and named H. M. S. Royal Arthur and many tens of thousands of recruits passed through the camp, including, as the war progressed, those from many other nations.

As the war drew to a close and the pace of entry slackened, and peace time National Service became of short duration, so the camp was handed back to Butlins, and the whole operation was moved down to spare accommodation on the outskirts of Corsham in Wiltshire whilst retaining the same name. Close by was a hutted camp that had been used during the war as living quarters for the workers of the underground Bristol Aircraft factory that lay underneath. Here the Navy started up a Petty Officer's Leadership School under a Commander in charge, who was responsible to the Central Commanding Officer. The whole concept of management training for supervisory rates, both in and outside the Navy was then considerably ahead of its time.

When National Service finally ceased and the main establishment closed down, the Leadership School retained the name and continued on its own under the independent command of the Commander. The staff officers, by nature of their work and example, were to a great degree hand-picked and the best known one was of course the Duke of Edinburgh, then Prince Philip and it was from here that he carried out his latter day courting of the heir to the throne. He is reputed still to hold the record from a standing start for the journey from Corsham to the gates of Buckingham Palace!

Another story that still survives from those days, which may be apocryphal but could easily be true concerns his engagement. It was an old custom and courtesy that when an officer got engaged he would first ask permission of his commanding officer, and accordingly the Duke went to his C. O. and said 'Request permission to get engaged sir, and my fiancee says that if you refuse it won't be very good for your career'!

The work itself was very absorbing and quite different to any other. The great advantage of having the place in the middle of Wiltshire was that the Petty Officers were not distracted by family matters and irrespective of their specialisation, they were all mixed up together doing a common course to improve their qualities of leadership.

H.M.S. Royal Arthur staff

The syllabus was an amalgam of a wide variety of approaches, which contained inter alia, theoretical lectures, public speaking, Naval History, practical exercises in taking charge, comparative religion and ethics, endurance tests, considerable physical exercise, and indeed the inevitable dose of parade ground to give confidence in giving words of command.

Every evening after formalised work, there were compulsory inter-course games in which the staff took part. In fact one of the features of the place was a very close liaison between staff and pupils, and a lot of benefit accrued simply by out of hours discussion. The endurance tests took the form of a sophisticated version of 'Cops and Robbers' with the course that were Robbers one week becoming the Cops the next and it usually covered rather over twenty miles around the neighbouring countryside. To keep all the local farmers sweet we would every term have them to supper and a contest against the staff, at cricket in the summer and skittles in the winter. The farmers were always led by a great character called Alan White who farmed just over the fence.

Apparently, early in the war, he was walking across his field and came across two men putting little pegs in the ground and on his asking what they were doing, was informed that they were marking out where a large hutted camp was about to be built. 'This is the first I have heard of it' he said and retired to lick his wounds. Notwithstanding this, he was a great friend of and an honorary member of our mess, and never missed the chance of some quiet humour. He was a keen proponent of home made wine and his wheat was particular dynamite.

It was a regular initiation for a newly joined officer to be asked down for a glass of wine, be given the wheat treatment and come back legless, quite under the impression that he had only partaken modestly. On the first occasion of being a robber myself, for staff including the Captain were expected to take part in everything, and resting after my twenty plus miles in a hot bath, I received a telegram of congratulation and asking me to be their President from the Trowbridge Walking Club. Guessing the origin I bided my time, but not for long, because a few days later his wife Doris lost all her smalls off the washing line, stolen by some local kinky citizen and she quickly received a telegram sympathising with her very sad loss from 'The Trowbridge Dhobying Club. '

Our establishment had a particularly close liaison with the town, partly I think because we were small and our activities could be seen by the locals and we also had a close link with the local British Legion. There were no less than eight Royal Air Force stations within fifteen miles of us, but of course they were large and scattered and it was difficult for them to strike up a close relationship with the community.

However, our great advantage was, not having married quarters, our officers got an allowance and then had to find their own accommodation and they lived scattered over a radius of ten miles. This resulted in not only their establishing their own circle of friends in the community, but the wardroom being more socially active because at frequent occasions such as after church on Sunday and many others, there were gatherings in the mess because they did not just go straight back to the married patch.

Our great character in the town was Alistair MacLaghan a very Scottish, very kind and at the same time very irascible dentist. He would regularly lose his temper and fire all his staff on a Friday, and they would turn up as usual as if nothing had happened on the following Monday! He was a very keen and able fly fisherman and a leading member of the Wylye Fly Fishing Club. It was a sport that I had longed to take part in, and as he had no car, I used to take him down to the river in exchange for having my first lessons in the art. It was from these beginnings that stemmed my abiding love both of fishing, and river management, which led in the end to twenty years of being Secretary and River Manager of the club, and now the privilege of being allowed to fish the club waters whenever I wish, as an honorary member. Visitors, high and low, began to arise thick and fast, and the only problem was that there was no fridge in the small kitchen, but there were hot water pipes.

I got permission from on high, and within a week two had arrived; that from the officers mess of an aircraft carrier labelled for me which would not even get in through the front door and was about the same size as the kitchen, and a delightful brand new domestic model destined for the N. A. A. F. I. to keep the beer cool for a couple of hundred thirsty

Petty Officers! I changed the labels round at the first opportunity after they arrived that no-one was looking, and all parties seemed happy thereafter.

We soon settled in and before long time had progressed to our August summer leave and we had Alison, for whom we were still acting as guardian to stay, and then took her down for two weeks by the sea at Polzeath. Driving back in the car Peggy suddenly turned round to me and asked me to drive carefully because she was sure she was pregnant! Not then having her confidence or faith I feared that this might be another bit of wishful thinking which might come to a sad end, but anyhow I expressed joy and astonishment and we duly arrived home safely.

We were registered in Corsham with a doctor of our own age, hereafter called 'Bill' and next day I asked if he could call and told him the whole story from the very beginning to which he listened with great interest.

He then took the customary tests and in due course returned with a beam all over his face to confirm that the miracle had happened, and there are no words that could express our delight.

Peggy at once phoned Dorothy Keren, who expressed not the slightest surprise and assured her that all would be well. Our first instinct was to get in touch thereafter with the original specialists in London, but Bill wisely advised against it saying that there was an excellent heart specialist in Bath and also a very competent gynaecologist and he felt sure that she would be better off living at home under his personal supervision and supported by the local specialists. The wisest thing we ever did was to take his advice.

It quickly became a bit of a wonder amongst all our friends and family, both in and outside the service who knew clearly that the whole thing was impossible! They were all extremely kind and supportive, and the difficult thing was to persuade her from trying to do too much because she not only wanted to achieve what had once seemed unachievable, but wanted the achievement to be as natural as possible, even though she still had the same cardiac defects as before.

We decided that the first thing to do was to get a young living in help, who could both do the majority of the cooking and help entertaining, support Peggy through the day to keep her work load to a minimum and then later help with the baby, and so we put an advertisement in the Lady.

Two days after publication we had over fifty replies! They included a few bizarre candidates, but I remember being particularly struck and saddened at the great number of what must have been lonely spinsters living in small south coast hotels desperately clutching at straws. The final selection was 'Marlyse'. She was Swiss and was an ex-stewardess from Swiss Air, who spoke six languages perfectly and had a great capacity from her previous training, for producing effortlessly dinner parties out of a small kitchen. She joined almost at once for a year and stayed two and was the forerunner, of nine continental girls who were to share our next ten years.

She travelled each week on her day off to London to meet her doctor boy friend, until after a few months she came back, sat down in the sitting room, burst into floods of tears and declared that if there was a third sex she would never speak to another man again, and that was the end of the trips to London!

The stream of visitors varied from most of the Sea Lords across to representatives from industry and a number of Commanding Officers before taking up their appointments. One of the more unusual groups was a bunch of Majors from the newly formed West German Defence Force and when I had them in for a drink before they left and asked them how they had got on, they metaphorically clicked their heels, gave a short bow and with boot faces solemnly stated that they had learnt one very important thing, that one must lead with a sense of humour!

There were considerable calls on one's time in local community demands and one of the less arduous was selecting and crowning the local carnival queen. At the other end of the scales mention will be made of but two. I received a request to address the Baptist Church Wednesday Afternoon Women's Bright Hour and was hard pressed to know what to do for the best when inspiration struck. I wrote off to the Ceylon Tea Institute in London and they kindly provided me with small tins of all the different kinds of tea and so after a brief talk on how tea is manufactured I was able to put all the good ladies to work, brewing up, and seeing if they could tell the difference between the different kinds.

The other occasion was when I was invited to address the annual conference of the Wiltshire Association of Women's Institutes and this really did pose a problem. The great thing to do was to think of a subject that they would find interesting but about which they would all be ignorant and after much thought I decided on 'Family life in the Falkland Islands", not a subject I had at my finger tips, but sufficient knowledge to keep one jump ahead of the audience. However, that turned out to be the easy bit. What I suddenly realised on arrival at the gathering was that I would be standing in front of every one as the only male present, singing two verses of 'Jerusalem' with them, when I am absolutely tone deaf and can not sing a note in tune. Everything after that was easy!

I also at about this time was invited to one of England's leading electrical goods manufacturers to spend two days on the shop floor, being totally free to discuss with the work force what problems they had with their foremen and vice versa, and this fascinating visit slotted in exactly with the same failings, misconceptions and potentials as we found with Petty Officers, newly promoted to positions of leadership but with hitherto no training in exercising these new responsibilities. It was of course not to be long thereafter that industry itself moved more and more to this field of training.

Meanwhile, on the home front, everything was proceeding with encouraging normality as month succeeded month and we were both very touched by the personal interest and good wishes coming from all the staff all the way down to the most junior sailor and on Good Friday 19th April 1957 Peggy moved into hospital. Things started happening on Easter Sunday and at 1 o'clock the following morning David was born into the world over fifteen years after Peggy was first determined not to take 'no' for an answer.

I went down in the early hours of the morning and got back about 5 a. m. only to be stopped at the guard house by the quarter-master who asked me if all was well and what the baby was because the lads all wanted to know as soon as there was any news. Totally overcome I retired to the house buoyed up by all this caring, but somewhat worried because there was some concern in the hospital over the baby's condition.

I rang Dorothy Keren straight away and within an hour she had rung me back to say that she had gone immediately to the chapel to pray and she knew that everything was all right. I then rang Bill, who although it was Bank Holiday Monday, had gone straight down to the hospital in Bath and was back reporting to me in the house that mother and son were both fine.

This is no place for going into all the personal emotions of the time; suffice to say that once the news got out amongst the family and friends, both in and outside the service the room in the hospital was hardly big enough to contain all the flowers and gifts that arrived. Not least among the gifts were delightful presents from both the staff and ships company which I valued as much as any.

The family returned home after a week, and routine returned to what could be described as normal, except that under the surface it was, of course to us, miraculous. David was wheeled round the establishment roads in his pram by his proud mum, except when this task was carried out by 'Chiefie Chapman'.

Chapman was our eighteen stone Chief Boatswain's mate who was an ex-Japanese prisoner of war, a great character who ruled his subordinates with a very successful mixture of good humour and rod of iron; they all considered him as a stern father figure who would at the same time guide them through troubled waters whenever necessary. He had been married ever since he returned from P. O. W camp and again after some ten years had no children and his paternalistic wishes had reached the point that nothing delighted him more than to be seen in his full uniform and all his giant stature, going round the camp seeing that his subordinates were doing their stuff, pushing David in his pram and showing him off to the 'Lads'. It gave us immeasurable delight when, shortly after this, incredible though it may seem, he informed us that his wife in turn was expecting a child, when they had given up hope, and they became proud parents of a son also.

Peggy had hardly been home more than a week before a bevy of Ministry of Works officials suddenly arrived in the house unannounced and asked us to move into the back rooms for a short time as they proposed to plaster the sitting room walls, which somewhat nonplussed us.

Although our glorified army hut which also acted as Commanding Officer's quarters was in fact very comfortable, warm and roomy, none the less the walls were plain brick, distempered over and when we asked why they suddenly had decided to plaster the living room, so came our first intimation via the back door that the Duke of Edinburgh was shortly to pay the first visit since he had left, to his old establishment. Indeed, this was confirmed two days later when I got a phone call from his equerry confirming his visit and stating his requirements.

He would arrive by helicopter, take the salute on parade, spend the rest of the morning looking round the instructional classes and then lunch in the wardroom. However, prior to lunch he would like to come to my house and meet his old skittles team from years ago, comprising, amongst others, Jo Daymond, the baker, Bill Ives, the butcher and Powell who I think was the local bookie. Peggy was duly instructed in the art of curtseying and in due course I brought the Duke down to the house where all the Commanding Officers of the other local service establishments and skittles team had been mustered.

Peggy did her curtseying and Your Royal Highnessing and showed him into the sitting room where all his old skittling team stepped forward, slapped him on the back, said ''Hello Philip' and retired to a corner with him whilst we all chatted in the other corner.

There was however a revealing example to me of the limits to which the press will go. Prince Philip noticed hanging on a hook the present the wardroom had given to David, which was a beautifully made mini rugby ball and boxing gloves and remarked that when he had recently visited Slazenger's he had been given similar gloves for his son Charles, but they had had to be taken away from him to stop him using them on his younger sister! To my acute embarrassment by tea time that day in the local papers and next morning in the national tabloids there were headlines saying ''Charles has boxing gloves removed to stop him bashing sister'' or variants on the same theme.

I was shattered to think how such a private remark Could get out into the press, and as soon as I heard about it, looked around the house and there was the

Sparring partners

Prince Philip tells: Anne and Charles have hung up their gloves

From STANLEY BONNETT

CORSHAM, Wiltshire, Thursday.

PRINCESS ANNE has been "learning to box" with Prince Charles. Their father said so today.

But their sparring has been so rough that the gloves have been hung up and will stay that way until both are old enough to understand the Queensbury rules.

"They nearly killed each other" said a laughing Prince Philip.

He told the "Palace secret" to Commander Patrick Hoare, captain of Royal Arthur, the Navy's "stone frigate" at Corsham, where Prince Philip served after the war as a £4 7s. 6d.-a-week lieutenant.

It was an informal day for Admiral of the Fleet Prince Philip.

Informal enough for him to arrive by helicopter in a dark lounge suit, instead of gold-banded uniform.

No knock-down

Informal enough for him to invite to Royal Arthur the village baker, bookmaker, butcher, and the rest of the team against whom he played skittles in his bachelor days.

It was a miniature pair of boxing gloves, presented by the men at Royal Arthur to Commander Hoare to commemorate the birth of *his* son, which brought out the story of the royal boxers as the Prince stood with his skittles friends in the Commander's home.

To Joe Daymond, the village baker, Prince Philip said : " D'you remember when my skittles team wanted only six to win ? Everything depended on me. My three woods went right through the pins, none of them went down ! "

evidence staring us in the face. Below the sitting room window, in the flower bed, were the unmistakable footprints where a reporter had crouched, writing down all that was said within and he was away in no time, and the story on its way.

After this interlude and with David now four weeks old, the time had come to take him down to see Dorothy Keren, who blessed him in the chapel and then we adjourned to her house for a few sherries and an excellent lunch. No aesthete her! However, in the

process of conversation, she mentioned it seemed a pity to have only one child and thought that it might be nice to have a second. My hair immediately stood on end and breathing almost ceased, but Peggy, totally unconcerned expressed the view that it was a splendid idea. On return home we consulted Bill, who did not exude instant enthusiasm, but could recognise a brick wall when he saw one, and finally said that if we were determined to go through with it; there were medical advantages in not leaving it too long.

Meanwhile everything went along steadily on both the professional and home fronts, but thoughts were beginning to turn to whether or not in our new circumstances I should seek retirement. By the following January it became clear that we were indeed to be blessed with another child and this led to even further thought. My two years was up in the spring of 1958 and the ships company did the whole family the honour of towing us off the premises in my car by attaching to it and manning gun ropes and hauling there on.

My next appointment was to be on the staff of the Commander in Chief Home and Channel in connection with planning the use and control of Merchant shipping in war and I was subject fairly soon to a number of professional cross currents. It had been a supremely happy two years, both professionally and domestically, in the heart of Wiltshire in a very unusual and rewarding appointment with a first class and relatively hand picked staff. Indeed every Lieutenant Commander except those who opted to retire under the 'Golden Bowler' scheme that was about to operate, subsequently got his brass hat.

Yet another major change was to take place in our lives.

24
Time of Decision

I N THE SPRING OF 1958, we moved to a very comfortable Commander's married quarter on the sea front at Southsea and I started my new appointment on the staff of C-in-C Home and Channel, war planning in a block that was a mini Fort Knox. The work was to prove very interesting and included much abroad, but there was now the continuous nagging feeling that I ought to call it a day. After I had been in the appointment for some months, and just as I had thought to take the plunge, Admiral Grantham, who had been our C-in-C, and who was going on to be Governor of Malta, on saying good-bye, shook me warmly by the hand and said he would look forward to my future career with interest and I drew back.

My Chief of Staff very kindly had a private word in London and the signal clearly came back that I could look forward to advancement if I transferred to the dry list but as this would mean that I would never go to sea, it made far more sense to call it a day, retire, and start again in the outside world. I accordingly put in for retirement, but as it was mutually convenient, I stayed on for nearly two years longer before final departure, and this chapter is of that time.

My first trip on taking over the reins was to go to a meeting in Washington with some senior Civil Servants in the Ministry of Transport with whom I regularly worked. When these journeys abroad took place it was normal for them to travel first class and Naval Officers tourist, but on this occasion I was to have the last laugh.

Our plane was delayed twelve hours and so a fellow Naval Officer and I went to the B. O. A. C. desk and explained how desperately important it was that we got to our meeting on time and we could brook no delay. The next thing we heard was our names being called over the Tannoy and we were hurried on to the Monarch flight which was the flagship of their line, and where there were two unbooked seats, leaving our Civil Service confreres floundering in the departure lounge.

The Monarch was a conversion of the old wartime Flying Fortresses, all first class with super luxury and in the old bomb bay was a little bar seating about four people. Everything was of course free and its normal clientele can be judged by the fact that an American, also using the free bar, assumed we were both Vice Presidents of General Motors! The pair of us certainly made the most of the time available to us.   It was an overnight flight, with the Monarch trundling along at a steady 110 miles per hour, and arriving at either Gander in Newfoundland or Goose Bay in Labrador in the early hours of the morning to refuel, arriving in New York at mid morning. I was to do many more travels over the next two years, but none as luxurious as this.

Meanwhile things were moving inexorably on the home front. We had settled into our attractive quarter facing the sea and joined up with a local doctor to whom we had been recommended who was satisfied that, providing all was going well, there would be no need for any specialists, and the target date was mid-August. Marlyse had been with us for two years and quite naturally wanted to move on and it was agreed that she would do so as soon as she could fix up fresh employment. This she did, but unfortunately it was to coincide with when just after the baby was due to be born. We made arrangements for a local trained nurse to follow Marlyse.

On 15th August 1958 at seven in the evening, Christopher was brought into the world weighing nine pounds, a good keeping size as we fishermen would say and all was unalloyed joy, and then things started going awry. A week after Peggy came home Marlyse departed and at the same time her intended relief slipped a disc and could not come. One week after this Peggy got a touch of pleurisy and returned to the nursing home for two weeks which left the forces on the ground at almost the irreducible minimum.

We hauled over my nearly octogenarian mother virtually to baby sit for the two of them whilst I took over feeding and nappy changing Christopher every four hours, slipping home in the morning break and after lunch to do the day time chores. Things seemed to be going along all right except that Christopher appeared consistently to be losing weight, and I was fearful that if this went on for a considerable time, he might disappear altogether rather like the Cheshire cat.

I accordingly telephoned 'her of the slipped disc' who was a specialist baby nurse and she recommended putting some brown sugar dissolved in the milk, and at once, with the aid of this and Mrs Somebody or others gripe water, he started putting on weight and never looked back. Meanwhile Marlyse had telephoned her mother in Switzerland to send over a replacement, and after two weeks of my ministrations, no doubt to Christopher's relief, his mother returned to the fold, although unable for a time to do very much.

Shortly after this, arrived 'Martha' from Switzerland who was all that we did not want. She was a fat inexperienced domestic of singular incompetence, no sense of dealing with babies and very unprepossessing appearance. She scarcely endeared herself to me on the first day after her arrival at breakfast, when sitting opposite to me, she took a quick sniff under each arm presumably to see if they fell within the acceptable limits of aroma! Purely coincidentally it transpired that her father was head of the Swiss Communist party but it was decided that this would not impinge on my secret work.

However, she had to go, and then a lucky break followed. There were a number of continental au pairs with Naval families in the area who met at the Technical College once a week for English lessons, and it was through their network that we found that a red headed German had her eighteen year old sister coming over looking for a post and so we booked her as it were on a blind date. And so arrived with us gorgeous eighteen year old Barbel from Hamburg. She professed not to be able to cook, but was fond of the babies and good with them and generally quite useful, and a great relief to Peggy. Soon Barbel was asking on most evenings if she could walk through the Royal Marine Barracks on to which our back entrances abutted at about nine p. m. in order to post a letter home to which we readily agreed.

The cause of this behaviour was soon made apparent. I got an irate phone call from the Colonel asking if I could get my redheaded au pair to desist from standing in front of the Bugler at 9p. m. each night as he stood outside the Officer's mess formally sounding the Last Post! Apparently a considerable feeling of mutual esteem had sprung up between them of which this was an outward and visible sign that had to be stopped forthwith, although no doubt other channels were established.

A few months after Barbel had joined us one of my many journeys took me to Cuxhaven via Hamburg and she asked me if I would visit her family which I was only too pleased to do, and very charming they were. I mentioned to her mother that we were very happy with Barbel but a little surprised that she could not cook. My surprise was as nothing compared with that of her mother at this news, and so the girls non-culinary career plan was blown.

The purpose of the visit was to open the first post-war operations room and headquarters for the new German navy at Cuxhaven and on the previous evening my German opposite number and his wife entertained Admiral Platirinck of the Netherlands

The opening of the first post-war German naval base at Cuxhaven

Navy and myself to supper. After supper our host took us down to the cellar, as they called it, and we drank not a little. The more we drank, the more our host, who had been a submarine officer in the war, reverted to type and started saying that Hitler was really rather a good chap and had unified Germany where no one else had succeeded, whereupon Platirinck blew a fuse and much fiery rhetoric followed, during which I kept comparative quiet; whereupon he turned to me and said 'It's all right for you, you were never occupied during the war'. The Germanic reversion to type and Platirinck's retort to me, have many times since given me food for thought. After the ceremony the following day I returned home, and Barbel was soon operating over the stove!

About a week later when I was sitting at breakfast and the mail had come, she was sitting opposite reading the newly arrived German magazine, and kept looking up at me and down again and then turned the paper round to face me, and there was a picture of me taken at the opening ceremony at Cuxhaven! Meanwhile, the interesting work took me off periodically, in addition to Germany, to Paris, Brussels, Washington, Virginia and Norway and the months rolled past.

My Admiral was kind enough to say that I could stay on in the appointment as long as I chose, but I was influenced both by the fact that the longer I stayed, the older I would be in transferring to civil employment and also one was only allowed to keep our very nice Commanders married quarter for three years. I accordingly asked to retire in the autumn of 1960, and started laying a plan. I had seen many of my friends retire full of the belief, quite wrongly, that with all their experience and acceptance of responsibility, industry would welcome them with open arms. In general only minor peripheral staff jobs awaited them. They had no experience inside the service of having to make a profit!

Certain facts were of influence. I would be aged 43 on retiring which was just too old to start retraining for one of the professions such as Chartered Accountant or Solicitor; my wife would not be fit enough to contribute a second income; it was important if at all possible, to send the boys to boarding school so that it would be easier for Peggy to cope for most of the year; we had no nepotic ready made entry into industry or commerce and lastly we neither had nor would have, any private capital or income other than the gratuity and pension which I would receive on leaving the Navy.

This led to the conclusion that the only salvation lay in entering industry at the bottom, learning the ropes, and hoping successfully, even though a late starter, to climb to the higher ranks of line management which should generate enough income to fulfil our plan. Accordingly, with a year and a half still to go in the Navy I started on a four year plan to take all nine intermediate and nine final exams to get the full degree of the British Institute of Management, starting with two exams every six months, learning by correspondence course and personal study, enhanced later by personal experience on the lower levels of industry.

A pleasant year had meanwhile passed and it was time for Barbel to return to Germany, and we were lucky enough to get Theresa through an agency in London. She was a German Swiss from Zurich who came for one year and stayed for two. She was highly competent and full of fun and became a lasting friend of the family. She spoke relatively little English to begin with but soon learnt and was to make her mark on her first evening. After supper she saw Peggy cutting out a summer dress pattern on the floor of the sitting room, and quietly took the scissors, pins and all the other impedimenta from her. After a flurry of some two hours, she handed back to Peggy the finished dress to our total amazement. It transpired that among her many achievements was that she was a fully qualified Haute Couturier and what she had just done was chicken feed! She was also to prove in the times ahead to have a considerable ability to attract the opposite sex!

By May 1960, not having taken a holiday since arriving, I consulted the doctor and he said it would be quite safe for Peggy to fly to Paris and back. I knew from my travels of a quiet hotel in a one way street close to the Champs Elysee with a little courtyard at the back, with a cherry tree that would be in bloom, and off it one ground floor double room. All that remained was what to do with the children, now 3 and 1. Such had become Peggy's faith in Theresa that she was happy to leave her on her own to look after the children, with a kindly neighbour keeping a watchful eye.

And so off we went and had an idyllic if fairly conventional four days stay in Paris. We telephoned Theresa at half time to find that the only crisis had been that she had gone out to make a purchase in the mobile greengrocers shop which was in the back of an old furniture van, and the owner had apparently tried to do her no good on top of a basket of sprouts. Her shouts were heard by the neighbour who rescued her before disaster struck. Knowing Theresa I just wonder whether the villain was wholly to blame!

We arrived back tired but happy to find everything again running smoothly and it was time to start making plans for the move. On the edge of Corsham was a lovely Elizabethan Cotswold farm house, which was rented to the head of the local doctor's partnership and where we had gone to dinner when at Royal Arthur. I remember Peggy emerging after dinner saying 'This is my dream house'.

It transpired that the doctor was retiring and moving in the autumn and we could not believe our luck when the landlord said we could take the house on, and at a very low rent at that. He was a farmer and was only interested in the land and was only too pleased to have a good tenant who would keep the house in order. However, it made the first alteration to the original master plan. That had been to be mobile and to move wherever was necessary to climb up the line management tree as high and as quickly as possible.

It was right, as she was denied so many of the pleasures available to the completely healthy that Peggy should at least have a lovely stable and permanent home, where she already had friends from our time at Royal Arthur. It only meant that I had to try and do an industrial Indian rope-trick from a base in the middle of rural Wiltshire. We were never to regret the decision, although once or twice the abyss was to loom dangerously close.

In September 1960 there was to be a world wide N. A. T. O. exercise conducted on paper concerning the control and protection of Merchant shipping in war, and to this end some members of the Ministry of Transport and myself with assistants made a plot of where every merchant ship in the Lloyds register was on a given day and transferred the details on to bits of paper. All the reserves for wartime appointments were called up and all places manned and the exercise conducted from our Home C-in-C's headquarters, underground near Portsmouth.

Bill Beloe, who had been our Commander in Jamaica, and who was now a Rear Admiral and was shortly to take up his appointment as Deputy Supreme Commander to SACLANT at Norfolk, Virginia, was roped in to be Flag Officer Falmouth at Pendennis Castle, as had many other senior officers between appointments, been allocated to different H. Q. all over the country.

It was soon clear that advancing seniority had not caused Bill to change his ways. It seemed that once all his reserve officers had joined him, he gave instructions for a liberal supply of brandy and ginger ale to be brought in, and if there were any attractive young ladies still on holiday on the beach below, he had no rooted objection to them being supplied as well.

The exercise was due to run for fourteen days and by the tenth not one signal had been received from Flag Officer Falmouth. In order to stir things up there our C-in-C made a signal to him to say that Plymouth had been knocked out and Falmouth was transferred to the responsibility of Flag Officer Brest, Bill then made his only signal of the exercise.

To C-in-C Home from Flag Officer Falmouth.

'Have come off the bottle and gone to Brest. '

The exercise over, I was asked what specific date I would like to leave and I suggested 21st October which was agreed without anyone noticing the significance.

And so on Trafalgar day 1960 I gave farewell drinks in the mess to all to which the C-in-C kindly came, had lunch, paid my mess-bill, changed out of uniform into civilian clothes and drove home out of the Royal Navy and into civilian life as if it was an everyday occurrence. I had been lucky enough to have a career of nearly thirty years in uniform in a large variety of interesting appointments and now came the challenge of a second career in industry for nearly as long. During this time I could be based at home without separations whilst our young children grew up.

A few months before leaving I had arranged to join an engineering company in Bath which was a public company selling products all over the world. As I had planned, I joined on the shop floor as the lowest of the low as 'Pump Spares Chaser' on the princely wage of ten pounds per week, and the only reason I got ten was because there was not a job at nine! It was an interesting and salutary experience after having had one's own command and I was to learn much.

25
Back to the Drawing Board

P EGGY, THERESA AND THE BOYS had gone on to 'Monks Farm House' which had been rented unfurnished and was to be our home for many years. It was the perfect place for the young to grow up in on a drive off a side lane, with a large garden, farm buildings on one side and fields in front. There was a vast playroom which had originally been the room where the Flemish refugee weavers congregated to do their work, and which still had the staples in the old beams. Over the years, it grew up with the boys, from farm yard lay out to table tennis to electric trains, to mini snooker table and finally to dancing to the disco, when on occasions I feared for the floor. There were two living rooms, a dining room, a large farm kitchen and enough bedrooms for all. It also had one unmodernised bathroom and no central heating.

As I drove there from Portsmouth, I found a great serenity where I had expected a mental turmoil. The die had been cast and the way ahead planned, even though it was far from adhered to in the event. We would be in one spot, in one community, in a lovely part of the country and the professional challenge in a new environment, if daunting, projected excitement. I gave myself two weeks holiday to help us settle in, and then set off on Monday morning for my new humble station, not really knowing what to expect.

I met my boss on arrival, who was the the Production Engineering Manager, a tall thin chap, who I found out that my fellow workers called 'Kapok' because in their judgement, he clearly needed plenty of stuffing , and then I was introduced to 'Jim' for whom I was to work on a day to day basis. He was the equivalent of a sergeant who was responsible for chasing up all bits for the pumps on order, whilst I, as one of his minions chased the flow of spares for him. Being totally non-technical in a world of technicians, I felt that quick action was required, so took to taking home the manuals for the different kinds of pumps and learning off by heart, the different bits and their functions!

The first human problem to overcome was some of my fellow workers, who knowing my background, thought I must be some management spy, or something else mysterious. However, when they finally realised that I was only a chap who was wanting to learn and had no ulterior motive, I was accepted into their fraternity and indeed became good friends.

My first major derailment was when, at the end of the first week, I got sent for by a lady in the wages department who threw down a piece of brown cardboard in front of me and asked if it was mine? I agreed that it had my name on it and she then asked how I

expected her to pay my princely wage for the first week when I had not clocked on once? I apologised profusely and asked what I was supposed to do, and almost distraught with disbelief she explained how I was meant to punch the clock four time a day. I returned with much food for thought, as I knew I would never regularly remember to carry out this task. There was a young impecunious chap who worked with me and was desperately saving up to get married, and we both came to a mutually happy arrangement where at the end of each week, if he had turned in a faultless performance in punching my card he would receive a ten bob note. The arrangement worked excellently.

There were odd little things one learnt in what to me was a new environment but which was of course common place to the others, as for example my normal habit of eating breakfast before going to work, whereas the work force in general tended to come to work on a cup of tea and then in the mid morning break had breakfast which they had either brought with them or they would purchase sandwiches off a perambulating trolley.

My modest work took me chasing to all the main shops, such as Foundry, Plate, and machine shop, all of whom had managers in charge. Each seemed to me to fall in to the same mould; very nice and helpful, absolutely expert in their own subject in which they had probably spent half a life time, and not the faintest concept of any modern management techniques. Meanwhile I found a surprising ally on the lower deck, one Pat Moran, who like Uncle Ropey of former days, almost deserves a chapter of his own.

He too was an Irish bachelor and had also once been a Lieutenant-Commander; he too had shed himself through life of one or two minor fortunes left to him by maiden aunts. He had also played wing three quarter for the Navy in the Inter- Services Rugby tournament. He had been a Submarine Engineer and one day was teaching a Petty Officer the drill in the escape tank at the submarine school when the Petty Officer panicked and pulled Pat Moran's mask off at some depth, causing damage to his lungs which resulted in his being invalided from the service. He now lived in a terraced house in Clifton with a housekeeper and was employed in a fairly modest capacity whence he conducted a desultory guerilla warfare against authority. Unlike me, he had because of his function, even though it was fairly ill-defined, to be a member of the Transport and General Workers Union, and each year he made a donation to Transport House, and to the Conservative Association in Clifton and invited both parties not to bother him for the rest of the year.

On the home front, a story of human interest was developing. Theresa had signed on at Bath Tech. for English lessons, and a couple of months after we had moved to Corsham, she received from her German fiancé in Zurich twelve red roses to which was attached a rejection slip! This caused her momentarily to be disconcerted, but she soon found a remedy to hand. On her next day off to travel to Bath for her lesson, she left a bit early to catch the shops, and put her engagement ring up the spout in exchange for a bit of the ready. She then proceeded to enter into a romance with a fellow student who was a waiter in the local Austrian restaurant, and it was not long before he had taken the ring out of hock and presented it back to her!

However the liaison was not to last long. After a few weeks, he telephoned one evening which was Theresa's day off to ask where she was. I had no idea and asked where he was and was informed that he was in Corsham waiting for her at the 'Heron Hunt' to meet as arranged. I had not the faintest idea what he was talking about so taxed her at breakfast next morning, she having returned late. 'Ah' she said 'I forgot that I arranged to meet him at the Hare and Hounds. Don't worry, there are plenty more fish in the sea. ', and the following week, the ring beginning to show a good profit, was back up the spout again!

Some months had now passed at work, and as I had bought shares in the company, I took time off to attend the Annual General meeting. There were two joint Managing Directors, (usually a recipe for disaster in itself); one, on the technical side was a retired Sapper Major General who was a personal friend of the owner of the company before it had gone public. He was a delightful person and no doubt a splendid soldier, who had not had a day's previous experience in business in his life and called all the employees 'lads' or 'chaps'. The other, in charge of the business side, was an unqualified Accountant, who had been with the company for many years, who may or may not have had expertise in this field, but had none at getting people to work for him.

I was the only employee to attend the A. G. M. , and somewhat to my astonishment the latter recognised me and came up after the meeting and said 'You are one of our work force, are you not? I suppose you think you could run the company better than us?' I could not resist the opening and said that that would not be very difficult and I was quite sure that I could! Nothing further was ever said, but I was finding it hard not to resist doing something about what I could see from even my humble position. Pumps and spares were getting more and more overdue and the material flow to the point of final assembly seemed chaotic. So, greatly daring, I wrote a paper to my boss, and ultimately the Works Manager, suggesting ways of chasing up missing parts and reducing delays so that products would more nearly finish on time.

To my astonishment I was elevated to £14 per week and told to implement my suggestions. There was of course instant resistance from departmental managers at someone starting to rock their boats which had ridden peacefully for so long, but after finding one was only trying to help it was surprising how quickly they co-operated, and indeed the overdue list came tumbling down. Parallel to all this I had been able to knock off the balance of my B. I. M. intermediate exams and started down the road to try and pass the eight exams for the finals.

In addition another extra-mural crisis brewed up on the home front. Having, relatively recently, been a Commanding Officer locally for two years, hardly had I moved back into the area in a civilian capacity before I was lured into every organisation you could think of. British Legion, Sea Cadets, Scouts, Church Council, School Governor to mention but some, and I found I was hardly ever free in the evenings. Peggy quite rightly read the riot act and I slowly dropped a lot of them and concentrated on starting up a youth club in our local village of Gastard, which is really a suburb of Corsham now.

I had also picked up the threads again of my increasing love for fly-fishing, started when at Royal Arthur, and it transpired that the Wylye Fly Fishing Club to which I had been introduced by Alistair McLagan were looking for a suitable new secretary and river manager to take over from the existing one who wished to retire. There was a long waiting list to join, but their committee were kind enough to think that I was suitable and so I jumped the waiting list and was elected a member for the 1962 season, and secretary the following year.

This took with it as payment a free rod for the season, and thus began my most absorbing hobby for all the years that followed. The club rented three miles of lovely water centred on Steeple Langford and being part of it was one of the luckiest breaks of my life.

Furthermore, inside Peggy had been for years the unrequited wish for love of water colour painting and so on many occasions of going fishing, she would come with me and set up her easel and have a no less pleasant day. From those small beginnings she was to advance to exhibiting on a number of occasions, including the International Amateur art exhibition in London and the Royal West of England Academy.

Our River Keeper was a great character and a true countryman who was also the Gamekeeper of the local shoot, and who had spent some years as a Petty Officer in the Navy. Fred Scott was to become a great friend of our family and was fascinating company on the river. He was in his middle sixties when we first knew him, of ruddy complexion, piercing blue eyes and a seemingly bottomless knowledge of the ways of the countryside, and he taught me much.

He also drank beer in vast quantities and if one was fishing on a Sunday afternoon, at about 2, 30 p. m. could be heard the stentorian voice of Fred singing on the conductors platform of the bus carrying him home to his dinner after turn-out from the Swan at Stoford which was his Sunday morning pub.

On one occasion Peggy and I were leaning over a field gate chatting to him, when I decided to go to the far end of the big field and start fishing, when I thought I saw a fisherman already there and was about to desist. Fred looked into the distance and announced that there was no-one there and I asked how he knew and he replied that if there had been anyone there that heron would not be standing in the water. How on earth he could see a heron at that range amazed me.

Soon afterwards he gave me a shout to say that a good trout of nearly a pound had run out of the river up an irrigation channel into a field and was staying motionless in a few inches of water. He accordingly directed me to go above the fish and stand astride the little runnel with my open net in the water between my legs. He then bunged a few stones into the water behind the fish which shot upstream into the net and was duly landed. It was not returned to the river!

Frequent visits to Steeple Langford down the years, either for attending to the river or seeing and paying the keepers enabled me to get to know the village very well, and a number of its inhabitants. It was not a village of great beauty, but stood for everything that I thought best in the British countryside. The village pub, which was our meeting place, was the club, with its Christmas club, and darts team and behind were the village football and cricket pitches.

Nearly everyone was engaged in agriculture and the village contained as it were two nobs and the village parson. The two former were our riparian owners and the latter was an ex- parachutist chaplain who would come into the pub on Sunday mornings after church and drink vast quantities of dry sherry and play the fruit machines. The charitable members of the congregation, who were also by then present, assumed that they were not watching the disappearance of the morning collection!

Nobody ever seemed to take much holiday and everybody seemed contented with their lot and did not seem to care which government was in power or even if there was a government at all. But once a year was the darts club outing, attended by a large quantity of the village. Sometimes it was to Weymouth and other years to the Lido at Barry. Wherever its destination, it always seemed to turn into a forty-eight hour wake during which everything came to a halt. My first visit to the pub each year was a couple of weeks before the season began at the beginning of April when I used to meet Fred and his son Stan who was his assistant and also the local poacher.

After much celebration at the passing of another winter we would strike a bargain with the poacher which he invariably kept, providing one refuelled his alcoholic tank at intervals through the season, that he would not poach our water and we would not harass him, but we were not bothered with what he did on any one else's water.

Old Fred had a very interesting form of piscine vermin control based on what he called his fishing rod, which was a piece of coiled up thin fencing wire with a noose, which he kept in his waistcoat pocket. When set on reducing the population of grayling of which we had far too many, he would attach the noose to the end of a hazel stick and crouching behind some cover, stick the hazel out over a shoal of grayling and gradually slip the noose over a fishes head, give a jerk and out it would sail on to the bank without disturbing its neighbours. He could clear a whole pool quickly in this fashion. On the rare occasion when he saw a pike he would use the same system only with stronger wire and longer noose. Alas, one day when he was in his twilight he was to misjudge the size of the pike which stayed where it was and Fred joined it in the river.

Meanwhile about a year had passed in my civilian life and life at home socially and in every way was very happy and the boys were expanding at the normal rate under Peggy's and Theresa's tutelage. By now Theresa had teamed up with a Persian architectural student from Bristol Tech: and to our slight worry she would return from her evening off ever later and the ring was once more out of pawn and back on her finger. It was somewhat to our relief that this romance was not of very long duration and the ring was back in its temporary accommodation once more. It must be said in all fairness to her, that whatever time she returned, she was always up on time, bright and breezy the next morning to attend to the children.

Back at work, the task I had been given to set up a better system for material flow was in place when my boss, the Production Engineering Manager, sent for me saying he had been told to carry out an investigation of some complexity and wanted me to do the job. On hearing what it was, I asked for an assistant and got Pat Moran! The company had produced a revolutionary tubular all welded dockside crane, a field in which they were one of the world market leaders, and the Port of London Authority had ordered eighty of them direct from the prototype stage and they were now being delivered. The only snag was that the crane had never properly been costed and it was feared that the business half of the Joint Managing Directorship had flogged the lot at a price that would make a loss. It was accordingly decided to cost accurately one of these cranes by taking every work ticket for every process of every part from the largest to the smallest, plus all the 'bought in' equipment and then add up the whole lot to get the true cost. This was the gargantuan task set before me and I moved into an office with my assistant, became a white collar worker and asked for a pay rise! And so I progressed up to £17 a week.

The office we moved into was already occupied by a remarkable character who is worthy of a digression. His name was Jack Donovan (Lonny Donegan behind his back), a fiery Irishman who had been a rabble rousing dockers leader in Bristol under Ernie Bevin. When the war ended and the Labour government was elected, and the ports nationalised, Jack was made General Manager of all the North Eastern ports, which appointment he held, with apparent distinction until he reached retiring age and returned to Bristol. He was recruited to our company on a part-time basis to help and advise the General on labour relations with the workforce, and was the owner of the office into which we had moved. He had somewhat mellowed with age but could still be very fiery if the occasion demanded, and was very interesting to listen to, having known Bevin well.

However, one day he started pontificating vigourously and at length on the fact that Britain should cease building nuclear weapons and markedly reduce its military forces, so that the money saved could be used to improve life for the less well off. I asked him gently if, as he deemed it right that Union Leaders should press for action on matters military, would he also support the view that Admirals and Generals should take part in negotiations on wages and working conditions for Dockers? There was a loud explosion and the plaster did not stop falling from the ceiling for some time! Our relations were never to be the same again.

The allotted task was never feasible and ought to have been conducted by the departmental line managers together with the large estimating department, and so it was reduced to examining one section in depth and this in itself was a formidable target, and all the relative work cards were piled onto my desk, one section of which was transferred to that of Pat Moran. After a couple of weeks, my pile was beginning to subside, but that of Pat appeared undiminished.

The cards were of a slightly absorbent paper, so I took two off his pile home, damped them and grew mustard on one and cress on the other. I then took this little garden back to the office and put one on each of his two piles. When he came in that day, he asked what the hell they were and I said they had just grown while he just looked at the piles each day and did nothing! This spurred him into some minimal level of action.

The job done, I was moved over to the Pump Estimating Department as a member of the team had gone sick. Their function was to take the details of a pump which the Technical Estimating Department adjudged to be the correct one to fit a particular enquiry and to calculate the cost to be quoted to the potential customer.

Some two years had gone past now and the exams were nearing completion, whilst on the home front Theresa had sadly departed, but not before one more adventure with the ring. This time it was an R. A. F. corporal who had taken out the ring and presented it back to her.

One evening he arrived at the house all spruced up in his uniform to take her out, but she was not quite ready so she gave him a Peter Rabbit book and told him to read his goodnight story to Christopher aged three, sitting on the sofa in his pyjamas. He ought to have known that all children of that age know them all off by heart, but when he got to the point where Benjamin Bunny had eaten too many lettuces and had got . . . . . he paused beaten by the next word. 'Sopo – Saro – Sorap' and so on he went until Christopher looked up at him and said 'Soporific, you big nit'. Whereupon the scarlet faced Corporal disappeared out through the front door never to be seen again, and shortly afterwards Theresa exchanged the ring for coin of the realm for the third and last time.

Peggy missed her much, but she continued to keep in touch to our horror, once she had got a new job in Zurich, by ringing Peggy up on the bosses phone in his lunch hour. This remarkable girl, besides being an exemplary au-pair with a somewhat overdeveloped romantic streak, had also during her time with us, become a good English linguist, had acquired a British driving licence and had been baptised and confirmed into the Church of England.

Marlyse the second, who followed and stayed for a year, was stolid, pleasant, adequately efficient and unremarkable. The only thing that sticks in the memory is when we took her to Bigbury on Sea for our first holiday for three years and as we breasted the final hill to drop down into the town, her gasp of disbelief when she saw the sea for the first time in her life.

Soon after joining the Estimating Department, it seemed to me to be amazing that, although there was tremendous duplication in a lot of the enquiries, the Technical Estimators solemnly recalculated from albeit quite complicated basic formulae separately for each enquiry the pump and motor that would meet the requirements. I enquired of the Pump Manager whether the whole thing would not be reduced to graphs and tables and he said he had discussed the matter with the Head of the Technical College and they had decided that it could not be done because there were too many variables, these basically being viscosity, pressure, volume of output, pump speed and motor horsepower.

Somehow this did not ring true and I took the formulae home with me and worked on them. Two months and many thousands of calculations later I produced a tome with graphs and tables which would do in five minutes what was taking the Estimators several hours. It was scarcely believable that they would not use it officially but they said it was not acceptable because it was not done by a qualified engineer and might make one or two Estimators redundant, but the salesmen took a photocopy on the quiet and used it all the time and my original stayed in my drawer and was used quietly off the record whenever a quotation was needed in a hurry.

The final time, shortly before my departure, was for all the relevant pumps for the Queen Elizabeth II, the quotation for which was needed in a hurry, which were done off the graphs in a couple of hours and the quotation despatched, days before the same result was produced by the system. When I left, I believe the magnum opus was destroyed as being too reactionary, but not before I had taken a photocopy which I still possess.

During this time there was a requirement to visit the Pump Fitting shop to see my good friend the foreman, who was always very helpful, but on this occasion was rather worried because there were four rayon viscous pumps for export to Russia and their representatives, who were very thorough had inspected two in the morning without difficulty, but he was worried about whether the two to be done in the afternoon were up to standard, and the Russians had meanwhile gone off to have a viscous lunch with the Pump Manager.

Pat Moran was with me at the time and this did not seem to present us with any problem. We suggested that the foreman went off to lunch too, and then swapped over the two identity plates and other markings, and the Russians quite happily inspected the two good ones all over again in the afternoon!

By now nearly three years had passed and I finally passed all the eighteen B. I. M. exams and had been elected a member and I had risen to the dizzy heights of £20 a week, about as far as one could get on the lower deck. I also by then had run into in Bath, Simon, my old Chief Engineer from H. M. S. Burghead Bay, who was still in the Navy and was seconded to Rolls Royce, working on gas turbines. He reckoned his company was the most inefficient in England and would be bankrupt ere long and I put up my lot as a challenger. He was to win his bet, but not by many years.

On the home front both boys had just started at the kindergarten of the local excellent and much sought after pre-preparatory school. The kindergarten had been ruled over for many years by a very well known character called Nanny Mutton, who had still been ruling when the mothers of a lot of the children had been there. She was highly respected by all; well nearly all. Soon after they arrived it was Nanny's birthday, and all the children brought her presents. There was a slight sensation when one little boy brought and gave to her his most precious possession, a live grass snake.

Shortly after that, Christopher who had never yet shown any tendency to pugnacity, achieved a brief period of infamy. He was apparently sitting peacefully, when for no known reason he entered into warfare with his neighbour. Nanny immediately called him out to the front of the class by himself and said 'Christopher, little boys do not hit other little boys' whereupon Christopher gave Nanny a fourpenny one right on the end of her nose and the world suddenly stood still. Nothing like this had ever happened to Nanny before and it took many a tea and sandwiches between Peggy and Nanny to restore diplomatic relations.

Painting was going along successfully and were beginning to creep into minor exhibitions and the fishing and fishery management gave much relaxation in season. However, none of these pleasantries were going to pay the grocer's bills and school fees, and I had been out of the Navy nearly three years. The time had come, now that I had qualified myself for a higher rung to find a means of taking that step.

I asked for an interview with the General who said that, apart from the Finance side, nobody, whilst he was in charge would become a Manager unless he was a qualified Engineer. I suggested that the Company might prosper more if he make a rule that nobody could become a Manager unless he could manage and we parted on a mutual lack of esteem. It was then that I got given an introduction to the Vice-Chairman of a very large Public Company who in turn passed me to the Managing Director of the Engineering division.

I was very impressed when I arrived for interview to find a notice on his door saying 'Come in, don't knock'', and on entering, found him behind a large desk without a single piece of paper on it. He knew my Christian name before I entered and simply said all in one breath ''Sit down Pat, what do you think of Trade Unions''! I had lunch with him and the Vice-Chairman, and I was very pleased that they wanted me to join them in a middle management capacity, but had no clear-cut vacancy at the moment. They suggested that I went back whence I came and they would send for me when an opportunity arose and so I returned.

There was no proper job for me because everyone knew I would soon be leaving, and after a short time I met a fellow member at the club who asked me if I would like to consider joining him to train as his assistant General Manager at the glove business which he owned in Westbury. My will power and patience broke down as I now was so fed up with where I had been for the previous nearly three years, that instead of waiting any longer for a summons from London I agreed to the proposal.

I often wonder what would have happened if I had hung on, for my potential London boss was later to become head of a nationalised industry, be knighted and become a household name. The path I was now to take had many pitfalls, but at least I now was to transfer on to the managerial ladder.

26
The Climb Back

N OW BEGAN THE JOURNEY from the shop floor up the management ladder once more. After some preliminary training, including on the glove counter of Harrods, I became the sales manager of a glove manufacturing company making top quality products for the leading stores of the country.

We produced both a spring and an autumn range, each comprising some two dozen samples, and many of the buyers came down and placed their orders directly with us. We employed a designer and also selected some half a dozen of the fashion colours for each season. The gloves were mainly leather and at the top end of the range, including Doeskin, Hogskin and various fur backed very expensive lines, in addition to the more conventional lines, but also forming part of our fairly large export market, which included the Arnold Palmer Golf glove.

My contribution to the actual designing was virtually nil, except for one success. In order to make a pair of mink gloves (£100 per pair), it took one skin per glove, which left a fair amount of trimmings left over. The larger pieces were made into babies mittens and sold through a large Texas store for rich American babies to wear in their prams! There were now even smaller bits left over, so we bought a number of large bottle openers, and stuck mink strips down the handles; they were sold at Christmas time through a large Midland store as a gimmick. 'The Mink Bottle opener' for the man who has everything! I had made my mark!

The company was a second generation small family business, which had succeeded in a top of a niche market, but, also as so often happens, the next generation head of the business, whilst having the required technical skills, had little of the management skills required in an increasingly competitive market. It also became clear that as he was now reaching the age of sixty, he was planning that I might take over his family business some time in the near future.

After some two years in the company, it was clear to me that, not only were they slowly losing their leading position, but the owner had no real skill in the human side of managing his work force. I therefore decided, after discussions with my wife, that this ladder had too many rungs missing to enable me to climb further and I gave three months notice to leave the company. I set about answering advertisements for middle management appointments with prospects.

By this time both boys were at preparatory school and problems loomed large. I drew unemployment benefit, and got short listed for posts as varied as assistant manager for a tanker fleet, management adviser to a trawler fleet, a consultant with a large firm of management consultants and general manager of a specialist firm of export packaging. All but the last fell at the final hurdle, and the other, just off the Sidcup bypass, was offered to me. After much thought, and to their anger, I took a deep breath and declined. , It seemed to me to suffer too much from the same malaise as the company I had left.

Meanwhile, we had just been down for half term, taking with us a cuckoo's egg which I had taken from a reed warbler's nest from by our fishing river which we had passed on the way down. Peggy kept it warm in her bosom and on arrival it was placed in the headmaster's pheasant hatching incubator, and duly hatched. The two Hoare brothers were made responsible for feeding the chick at frequent intervals with worms. However, they must have taken their responsibilities too keenly, because not long afterwards, Christopher's weekly letter home read; 'dear mum, the cuckoo has burst'!

However, then, just as things were beginning to look really serious, came news which was to change everything. A distant relative of mine, who owned a small company running five coastal ships, phoned me and asked if I would like to come and fill a vacancy as his shipping manager.

In February 1967 on a rainy Monday morning, six and half years after leaving the Royal Navy, I set out to be the shipping manager of Osborn and Wallis Ltd. in Hotwells Dock; it had to be right this time. Our five coasters were employed extensively in transporting coal from south Wales and Scotland to the power stations of Devon and Somerset, and we also employed six registered dock workers at Portishead for discharge. The company was now 51% owned by United Dominions Trust, owing to death duties problems, and our chairman was also Aldermanic sheriff of London, and let the original owner, Dennis Osborn get on and run the company without interference. He related the anecdote, when we first met, that he attended as sheriff, a formal lunch at the Old Bailey and was sitting next to Mr Justice Melford Stevenson who was in the process of trying the Kray twins.

He asked the judge how the trial was proceeding to which the judge replied that he had sat opposite one of the twins throughout the trial and he had only heard him speak the truth twice, once when he had called the prosecuting council a big fat slob, and the other time when he had said that the judge was biased against him! My specific function as shipping manager was to arrange the timetables for the ships to match the cargos that needed to be moved to the power stations, and to manage our six dockers who carried out the unloading.

The planning of the ships movements was relatively simple, but managing six dockers was anything but. This was a time when 'Docker Power' was very much in the ascendancy, and it was very difficult with my 'six' to do other than operate within the agreed manager-unions' rules.

A typical example was that if a ship was being discharged on a Friday and could easily have been finished, the dockers would leave say fifty tons still to be discharged. That meant that they came in for half an hour on Saturday morning, which in turn meant that they had to be paid for the whole day at double time for their half-hours work! It might be said that they should simply be told to come back on Monday after finishing work on Friday, but this was made impossible by what is called 'Dispatch and Demurrage'.

A time is agreed for the length of time needed to discharge a cargo between the cargo owner and the deliverer. If the ship was forced to stay over until Monday to out wit the dockers, then considerable demurrage would be paid for delaying the discharge, and so it was cheaper to pay the dockers.

This is simply quoted as an example of the endless battle of wits between the employer and the dockers, with hardly a week passing without some problem. Two happy, if sometimes frustrating years had passed at Osborn and Wallis Ltd, during which time they had kindly made me a director, when there was a bombshell in our midst. The Central Electricity Generating Board, who were our single employer, announced that they were going to change the Portishead Power Stations over to burning oil, and that of course meant that the reason for our coal carrying coasters would cease to exist. It was accordingly decided to sell all the ships, and Osborn and Wallis would simply become a holding company for developing the very valuable land in the heart of Bristol which they owned around the area of their offices.

I was now nearly fifty two years old, and the thought of returning once more to the dole, at that age, with one's aspirations in ruins, and two boys at boarding school was almost too much to contemplate.

. . . And then a remarkable thing happened.

Occasionally, we had let our derelict dock outside the office, so that coasters could periodically discharge cargos of gravel from the channel islands, and the ship owners hired a haulage firm called A. H. Gore Ltd. to haul the gravel to its final destination. The partners in this very successful little business were getting old. They knew Dennis Osborn well and approached him with the suggestion that he might like to buy their business to complement the ships, unaware that they were about to be sold. It seems that Dennis Osborn had become very concerned that there had always been a family business ever since his grandfather's time and this was about to cease. He now wondered whether this might be a way of recreating a family business once more, but concerned that he was getting older and in increasing ill health. Then apparently an idea struck him and he agreed a date and price for taking over the haulage business.

I was then sent for; the whole transaction would be completed providing I agreed to become the managing director. I could scarcely believe what I had heard, and once more I had been pulled back from the brink at the eleventh hour and providing I could successfully operate a company of which I had no experience, the way ahead looked more secure.

27
Back in Command Once More

O N 1ST MAY 1969, one day after my fifty second birthday and eight and a half years after leaving the Royal Navy, the ladder had finally been climbed once more and I was again as it were Captain of a ship, only this time it was thirty lorries. I sat down behind the large Managing Director's desk and pondered the fact that I knew nothing about running lorries, but had a profound belief that the principles of successful management leading to healthy profit are the same whatever the basic commodity or service, namely to produce at the most efficient cost and sell at the best price the market would pay. If the latter was more that the former you made a profit! Our company were leaders in the field of Bulk tippers which represented some two thirds of our fleet the remaining being 'flats'.

I was very lucky from two main sources of support. Mr West, one of the partners from whom we had bought the company, was only too ready to give advice on the financial side whenever I asked him, and Gordon Lumber, the Transport Manager, and my second in command, was a master at superintending the best matrix each day in order to ensure that each lorry operated to the best advantage for completing the days work with the minimum of dead mileage running empty.

He had two assistants, one planning the flats and the other the tippers, on a detailed basis. Whilst customers were varied, the main ones on the tipper's were the Port of Bristol, B. O. C. M., Pauls & Whites and the like, dealing in bulk grains and feeding stuffs, and on the flat Spillers, Fisons, I. C. I. and similar firms, caring finished products.

Twice a year came the remorseless battle of visiting all our customers to agree rates for the ensuing six months. One of the problems was that we had to be totally unionised, because there was a restrictive practice by which no lorry could enter the Port of Bristol unless the driver had a T & G W card, and a considerable proportion of our business lay with the Port or companies that lay therein, whilst lots of smaller hauliers, paying less than union pay could run round the country quoting much reduced rates.

We had to rely entirely on service and reliability to beat the under cutters. In practice we only used the union rates to guarantee minimum weekly wages and operated a very sophisticated payments by results scheme which provided high wages for high lorry earnings, but needed watching to ensure that the laws on speeding and driving hours were not exceeded in an endeavour to get higher wages.

Each driver and his vehicle was an integral unit and much effort was spent in making the vehicle 'tidy' and they would travel across the length and breadth of the United Kingdom, sometimes being away for almost a whole week, all journeys being precisely planned by the Assistant Transport Managers to ensure always the minimum of dead running.

Most of the drivers, whom, together with their families, I got to know personally very quickly, had backgrounds emanating from the local coal fields which had all recently closed, and indeed A. H. Gore Ltd. was over the top of Greyfield Colliery which closed in 1912. It was still possible, but hazardous, to go down into the old flooded workings and it was necessary to be very careful, when putting up new buildings, to avoid any subsidence. By the time we took over, Mr Gore had had a bad stroke and was no longer active, but not so Gilbert West. Although over eighty he was still as sharp as a razor blade with a very active mind and wished always to know what was going on and to hear any news of his ex-employees. He had built himself a nice house next to the depot, and apart from coming into my office weekly to see what my problems were and if he could be of any help, we started a routine by which I walked up to his house every Tuesday at noon for a gossip and a drink with himself and his wife to talk about the firm and any ideas I had had for its future, and to convey any messages to them from the staff or drivers, for they were

Holidaying in Solva

meticulous, now the firm had been sold, in their rules of never coming down and talking to any of their old cronies now that they had left.

The one draw back was that Gilbert West was a very generous host and had never seemed to cotton on to the fact that beer and gin demanded different size measures! The outcome was that the staff knew better than to ask intelligent questions of me on Tuesday afternoons!

Not long after taking over, we were lucky enough to obtain from the Port of Bristol a lucrative contract for the bulk discharge of fish meal and other animal feeding stuffs from South Africa which would entail bringing the tonnage to a warehouse and then distributing it to the final customers as required. The warehouses needed to have strengthened side walls to withstand the outward pressure of bulk. Taking a deep breath I approached my masters for permission to build not one, but two such warehouses and all they said was 'go ahead if you can make a profit'.

It was the best thing I ever did for the company. They were semi-detached, each 100 feet by seventy five, with strengthened sides, and because of the old mineworkings and the made up ground, the floor had to be one reinforced concrete raft on which the rest was built. The year was 1970 and it is incredible to think now that the whole lot cost under £100, 000!

They only brought one problem in their wake. When loading or discharging there was bound to be a small amount of spillage of grain or whatever.

We lived alongside the Somerset mining community whose hobbies, as in other parts of the country, were whippets and carrier pigeons. Indeed one of our drivers was runner-up in the British National Championships. It appeared that every pigeon was getting its sustenance in or just outside our warehouses and they were a perishing nuisance. It was more that my life's worth to destroy even one pigeon by any method and no solution was ever found. The pigeons just got on with it!

1970 also marked the time when David was ending his time at prep school and sitting common entrance for Sherborne. He had reached the point where he was Deputy Head of School, Head of House and Captain of rugger, but now came the all important test and we were delighted to hear that he had passed in well and would be on his way to Abbeylands House in September.

During this time Christopher, taking after his mother in anyhow this respect, was showing clear signs of exceptional intellectual talent, as well as enjoying his games. He had moved into the upper sixth early on in his time there and was to aim later, when his time came, for a Sherborne scholarship.

At Gore's, it seemed to me that, with our fleet of thirty vehicles, the facilities and staff were under-used and we should start increasing our fleet. This was to take a gradual advance over the years, until it finally reached a maximum of forty two. It needed an increase only in re-fitting staff.

They were of course a vital part of the organisation which needed careful planning for regular servicing, daily rectification of reported defects and not infrequent visits all over the country to get broken down lorries rolling again.

I remember clearly very early in my time answering my phone one evening to be informed by the Metropolitan Police that our biggest articulated lorry had broken down right in Hyde Park Corner in the rush hour and would I kindly have it removed at once. As ill luck would have it the vehicle was our only one with an automatic gearbox and so could only be removed by suspended tow or taking out the box. The nearest Leyland agents who could do it were at Watford and there our lorry sat holding up the traffic until the rescuers arrived whilst the ever more irascible Police rang at frequent intervals. After that all the other crises seemed easier.

Some of our drivers, who were all absolutely splendid and whom I was to grow to know very well, together with most of their families, were not of great literacy, and their defect reports sometimes required a little translation. One I particularly remember from none other than the Pigeon champion, just had one word on the report; it was 'Puncher'!

We had made quite a good profit at the end of the first year and so I got agreements to pay everyone a bonus paid in proportion to their earnings, and when it came to doing the same at the end of the following year I had found out that nobody had seemed to tell their wives the previous year of the fact that they had received anything.

The wives goodwill were very important to us with drivers having many nights away and indeed often being collected by the wives if not too far away. Accordingly, at the end of the second year I told everyone that I was going to dock all bonuses by £10 and give everybody a Christmas dinner to take home to their wives. I thought I would get shot but to my great surprise they thought it was a splendid idea and the idea was perpetuated thereafter.

They were given the choice of:-
A.   Turkey plus Sherry
B.   Chicken plus Whiskey
C.   Turkey plus Plum pudding and crackers (for the tee-totallers.)
      P. M. on Christmas Eve they would collect their parcels, have a drink with me and go home delighted.
      A simple little innovation that luckily scored a bulls-eye.
      At about the same time we started a social club which held functions a few times a year including giving farewells to our long serving and elderly drivers when they retired and a big family Christmas party which gave an excellent opportunity to meet every one, even if it sometimes resulted in a perilous journey home!
      In the late spring of 1972 Peggy and I treated ourselves to a couple of nights at the Lamb at Hindon for painting and May fly fishing whilst Christopher went to Sherborne for interviews and exam papers for the scholarship. On the last day of our stay, and to his great credit we heard the wonderful news that he had been awarded the top scholarship of £200 per year.
      We rang the Headmaster and arranged for Champagne in his drawing room for all the masters that had taught Christopher and went straight down ourselves. It was a splendidly cheerful gathering and we were astounded to hear that this was the first time ever that any parents had ever thought to do such a thing.
      It is interesting to ponder that when Christopher went to Sherborne the normal fees were £500 per year, when he left five years later to go to Cambridge the fees were £3, 000 but the scholarship remained at £200. Now, I understand, scholarships are index linked to fee increases in most cases.
      We got bitten in the same way, only in reverse at about the same time. As I was no longer connected with ships, and the money for school fees was always a pressure on our resources, we decided to sell our cottage, the Anchorage, at Chew Magna. We had paid £1, 200 and spent the same again in modernising it and so were pleased to sell for £3, 950.
      Hardly had we sold than the 'Barber' cheap credit house boom, the first of many, took off and six months later the Anchorage was sold on for £9, 500, one presumes that now the price would be about £70, 000!
      This coincided with a major development at work. Unigate had bought Cow and Gate and there arose a requirement to distribute all over the U. K. their bottled baby foods which were manufactured at near-by Wells. It was agreed that if we could provide a warehouse to carry out the operation the contract could be ours. Back to the drawing board again, and inside eight months up had gone another warehouse the same size as the other two combined, but put end to end, so that an articulated lorry could back in and load under cover.
      We brought up all the finished products, not the famous 57 but more like 80 varieties on small flats from Wells and had to store and arrange them so that all could be got at, and

keep an exact stock list. Then each week we would get a list of parcels of from 5 to 20 tons to be made up in each of about fifteen depot drops ranged across the United Kingdom with any combination of the varieties and off would go all the vehicles. This was great work for us and Cow and Gate were delighted at the way their goods were now arriving at their correct destinations on time and with accurate cargoes. Together with good contracts in the Port of Bristol and elsewhere, these were the Halcyon days of A. H. Gore Ltd.

We also made one mistake, we did it too efficiently! After a couple of years Cow and Gate said to themselves 'If its that damn easy, why don't we do it ourselves and save money?' They also said it to us, and they promptly built themselves a warehouse and took all the work back!

Problems of marketing were from time to time bedevilled by the intrusion of the Bristol dialect, from which even our transport manager was not immune. He came to me with great delight one day to say that we had won an order for taking nearly 1000 tons of soil from the Mendips to Lancashire, a contract which puzzled me, unless it was for constructing a crown bowling green or something similar. Further questioning at last elicited the true nature of the job which was to carry soya.

The boys, ably taught to cast by a master at school, had become keen fishermen, and in addition to the visit to Solva we had much pleasure going down to the river in August, when the trout were not on the fin, and catching grayling, which, if put straight into a smoker and immediately eaten thereafter, provide excellent fodder.

Peggy, at the same time, reached her zenith with her painting. She had thrown down in disgust a water-colour of the river with morning mist coming off it exclaiming that she did not think she would ever paint a decent picture. I took it away and had it framed and it finished up being one of the only two pictures from Wiltshire to be hung in London at the International Art exhibition. Shortly afterwards, in the early Autumn another water-colour was presented for exhibition, this time for the Royal West of England Academy annual exhibition in Bristol and was of Christopher doing a jigsaw puzzle. Water-colour portraits are notoriously difficult to execute, because there is no chance of rectifying mistakes, and so there was a great delight among us when it was chosen for hanging.

By the summer term of 1974 both boys had completed their 'O' levels and David was down the road of 'A' levels. There had been a brief hiccup when he twice failed 'O' level maths, and when I remonstrated with him, he asked why I was getting on to him, Smith had failed three times, to which I had no answer! That was the only educational slip to date. David was also showing a particular propensity for athletics and was captain of the school at this, his forte being hurdles and high jump.

The story goes, which may be apocryphal, but which I hope is true, it deserves to be, that shortly before David joined, there was a triangular athletic match between Sherborne, Bryanston and the Borstal from Portland, the latter being instantly recognisable by the fact that they were the only one's in clean kit. Their masters were instantly recognisable too for looking exactly what they were, retired warders!

A reputation arrived in advance that the Borstal team included a lad of lightning speed who would clean up all the sprints. The first race was the 100 metres and indeed the lad's reputation was not false. He dashed down the straight winning by a distance, and then kept on running, down the playing fields across the road, through the shopping centre and up the hill the other side! He was cheered on by all the Sherborne boys, who only interrupted their encouragement to try and trip up the warders as they set off in hot pursuit. Alas, some hour later the lad was captured and the contest proceeded.

We were lucky in that both boys already knew what careers they wished to follow. David was doing his 'A' levels to lead him to the Royal Agricultural College at Cirencester, whilst Christopher was about to set out on the long journey that it was hoped would lead to Veterinary degree at Cambridge. Meanwhile, he was enjoying some gentle non-competitive cricket.

In early July Peggy complained of some cardiac irregularity and was clearly in some distress and her state rapidly deteriorated. The fear had always been present that with advancing age, she was now fifty six, there might be a sudden deterioration, although in spite of two damaged valves, her health had stood up so remarkably well that the fear had to some degree receded.

However the symptoms rapidly reached the point where she had to be moved in some haste to a hospital intensive care unit where her condition was stabilised, but it was necessary to make some major decisions.

28
The Final Chapter

ONCE SHE WAS STABILISED, I was able to take Peggy in the car to the Nursing Home in Bath where she could be seen by the original Cardiac Specialist and Bill Burrowes, our family Doctor since before the boys were born. The decision was made, as valve replacement under open heart surgery had advanced so rapidly, that the only solution to give Peggy further quality of life, was to go down this route. The alternative, because of the rapid deterioration that had suddenly taken place would have been that she would virtually have been confined to her bedroom for the remainder of her life, which she would have never have wanted, and nor would one have wanted it for her.

Accordingly, an appointment was made to see Donald Ross in his Harley Street consulting rooms. He, it was at that time who, had carried out the first successful heart transplant in the country and was the leading open heart surgeon at the National Heart Hospital.

Peggy had sufficiently recovered, with the aid of drugs, for me to be able to take her to London gently in the car, and after examination, Ross agreed that valve replacement was the right course and was very guardedly optimistic of total success which would make Peggy better than she had been for the previous thirty years.

There was to be a period first of some two months when her heart was to be built up in various ways and this coincided with the summer holidays.

It was arranged for Peggy to be taken to the National Heart Hospital at the beginning of October, by which time the boys were back at school, and there was in general little cause for alarm and despondency because all the medical prognostications pointed to the great likelihood of success.

The operation started at 8 a. m. on 7th October 1974 and the two new valves were successfully placed. However great difficulty was being found in restarting the hearts natural pace-maker, which had apparently been the cause of all the recent trouble. After twelve hours of fighting for her life Peggy finally lost her last battle, all the harder to bear when hopes had run so high. The path that had begun thirty-five years before in an oxygen tent had come to an end, but what rewarding years of achievement they had been for us both.

Family backgrounds are often quickly lost with time; this little effort has been in the hope that my grandchildren, and beyond, will like to know of the somewhat unusual circumstances that preceded them, and the life of a very brave woman which made it possible.